The

DEATH

and

RESURRECTION

of

ISRAEL

D1452245

The

DEATH

and

RESURRECTION

of

ISRAEL

REVISED EDITION

*A Message Of Hope For A Time
Of Trouble*

ARTHUR W. KAC

BAKER BOOK HOUSE
Grand Rapids, Michigan

By the same author:

THE REBIRTH OF THE STATE OF ISRAEL:
IS IT OF GOD OR OF MEN?

THE SPIRITUAL DILEMMA OF THE JEWISH PEOPLE

THE MESSIANIC HOPE

Biblical texts used in this book are from the Hebrew version of the Old Testament; from the Revised Standard Version, copyrighted 1946 and 1952 by The Division of Christian Education of the National Council of the Churches of Christ in the U.S.A.; from the American Standard Version, copyrighted 1901 by Thomas Nelson & Sons; from the New American Standard Bible (New Testament), copyrighted 1960, 1962, 1963 by the Lockman Foundation; from The New Testament in Modern English, copyrighted 1958 by J. B. Phillips.

ISBN: 0-8010-5380-3

PREFACE

In 1948 the Jewish people reestablished their national home in the Land of Israel after the lapse of nineteen centuries. In all of world history there is no other instance of a people which, though dispersed from its native land for some two thousand years, managed to survive and at the end of this long period returned to the country of its origin to resume its national existence. An attempt to explain the significance of this unique and unparalleled phenomenon was made by this author in a book entitled *The Rebirth Of The State Of Israel: Is it of God or of Men?* That book made its appearance in 1958 and passed through three printings and one special edition. It was favorably accepted in the English-speaking world. In the present work the author seeks to complete the story begun in *The Rebirth Of The State Of Israel.*

Among the aims which the Allied nations sought to achieve in the First World War were the liberation of the Arab peoples, and the resettlement of the Jewish people in Palestine. In the years following the First World War one Arab nation after another acquired political independence. Moreover, by investing its know-how and its money in Arab countries, by developing the huge oil resources in Arab lands, the West has given the new Arab states an opportunity to become economically viable.

And yet, in spite of all these benefits reaped by the Arabs as a result of the Allied victory in the First World War, and notwithstanding the fact that Palestine is poor in natural resources and constitutes a mere nook in the vast area of the Middle East, all Jewish attempts to resettle in Palestine and terminate their age-long national homelessness have been fought by the Arabs tooth and nail. So intense has been Arab hatred of Israel that the self-appointed and irresponsible Arab leaders have turned their backs on the Western benefactors of the Arab peoples and have opened up the gates of the Middle East to Russian penetration. They have done this in reckless and heedless disregard of the tragic experiences of the peoples in Europe which have been under Russian domination since the end of World War Two.

The Jewish people in and out of Israel and a large part of the non-communist world have been baffled by this strange Arab behavior and perplexed by Arab intransigence and the growing explosiveness of the Middle East conflict. The Jewish people have often asked, how Jesus Christ can be the promised Messiah, seeing that He brought no peace to the world. Since their resumption of nationhood the Jews are discovering for themselves that true peace cannot be imposed from without, but must come from a change of the human heart. This, of course, has been the consistent teaching not only of the New Testament but of the Old Testament as well (Isaiah 2:1-4; Micah 4:1-5).

But a change of man's heart will not take place until man has been permitted to go all the way in his determination to work out his salvation by human resources alone, and until he has arrived at a dead-end point in human history. Mankind has desperately been striving to bring in the Millenium with God left out of it. But a Millenium without God and with unregenerated human hearts can only end up being the kingdom of Satan rather than the Kingdom of God.

History is an interaction of Divine and human elements and a preparation for the establishment of God's Kingdom on earth. There are many signs today that this process of preparation is fast approaching its completion.

In the Biblical period great events, coming at critical points of history, were attended by equally great Divine revelations aiming to interpret those events. Israel was the channel through which the Word of God was then communicated to the world. During the nineteen centuries of Jewish dispersion Heaven remained silent. Does the present reconstitution of Jewish nationhood in the Land of Israel portend the nearness of the day when the long silence of God will at last be broken?

✦ ✦ ✦

The author wishes to thank all publishers and owners of copyright material for permission granted to use excerpts in the following pages. If any acknowledgment has inadvertently been omitted apologies are offered.

PREFACE TO THE SECOND EDITION

The present edition of this work has been enlarged by the addition of new material. While this book may be regarded as a companion volume of *The Rebirth of the State of Israel*, it is not, strictly speaking, a continuation of that work. It would, however, be advisable for those contemplating reading both books to begin with *The Death and Resurrection of Israel*, as it gives the reader a bird's eye view of the whole subject, and thus prepares him for the more detailed study of *The Rebirth of the State of Israel*. Together, both books seek to interpret the meaning of this extraordinary phenomenon of the resumption by the Jewish people of their national existence after a lapse of eighteen centuries.

A. W. K.

July 1976

CONTENTS

PART ONE

Israel's Death

"But if you will not hearken unto me, and will not do all these commandments . . . I will devastate the land, so that your enemies who settle in it shall be astonished at it. And I will scatter you among the nations, and I will unsheathe the sword after you; and your land shall be a desolation, and your cities shall be a waste" (Leviticus 26: 14, 32-33).

"And you shall become a horror, a proverb, and a byword, among all the peoples where the LORD will lead you away . . . And the LORD will scatter you among all peoples, from one end of the earth to the other; and there you shall serve other gods, of wood and stone, which neither you nor your fathers have known. And among these nations you shall find no ease, and there shall be no rest for the sole of your foot; but the LORD will give you there a trembling heart, and failing eyes, and a languishing soul. Your life shall hang in doubt before you; night and day you shall be in dread, and have no assurance of your life. In the morning you shall say, 'Would it were evening!' and at evening you shall say, 'Would it were morning!' because of the dread which your heart shall fear, and the sights which your eyes shall see" (Deuteronomy 28: 37, 64-67).

"But if you* turn aside from following me, you or your children, and do not keep my commandments and my statutes which I have set before you, but go and serve other gods and worship them. Then I will cut off Israel from the land which I have given them; and the house** which I have consecrated for my name I will cast out of my sight; and Israel will become a proverb and a byword among all peoples. And this house will become a heap of ruins; everyone passing by it will be astonished, and will hiss; and they will say, 'Why has the LORD done thus to this land and to this house?' Then they will say, 'Because they forsook the LORD their God who brought their fathers out of the land of Egypt, and laid hold on other gods, and worshipped them and served them; therefore the LORD has brought all this evil upon them'" (I Kings 9: 6-9).

---

* i.e., King Solomon
** Jerusalem Temple

1

"O Jerusalem, Jerusalem, who kills the prophets and stones those who are sent to her! How often I wanted to gather your children together, the way a hen gathers her chicks under her wings, and you were unwilling. Behold, your house is being left to you desolate. For I say to you, from now on you shall not see me until you say, 'Blessed is he who comes in the name of the Lord' " (Matthew 23: 37-39).

"And when he approached, he saw the city and wept over it. Saying, 'If you had known in this day, even you, the things which make for peace! But now they have been hidden from your eyes. For the days shall come upon you when your enemies will throw up a bank before you, and surround you, and hem you in on every side. And will level you to the ground and your children within you, and they will not leave in you one stone upon another, because you did not recognize the time of your visitation' " (Luke 19: 41-44).

"But when you see Jeruslaem surrounded by armies, then recognize that her desolation is at hand. Then let those who are in Judea flee to the mountains, and let those who are in the midst of the city depart, and let not those who are in the country enter the city. Because these are days of vengeance, in order that all things which are written may be fulfilled. Woe to those who are with child and to those who nurse babes in those days; for there will be great distress upon the land, and wrath to this people. And they will fall by the edge of the sword, and will be led captive among all nations; and Jerusalem will be trodden down by the Gentiles until the times of the Gentiles are fulfilled" (Luke 21: 20-24).

CHAPTER 1

HISTORICAL SURVEY OF PALESTINE:
The Era Of The Great Dispersion, 135-1917

I. The Land Of Israel Under Foreign Rule

1. The Roman Period
2. The Arab Period
3. The Latin Kingdom of Jerusalem
4. The Period of the Mamluks
5. The Period of the Ottoman Turks
6. The Obliteration of Palestine's Political Identity

II. The Economic Decline Of Palestine

1. The Economic Position of Palestine prior to the Destruction of the Second Jewish Commonwealth.
2. The Economic Deterioration of Palestine under the Arabs.
3. Reasons for the Economic Deterioration of Palestine.
   a. The low cultural level of the Arabs
   b. External wars
   c. Administrative inefficiency
   d. Civil strife and internal disorders
   e. The land tenure system
4. Conclusion

III. The Position Of The Jewish Community

1. The Roman Period
2. The Arab Period
3. The Period of the Crusaders
4. The Mamluk Period
5. The Turkish Period
6. Conclusion

CHAPTER 1

HISTORICAL SURVEY OF PALESTINE:

The Era Of The Great Dispersion, 135-1917

The full significance of the re-emergence of the State of Israel and of the Arab-Israel problem cannot be fully understood without some knowledge of what happened to Palestine during the time of the Great Dispersion of the Jewish people. The beginning of the Great Dispersion dates from the year A.D. 135. We have selected the year of 1917 as the end of the Great Dispersion era, as the promulgation of the Balfour Declaration in 1917 became the basis for the political reconstitution of the Jewish National Homeland.

I. THE LAND OF ISRAEL UNDER FOREIGN RULE

1. THE ROMAN PERIOD, 135-640

In A.D. 66 the Jews in Palestine rose in revolt against Rome in an effort to free their Homeland from Roman rule. Jerusalem fell and the Temple was destroyed in A.D. 71, but it took two more years of mopping up operations. With the capture of the fortress of Masada in A.D. 73 the war against Rome came to an end.[1] The total number of killed in that war is estimated to have reached 1,356,460, and the number of prisoners taken was 101,700.[2] When emperor Hadrian published in A.D. 132 new restrictive laws against the Jewish religion and decided to build a new city on the ruins of destroyed Jerusalem and erect a pagan temple on the site of the burned-down Jewish Temple the Jews in Palestine rebelled once more under the leadership of Bar Kochba. It took three years before the Romans succeeded in putting down this bloody uprising. Don Cassius states that about 580,000 Jews fell by the sword, not counting those who perished from starvation, disease and other related causes.[3] Many others were sold as slaves. Hadrian now carried out his plans in the belief that these will extinguish forever all Jewish hopes of the restoration of the National Homeland. A new city was built on the ruins of Jerusalem and called Aelia Capitolina and peopled by foreigners. A pagan temple was reared on the site of the old Temple. An edict was issued prohibiting on pain of death any Jew from entering or even approaching the vicinity of the new city. The name of the province of Judaea was changed to that of Syria Palestina. Thus the name "Palestine" was given to the Land of Israel following the failure of the Bar-Kochba rebellion.[4]

In the interval between the end of the Bar-Kochba revolt and the Muslim invasion Palestine enjoyed peace from outside invasion and a measure of prosperity. In 364 the extensive territories of the Roman Empire became divided into an eastern and western part. For the next 250 years Palestine was part of the eastern half of the empire ruled from Constantinople.

In 614 Palestine was invaded by the Persians. The Persian empire formed the easternmost boundary of the Roman empire and it had never been subdued by Rome. The Jews who threw their support on the side of the Persian army had high hopes of gaining permission to restore their National Homeland. It is quite possible that their hopes would have been realized. But Persian occupation of Palestine ended after fifteen years at which time it reverted to the authority of the Eastern Roman Empire. But it remained under Roman rule only for another eleven years. In 640 the Arab followers of Mohammed invaded Palestine and the Roman period in the history of Palestine came to a definite end.

Up to the time of Diocletian the Roman province of Palestine consisted of Judaea, Idumaea, a strip of Peraea across the Jordan, Samaria, and Galilee, exclusive of the sea coast north from Dora and the westerly cities of the Decapolis. Diocletian (284-305) detached from it Idumaea, but added to it other parts of the Decapolis territory. At some later date Dora also became joined to the Palestine province. During the reign of Constantine or one of his successors the political boundaries of Palestine underwent another revision into two parts: Palestina Prima which took in Judaea, Samaria and the northern part of Idumaea; while Palestina Secunda was made up of Galilee and the Decapolis.

2. THE ARAB PERIOD, 640-1090

With the exception of the Persian incident mentioned above Palestine experienced no foreign invasion for some 700 years since Rome had extended its power over the Jewish National Homeland in 63 B.C. This long era of external peace and relative prosperity came to an end in 640 with the conquest of Palestine by the Arabs. The Muslim followers of Mohammed poured out of the deserts of the Arabian peninsula and within a hunded years they overran vast spaces extending from central Asia, through northern Africa, the Spanish peninsula, to the very borders of Southern France. There the Arab onrush was brought to a halt by the French forces under Charles Martel. While material motives and lust for power were undoubtedly among the primary forces which energized the new invaders, their newly acquired religious zeal largely accounted, in the first century at least, for the determination and fury which marked the Arab conquests. On the other hand, Arab victories were in no small measure due to the physical exhaustion of the Middle East world brought about by the frequent wars between the Byzantine and Persian empires.

The effect of the Arab conquests upon the destiny of Palestine was to prove disastrous in many respects. Since Alexander the Great until the Arab invasion Palestine was part of the Mediterranean Middle Eastern world. For a thousand years Palestine had been in intimate contact with Graeco-Roman civilization. With the exception of the brief Latin period this link between Palestine and the West was broken, and the unity of the Mediterranean world was destroyed by the rise of Arab power. In fact, Palestine would have been all but forgotten if not for the Jewish immigrants and Christian pilgrims. The love for the land of their forefathers of the former and the religious devotion to the Holy Land of the latter brought numbers of them to Palestine in every century and maintained a bridge between Palestine and the West.

Mohammed's successors were called caliphs. Following Mohammed's death in 632 the first of these caliphs, Abu Bakr, extended his authority over the rest of the Arabian peninsula, as during Mohammed's life only a third of the Arabian peninsula is said to have submitted to his religious and political leadership. It was during the reign of Umar, the second caliph, that Arab power extended outside the Arab peninsula. Palestine and Syria were among the first foreign territories to be swept into the net of the advancing Arab armies.

After the second caliph the seat of power in the Muslim world was frequently vacated through murder. At first the capital of Arab rule was located in Medina. Ali (656-661) removed the capital to al-Kufah on the Euphrates. After assassination by one of his army men he was succeeded by Muawiyah (661-680) who transferred the capital to Damascus. Muawiyah was a descendant of Umayyah, a nephew of the Great-grandfather of Mohammed. But the followers of Ali refused to accept Muawiyah's religious supremacy and brought about the oldest schism in the Islamic religion. They founded the Shiite sect, while those who recognized Muawiyah's leadership gave rise to the Sunni sect. The Caliphate became hereditary in the house of Muawiyah. His descendants ruled the Muslim world less than a century, but it was during this period that Arab power reached its greatest height, extending its rule from India to Spain.

It was during the reign of the Umayyad dynasty (661-750), less than one century, that the Arab empire was really Arab. In the years following the end of this dynasty the Arab element lost its dominating position. In fact, Arab power began to decline even before the fall of the Umayyads. In the eighth century the old feuds between the Arab tribes began to reassert themselves, and civil wars and intermittent revolts were erupting here and there. One such revolt was staged in the east by Abu C. Abbas al-Saffah in 750 whose general murdered the last Umayyad. This gave rise to the Abbasid dynasty. Al-Saffa (750-754) set up his capital at al-Kufah, but his successor, al-Mansur (754-775), moved his capital to the newly built city of Baghdad. Beginning with the Abbasids it was the Muslim, not the Arab, element which was the dominating component of the empire. The Abbasids, however, were not the sole rulers of the whole Muslim empire. Representatives of the Umayyads retained power in Spain, while local dynasties established themselves in the extreme East.

From the ninth century on the Abbasid caliphs began to depend on Turkish mercenaries from central Asia to keep them in power. These mercenaries, who were Muslim converts, in time became the real rulers of the empire. One of these Turkish generals, Ahmad ibn-Tulum, at first was governor of Egypt, one of the provinces of the empire. He soon made himself an independent ruler and in 877 he conquered Palestine and Syria. After his death in 884 there followed a period of misrule and confusion lasting twenty years, and in 905 Egypt, Palestine and Syria reverted nominally to Abbasid power, but actually they were ruled by the Turkish mercenary generals.

In 935 Turkish General Mohammed ibn-Tughj was sent to Egypt to restore order. He then made himself ruler of Egypt, and in 940 he annexed Palestine and Syria to his kingdom. After his death in 946 another period of confusion began. Taking advantage of the weakness of the Abbasid dynasty, the Byzantines invaded Syria and northern Palestine for the first time since the rise of Arab power. During this period Palestine, which was under the nominal rule of the successors of Mohammed ibn-Tughj, was actually governed for twenty years by an Abyssinian Negro slave.

Following this Palestine came under the rule of the Fatimid dynasty. The Fatimids claimed descent from Fatima, daughter of Mohammed. In 909 they established a Caliphate of the Shiite sect in northwestern Africa. The Fatimids built Cairo and one of their number, al-Aziz (975-996), conquered Palestine and Syria. After his death civil war broke out between the rival generals of his successor al-Hakim.

About the end of the tenth century the Seljuk Turks were converted to the Islamic faith while in the employ of an Islamic dynasty, the Ghaznavids, who then were the rulers of Persia and Northwest India. These Turkish mercenaries in time became independent rulers. One of them, Tughril Beg, occupied Baghdad in 1055, proclaiming himself Sultan while leaving supreme religious authority in the hands of the Abbasid Caliph al-Kaim. In 1071, Aziz, a Seljuk Turk, overran Syria and Palestine. In 1098 the Fatimids reestablished their authority in Palestine, but in a few months this was terminated by the arrival of the European Crusaders.

Following the Arab invasion Palestine became divided into two provinces: the northern part became the Jund of al-Urdunn, with the capital at Tiberias; the southern part was called Filastin, extending down to the border of Egypt, with its capital at Lydda, and later at Ramleh.

3. THE LATIN KINGDOM OF JERUSALEM, 1009-1291

A two-fold historical process began in Europe following the fall of the western branch of the Roman empire in 476. On the political side Europe saw the formation of a number of new States by the Franko-Germanic tribes, and the rise of a federation of certain cities bordering on the Mediterranean. On the economic and social side Europe witnessed the emergence of the feudal system of the Middle Ages. By the eleventh century both these historical developments reached maturity. Having set its own house in order and having begun to feel its strength Europe was turning its gaze in the direction of the Middle East. The increasing farm population of Europe and the growing maritime power of the commercial cities of Italy intensified the lure of the East both as a possible source of new agricultural lands and a valuable trading area.

While Medieval Europe was reaching full growth successive waves of Turkish tribes from central Asia were streaming westward and southward into the possessions of the Caliphs, reinvigorating their decaying empire in the East and gradually supplanting them as its real masters. In order to consolidate and expand the territories of

Islam these new masters increased their pressure against the Byzantines, Islam's archenemy in the East, and imposed fresh obstacles designed to stop the flow of Christian pilgrims from the West. Confronted with this new danger the Byzantine empire appealed to Western Christendom for help. Outwardly, at least, the European Crusades were Europe's response to this appeal. Actually, however, the Crusades were motivated by three sets of circumstances: 1) Political—Europe's readiness for territorial expansion; 2) economic—the desirability to establish commercial relations with the rich East; 3) religious—the sense of solidarity felt by Christendom of the West towards the Byzantine State representing Christendom in the East; and the highly emotional factor involved in the desire to deliver the Holy Land of Christendom from the hands of the Muslims.

There were several Crusades, the first of which began in 1096. Jerusalem was captured in 1099. As a result of the victories of the Crusaders a number of Latin colonies were established. These were from north southward: the country of Edessa, the principality of Antioch, the county of Tripoli and the kingdom of Jerusalem. The Kingdom of Jerusalem was offered to Godfrey of Bouillon, one of the leaders of the First Crusade, but he declined. He consented to accept the title of the Defender of the Holy Sepulchre. Upon Godfrey's death which took place within one year his brother Baldwin became king of Jerusalem as Baldwin I (1100-1118). He was followed by Baldwin II (1118-1131). After his death the crown passed on to his son-in-law Fulk of Anjou (1131-1143), grandfather of the English King Henry II. Under these three kings the Kingdom of Jerusalem attained its greatest territorial limits.

After Fulk's accidental death the throne passed on to his son Baldwin III who, still a minor, remained under the regency of his mother. Baldwin III ruled from 1152 to 1158 when he died of poison. He was succeeded by his brother Amaury (1162-1173). He in turn was succeeded by his son Baldwin IV (1173-1185). At the age of nine he became infected with leprosy. He was only thirteen years when his father died. All his public life, which ended at the tender age of twenty-four, he spent trying to block Saladin's expansionist movements. Upon his death Guy de Lusignan became the last king of the Latin Kingdom of Jerusalem. After his defeat by Saladin in 1187 in the battle of the Horns of Hattin Palestine became divided into a Christian and Muslim part. Jerusalem surrendered to Saladin in October 1187.

Saladin died in 1193 and his empire was divided among his sons, among whom there was the usual rivalry. The German king, Frederick II of Hohenstaufen, landed in 1228 in Acre. Fearing that Frederick may form an alliance with the ruler of Damascus, al-Kamil, one of Saladin's heirs, concluded with Frederick a treaty in February 1229 and handed over to him Jaffa, Jerusalem, Bethlehem and Nazareth. Frederick subsequently crowned himself king of the Jerusalem Kingdom. But soon after his coronation he returned to Europe.

In 1239 Jerusalem was seized by the Muslim lord of Kerak and regained by the Latins who held it for a brief period. In 1243 the whole of Palestine was raided by the Khwarizmian Turks. The Mongols invaded Syria and northern Palestine in 1260.

In 1271 Prince Edward, who later became Edward I of England, arrived at Acre and concluded a ten years' truce with the Mamluk Sultan Baibars. In 1291 Sultan al-Ashraf Khalil (1290-1293) undertook the final campaign of liquidating the Latin holdings in the Near East. This was accomplished in 1303 when the Island of Ruad, off Tortosa, was cleared of the Latin forces. "With this evacuation, an enterprise, which might have done much to build a permanent bridge between East and West, ended unhonored and unlamented, leaving behind it nothing of which Christendom could be proud."[5]

4. THE PERIOD OF THE MAMLUKS, 1250-1517

Saladin, a Seljuk Turk, founded the Ayyubid dynasty which lasted for about fifty years. After his death one branch ruled Egypt, while the other branches ruled in Damascus and in other parts of the empire. Al-Kamil, mentioned above, was Saladin's nephew. When his son Ayyab died his widow ruled in his place until her amirs advanced one of their own number to the throne. She married this amir whose name was Aybak, but later murdered him. This Aybak became the founder of a line of Mamluk Sultans. The word Mamluk means slave and the reason for this name was that they were foreign slaves. Some of them were of Turkish, others of Circassian descent. There were forty-seven of these Mamluk Sultans reigning in the space of 267 years. Only one family retained power for four successive generations. Most of the others lasted only a few years. Some of them were insane; others, illiterate. Many came to the throne by assassinating their predecessors, and were in turn murdered themselves. And yet these Mamluks repelled successive invasions of the Mongols, and completed the liquidation of the Latin colonies in the Near East.

It is said that Egypt, Palestine and Syria lost about two-thirds of their population during the reign of the Mamluks. Palestine, in addition, suffered much damage from the lack of an effective administration, from the frequent quarrels of rival amirs, and the perennial depredations of the countryside by the desert Bedouins.

5. THE PERIOD OF THE OTTOMAN TURKS, 1517-1917

While the Mamluk empire was decaying from within, the Osmanli Turks, better known as the Ottoman Turks, were moving up to the forefront of events in Asia. In 1453 Constantinople fell to their arms, and thus came to an end the eastern division of the Roman empire which had outlived the western division by a thousand years. In 1517, under the leadership of Selim I, Syria, Palestine and Egypt were overrun. In Egypt, however, the Mamluks continued for some time to rule as the appointees of Constantinople, which was the seat of government of the Ottoman empire.

In the beginning of Ottoman rule Syria and Palestine were rearranged for administrative purposes. Palestine, as under previous regimes, did not form a single administrative unit. Jerusalem, Nablus, Gaza, Sidon and Beirut constituted one unit, while Galilee became part of the pashalik of Sidon. For defensive reasons Suleiman the Magnificent (1520-1566) rebuilt the walls of Jerusalem which are said to be the same walls surrounding the old city to this day.[6]

The provincial Pasha was the highest governing authority of a province. While theoretically his function called for maintenance of law and order, in practice his duties were limited to the maintenance of the forces under his authority and the collection of the taxes from the province. Once a year he visited the whole province for tax collection. His actual and effective authority was limited to his own provincial capital and its immediate environs. The rest of the province was left in control of the landowners.

In the first two hundred years of Turkish occupation Palestine, while ravaged by incessant internal wars, experienced no invasion from the outside. The first such invasion came at the very end of the 18th century during the Napoleonic wars. After occupying Egypt in July 1798, Napoleon crossed into Palestine in the beginning of 1799. He took Jaffa and moved on to Tyre where he laid siege to the city, but he failed to capture it. Jerusalem was never attacked. In June Napoleon recrossed into Egypt and in August 1799, he left for Europe.

About thirty years later Palestine was invaded by one of the Sultan's governors, Mehmet Ali (1769-1849), an Albanian, was in command of an Albanian regiment. In 1801, taking advantage of the confusion which followed the departure of Napoleon, he made himself Pasha of Egypt with the help of the Mamluks. The Turkish Sultan confirmed him in his office in 1805. He was energetic and ruthless. He reorganized the administration and economy of Egypt, and built up a strong armed force. For his military exploits in Arabia he demanded from the Sultan the pashalik of Syria. When refused, he sent his son Ibrahim on an expedition, and Palestine was taken in 1831 and Syria in 1832. He then marched on Constantinople. He was stopped by Russian intervention and returned to Syria. New disturbances broke out six years later when the Turkish Sultan attempted to reconquer Syria and Palestine. Under pressure from the European powers Mehmet Ali was forced to abandon Syria and Palestine and content himself with the hereditary pashalik of Egypt.

Toward the end of the 19th century certain administrative changes were introduced in Palestine. Abdul Hamid II (1876-1908) created the pashalik of Beirut which took in the sanjak of Acre including all of Galilee, and the sanjak of Balfa which included Samaria. The territory corresponding to ancient Judaea became the independent sanjak of Jerusalem under the direct supervision of the central government in Constantinople. The reason for this change is said to have been the increasing European population, the growing European interest in Palestine, and the renewed colonizing activities of the Jews.[7]

Following the Mehmet Ali adventures Palestine sank back again into international obscurity until the First World War. In 1917 the British army entered Palestine and the 400 years of Turkish occupation came to an end.

6. THE OBLITERATION OF PALESTINE'S POLITICAL IDENTITY

The reader will recall from previous pages how Palestine lost its status as a political unit in the years following the dispersion of the Jewish people which had taken place after A.D. 135. To be sure, even after the death of Herod the Great the country was subdivided among his sons, while one part was administered by a Roman official. But these subdivisions had something of an artificial character. Whether in the days of Herod the Great or of his heirs, the real masters of Palestine were the Romans. Furthermore, the Jews lived in the whole country and these subdivisions had no practical significance for them. As far as they were concerned the whole country was the land of Israel in which they constituted the vast majority of the population and which was dominated by the power of Rome.

A significant change had taken place in this respect after A.D. 135 when due to extermination and exile the Jewish population in the Land of Israel sank to a mere fraction of the total population. The name of the country was changed to that of Palestine, the name of the rebuilt city of Jerusalem became Aelia Capitolina, and Palestine was split up into two political units. Under Muslim rule these subdivisions became further multiplied.

But it was especially during the long centuries of Muslim rule that Palestine lost all political identity. "The country was divided, according to convenience, between different provinces, whose frontiers were continually altered. Jerusalem was never a Muslim capital. Even the two Umayyad caliphs who were most closely associated with the country, Muawiyah and Sulayman, showed no special regard for it. Muawiyah, who was proclaimed caliph at Jerusalem, made Damascus the seat of his government; and Sulayman, who chose Palestine for his residence during the three years of his rule, built himself a new capital at Ramleh. Nor had it a paramount religious position, save for brief periods when Mecca was, for some reason, inaccessible to the Muslims of Syria. When the crusaders were approaching the city in 1098 the Abbasids were unmoved by appeals from their fellow-Muslims for assistance. The Ayyubid al-Kamil exchanged it for a treaty of alliance against Damascus with Frederick II. On two occasions in the thirteenth century, when the Christians captured Damietta, al-Kamil and his successor as-Salih were prepared to exchange this port for the holy city of Jerusalem."[8]

"During all this period of nearly two thousand years, Palestine was not even a name on the political map of the world. It was a portion of a larger province, whether Roman, Byzantine, Arab or Turkish: and its people were never conscious of themselves as a national unit, nor did they ever attempt, as they had done in early and later Israelite days, to form an independent kingdom."[9] At no time in the whole recorded history of Palestine was the country one independent political state except under the Jews. Palestine's political identity was destroyed when the Jewish National Homeland was destroyed. When at the end of the 19th century the Jews began to return to the country with a renewed determination to rebuild their National Homeland

Palestine once more re-emerged from obscurity. And when in 1948 the State of Israel was re-established Palestine became again, after a lapse of more than two thousand years, an independent State.

II. THE ECONOMIC DECLINE OF PALESTINE

1. THE ECONOMIC POSITION OF PALESTINE PRIOR TO THE DESTRUCTION OF THE SECOND JEWISH COMMONWEALTH

Before the destruction of the Jewish National Homeland by the Romans, Palestine, which then included part of Transjordan, had a population variously estimated at between two and a half and five million. A figure of three and a half million people is probably a correct estimate.

The basis of Palestine's economy was a varied and thriving agriculture. It grew sufficient food to take care of the country's needs and even some for export purposes. The main agricultural products exported were oil from the hill country, wine from the plains, dates from the Jordan valley, and wheat from Transjordan. One observer states that "its hills were richly forested, as in early Greece and early England. Its valleys were fertile enough to produce ordinary crops of grains, to support the vine, the fig, and the olive."[10]

Palestine's commercial advantages stemmed from its geographic position. It should be noted that the Near East at the time of the Roman Empire was the industrial and commercial center of the Empire. Manufactured goods produced there were exchanged for the raw materials from the less developed and backward western part of the Roman empire. Palestine shared fully in the economic prosperity of those days because of its position as a land bridge between three continents and because of its situation on the crossroads of trade routes from Central Asia to Egypt, and from India to Rome. Various inland trade routes passed through the country carrying the commercial exchange between Syria, Arabia, Egypt, Greece and Rome.

The chief industrial item which Palestine exported were textiles. Beisan was the center of the linen industry. Whole villages in the south were busy weaving and dyeing silk. Dyed silks and cotton were produced in Gaza. Cotton was growing in the Jericho area. In the Jericho district were also the balsam groves. In fact, the manufacture of balsam is said to have been the monopoly of the Jericho region, it being the only place in the whole of the Roman empire where balsam was produced.[11]

Palestine also had a profitable fish industry. Fish caught in the Sea of Galilee, salted, dried and packed in jars, were exported to Rome and Spain. The town of Tarichaea, whose name in Greek means Pickletown, must have been the center for the fish industry.

Salt and asphalt were exploited from the Dead Sea. Large quantities of asphalt were sent to Egypt where it was used in embalming operations. Asphalt was also used for pitching ship bottoms. From statements in Josephus, the Jewish historian of the first century A.D., and in the Talmud one is led to believe that there existed in those days a well developed shipbuilding industry.

Another indication of the prosperous state of Jewish Palestine in the first century A.D. was the discovery by archaeologists of the ruins of a large number of village sites in the Negev part of the country. Hundreds of these thriving villages dotted the southern part of Palestine where both agriculture and industry flourished in those days. This is the same Negev which under Arab occupation became desert country.

The destruction of the Jewish Homeland in the wars of A.D. 70 and A.D. 135, and especially the dispersion of the Jewish people from Palestine, did not augur well for the economic welfare of the country. Nevertheless, under Roman rule Palestine still enjoyed a high measure of prosperity. The Romans built good roads, constructed efficient irrigation systems, and maintained law and order—all of which helped keep the country in a relatively good economic condition. The real decline began with the conquest of Palestine by the Arabs.

2. THE ECONOMIC DETERIORATION OF PALESTINE UNDER THE ARABS

What did the Jews find when the modern Return began in the second half of the nineteenth century? It is estimated that the total population of Palestine in 1850 numbered about 200,000. Compare this figure with the population of about three to four million at the time of the destruction of the National Homeland of the Jewish people. Travelers in Palestine were impressed with the underpopulated state of the country and with the barbarous, lethargic and despondent state of its peasants, many of whom suffered from malaria and blindness-producing trachoma.

The size and condition of Palestine's population was of course directly related to the state of the country. When the Jews returned in the nineteenth century from their Dispersion they found a land denuded of trees, hillsides turned into bare rocks, terrace walls and water conservation works broken down, river channels clogged—resulting in malaria breeding swamps—the cities destroyed, the whole country a silent desert. These are a few observations by two visitors to Palestine in that era: "Outside of the gates of Jerusalem 'we saw, indeed, no living object, heard no living sound, we found the same void, the same silence . . . as we should have expected before the entombed gates of Pompeii or Herculaneum. A complete eternal silence reigns in the town, on the highways, in the country . . . the tomb of a whole people.' "[12] 'Palestine . . . is an island in a desert waste . . . also an island in the midst of pirates. The Bedouins are the corsairs of the wilderness . . . [Jerusalem is] a city of ruins. Here and there a regular street, or a well-built European house emerges from the general chaos, but the general appearance is that of a city which had been burnt down in some great conflagration.'[13]

3. REASONS FOR THE ECONOMIC DETERIORATION OF PALESTINE

a. *The low cultural level of the Arabs*

The principal cause of the economic deterioration of Palestine may be traced to the Arab conquest of the country in the seventh century. The fate of a conquered territory is often determined by the cultural level of the conqueror. In the case of the Arabs their level of civilization was in every respect below that of the areas of the Persian and Byzantine empires which they overran. The Arab invaders were mostly nomads from the wilds of Arabia. Consequently, the cultural level of the lands which the Arabs subjugated was in due time dragged down to that of the Arabs themselves.

b. *External wars*

With the exception of the short occupation of Palestine by the Persians in the first half of the seventh century A.D. Palestine had been free from external wars for about seven centuries under Roman rule. The Arab occupation of Palestine in 636 was the beginning of a long era of intermittent external wars. "At short intervals, for all of sixteen centuries, Palestine felt the steady tread of serried ranks of soldiers and the stamping hoofs of undisciplined cavalry; all marching and countermarching in obedience to sanguinary imperial interests. Within this period and even afterwards it suffered from foray and incursion, from ruthless civil war, and from the brutalities of tribal strife. In its endless changing experiences it had borne the wasteful pressure of the armies of all nations from the North Sea to the Great Wall of China, from the Baltic to Abyssinia."[14]

c. Administrative inefficiency

This was one of the great factors which contributed much to the ruin of Palestine. The Arab conquerors put the administration of their conquered territories under the rule of military governors. The main function of these governors, who were primarily soldiers, was to assure the collection of taxes. Under the Abbasids the long distance between Palestine and the capital in Baghdad increased the state of disorder and lawlessness in the country. Under the Mamluks the tempo of Palestine's economic decline was accelerated. The ports of Palestine lay in ruins, and foreign commerce was virtually at a standstill. An additional factor in the increasing worsening of Palestine's economy under the Mamluks were the many new geographic discoveries in the fifteenth century, such as of the American continent, and the ocean way to India. This had led to a gradual diminishing of the commercial importance of the Mediterranean countries. The administrative system in the provinces under the Mamluks was no more effective than under the Arabs.

Under the Turks provincial officials called Pashas were appointed annually by the Sultan. These Pashas, many of whom were old men, were either indifferent to the fate of the provinces or incapable of maintaining law and order. This was especially true of Palestine where they left the actual supervision of the country in the hands of local amirs, tribal chiefs, and rich and corrupt Arab effendis. The main function of the Pashas was to maintain the forces under them and to collect the taxes from the provinces. The Turkish tax system substantially added to Palestine's impoverishment. The taxes were farmed out to the highest bidder, who were usually the rich landowners, the so-called effendis, many of whom lived in the cities. While the law set the tax at fifteen per cent to be paid in kind, the tax-collecting effendis used to assess the produce at a higher than the real value and insisted on cash payments. Many of the peasants eager to prevent conscription of their sons into the Turkish army would buy release from the service. As they were poor they were forced to borrow money from the effendis. This meant that a large share of the meager crop which the peasants harvested went to the effendis leaving the peasant barely enough food to survive till the next harvest. This system made the peasants virtual life-long slaves of the effendis.[15]

One of the worst features of the Turkish tax system was the taxing of every tree, whether woodland, orchard or forest, and every vine. To evade this ruinous taxation the Palestinian peasants would dig up or cut down their trees. This was one of the factors responsible for the tree-less state of the country which the Jewish colonists found when they returned in the nineteenth century.[16]

d. Civil strife and internal disorders

Almost from the very beginning of the Arab conquest of Palestine internal security disappeared. Even in the days of the illustrious Harun al-Rashid (786-809) wars between the Southern and the Northern Arab confederacies devasted wide areas of Palestine.[17] Wars between families, between villages, between tribes, and the incessant raids by the desert Bedouins, were a frequent occurrence. In the course of these disorders trees were cut down and wells stopped up with stones as a matter of revenge. The Bedouin tribes in raiding the countryside thought nothing of destroying the crops, killing or carrying off the cattle. These Bedouins were perfectly willing to sell their services and raid one village if paid to do so by another grudge-bearing village.

e. The land tenure system

Many of the Arab peasants were landless and lived on the land as tenants. One of the worst features of the Arab landholding system was the collective cultivation of the land prevalent in many villages and the periodic redistribution of the land among its tenants. This policy tended to discourage the individual tenant from making any improvements on the land which he tilled only temporarily. The obsolete farming methods of the Arab peasants were another factor in the low farm yield.

Added to this inefficient land tenure system were the ruinous money lending practices. The landowner not only owned the peasant's land, he was also his money lender. Interest charges on loans were exorbitant, amounting often to fifty per cent or more. The peasant was in perpetual indebtedness to the landowner, to the professional money lender, and to the tax farmer.

Under these circumstances many peasants abandoned their farms and took to Bedouin life. Whole areas of farmland were left uncultivated. Land terraces in the hill country were permitted to break down and remain unrepaired. Rivers and streams became dammed up, forming large malaria-ridden swamps. The desert was moving in from the east and south, while the sand dunes were rolling in from the seacoast.

4. CONCLUSION

In the whole era, from the dispersion of the Jews from Palestine in A.D. 135 until their modern Return in the nineteenth century, Palestine had known a measure of prosperity only in the Roman period and under the European Crusaders. The reason for this was the enforcement of law and order which made life secure and the trade routes safe. An added factor in the revived prosperity under the Crusaders was the considerable increase in the country's foreign trade.

But as one reviews the economic history of Palestine during the entire era in which the bulk of the Jewish people was in worldwide dispersion one cannot escape the conclusion that of the many and varied factors which had brought about the awful devastation of the Holy Land, the absence of the Jews was the most important single element in the whole picture. Had the Jews not been exiled from the country in the wars of 66-70 and 132-135 Palestine could hardly have experienced all this physical desolation and material destruction. Be that as it may, Palestine was not destined to prosper while her children were groaning in the oppression of the exile.

III. THE POSITION OF THE JEWISH COMMUNITY

1. THE ROMAN PERIOD

After the division of the Roman empire in the fourth century into an eastern and a western half, Palestine became part of the eastern or Byzantine half. The Jews in Palestine were concentrated in this period in Galilee where they still formed the majority of the population. Few Jews remained in the hills of Judaea. During the reign of Empress Eudocia the ban on Jewish residence in Jerusalem was revoked. The number of Jews in Palestine in the seventh century is estimated at about 200,000. When the Persians invaded Palestine in A.D. 614 the Jews are said to have aided the Persians by supplying some 20,000 Jewish soldiers to the Persian army. They were confident that in case of a lasting victory the Persians would permit them to re-establish their National Homeland. Persian occupation of Palestine was, however, short-lived and it ended after fifteen years.

With the rise of Islam in Arabia many Jews were driven from the Arabian peninsula by Mohammed whose aim was to rid Arabia, his new holy land, from all non-Muslim people. Six hundred Jews left Kainukaa, in Arabia, in 624 and settled at Adrat and in Jericho. A year later another group of Jews came to Jericho from Nadhir.[18]

2. THE ARAB PERIOD

During the Arab period the Jews lived in all parts of Palestine and derived their livelihood from agriculture and handicrafts. Tiberias was the Jewish center in the seventh and eighth centuries. There were important Jewish settlements in Lydda, Ramleh, Ascalon, Caesarea and Gaza. Some Jews took up their residence in Jerusalem. There was a revival of Jewish religious life in Palestine in this era, probably under the stimulus of a vigorous intellectual activity encouraged by the Umayyad and Abbasid Caliphs. This period saw a revival of interest in the study of the Hebrew language, a fresh outpouring of Hebrew poetry, and the activities of the Masoretes which culminated in the production of the all-important Masoretic text of the Old Testament. Many of the Synagogue hymns, still in use today, were the works of Palestine poets of that period, the greatest of whom is probably Eliezer b. Kalir.

After the decline of the two great Talmudic centers in Babylonia and the expiration of the Babylonian exilarchate Palestine became once again, temporarily at least, the spiritual center of Jewry. The head of the Jerusalem Yeshivah* assumed the title of Gaon of Jacob and was recognized as the religious authority for all Jews living in the territory ruled by the Fatimid dynasty. The Jewish sect of Karaites, who rejected the Talmudic regulation of Jewish life, established in Jerusalem an ascetic brotherhood of the Mourners of Zion and made Jerusalem the center of their movement. However, the number of Jews in Palestine in the Arab period was not large. The political unrest and the natural catastrophes which visited Palestine in that period impoverished the economic resources of the Palestine Jews and reduced their numbers.

3. THE PERIOD OF THE CRUSADES

The conquest of Palestine by the Crusaders was followed by massacres of the Jews. But as the initial fury had spent itself, and the government of the country became organized, a lenient attitude was adopted to both Jews and Muslims. In fact, the legal position of the Jews was better in Palestine than in Medieval Europe at that time. Jews who came to Palestine in the period of the Crusaders preferred to settle in the Christian rather than in the Muslim part of Palestine.[19]

---

* Yeshivah—center for Talmudic studies

4. THE MAMLUK PERIOD

Under the Mamluks the Jews of Palestine shared with the rest of the population in the further general decline of the country's economy. Notwithstanding this, there was a constant trickle of immigrants to Palestine in the Mamluk era. Some came from Europe, others from Muslim countries. It was in this era that a custom is said to have come into use whereby the better-to-do Jewish communities in the Dispersion were sending contributions to help support the Jews in Palestine.[20] Bad as the economic situation of the Palestine Jews was at that time, their intellectual life showed signs of a new vitality largely due to the activities of outstanding Rabbinic authorities, a number of whom had settled in Palestine in this period. About three hundred Rabbis and Talmudic scholars are said to have arrived in Palestine in 1211 from England and France, while the aged and venerable Rabbi Nachmanides came from Spain.

5. THE TURKISH PERIOD

The conquest of Palestine by the Turks augured well at the beginning for the Jewish inhabitants. Turkish policy was favorable to Jews in general. The Turks probably aimed to attract the Jews from the oppression of the European countries in order that the Turkish empire may benefit from Jewish economic activities. Accordingly, Palestine received a sizable influx of Spanish Jews when the Jews were driven from Spain in 1492. Galilee was still the center of the Jewish population in Palestine and Safad was the most important city where the Jews developed a thriving wool-weaving industry. Safad was also known as the center of Jewish mysticism. In Safad lived Joseph Caro, a Spanish-born Jew but raised in Turkey. Caro combined with his Jewish mysticism a profound knowledge of the Talmud, and it was he who composed the Shulhan Arukh designed to regulate the daily life of the Jew in accordance with Rabbinic teachings. The Jerusalem Jew, Isaac Luria, was also active in Safad, and under his leadership the Zohar became the absorbing study of the Jewish mystics. Safad had a Jewish population of some 15,000 by the middle of the sixteenth century.

The city of Tiberias was rebuilt with the help of Dona Gracia Mendes and her son-in-law, Don Joseph Nasi, who were wealthy Spanish Jewish refugees residing in Constantinople. They received permission from Suleiman the Magnificent to rebuild the city of Tiberias and to populate it with native and foreign Jews. Don Joseph

Nasi hoped to create there an autonomous refuge place for distressed European Jews. But the opposition of the powerful Franciscan order and the hostility of the local Arab tribes combined to wreck his plans. An attempt to revive the scheme of Don Joseph Nasi was made by an influential Jewish courtier at the court of Constantinople whose name was Solomon ibn Ayesh. He secured for his son a concession to develop the city of Tiberias and the commercial possibilities of the warm springs and its fishing industry. But Tiberias never attained the commercial significance of Safad.

Jerusalem occupied the third place as a center of Jewish residence and intellectual activity. Hebron had but a small Jewish community which was struggling for survival amidst a powerful and hostile Muslim populace.

During the era of the Great Dispersion the Jewish position in Palestine reached its lowest point in the first half of the nineteenth century. According to a report by the British consul in Jerusalem in 1839 the Jewish population in Palestine was distributed as follows: Jerusalem had 5000 Jews; Safad, 1500; Hebron, 750; Tiberias, 600; Acre, 200; Haifa, 150; Jaffa, 60; Nablus, 150. The villages were said to have some 400 Jews. The total Jewish population in Palestine in 1839 amounted to some 10,000. From then on the number of Jews in Palestine began to increase. In 1880 there were some 25,000 Jews in Palestine.[21]

Palestine had four groups of Jews according to their point of origin. There were the Jews who took pride in the fact that they were the descendants of Jews who had never left the country and, consequently, had never known the meaning of exile. At the time when Britain received the Palestine Mandate there was one group of these Jews left in the whole of Palestine, who were living in the village of Pekiin and who were like the surrounding Arabs in all ways save their religion. Then, there were the so-called Sephardic Jews, who were descendants of Jews driven out of Spain and Portugal. They constituted the largest Jewish community in the beginning of the nineteenth century. The third group were the Askenazi Jews who came to Palestine from parts of Christian Europe other than Spain and Portugal. They gradually increased in numbers and importance. The fourth group were the Jews from Muslim countries, i.e., Turkey and Arabic-speaking lands.

At this juncture mention should be made of the part which the British Government played in the improvement of the Jewish position in Palestine in the second half of the nineteenth century. On January 31, 1839, Mr. Young, the first British Consul in Jerusalem, received from the British Foreign Office the following note: "I am directed by Viscount Palmerston to state to you that it will be a part of your duty as British Vice-consul at Jerusalem to afford protection to the Jews generally: and you will take an early opportunity of reporting to his Lordship upon the present state of the Jewish population in Palestine."[22] In November of the same year Mr. Young received further instructions authorizing him to take under his protection Jewish subjects of other European powers if requested to do so by the consuls of these powers whose offices were at that time located in Alexandria. The importance of this measure may be seen from this that while the various Christian religious groups were under the protection of France and Russia, the Jewish group had no governmental representation to defend its interests. These functions of the British Consulate played an important part in the local history of the Jews from 1839 to 1893.[23]

About the same time British and French Jews began to interest themselves in the condition of the Palestine Jews. Moses Montefiore, a prominent British Jew, made seven trips to Palestine and had done much to bring the plight of Palestine's Jews to the attention of world Jewry. In 1860 the French Jews founded the Alliance Israelite Universelle and this society came in time to represent the philanthropic interests of French, British and American Jews on behalf of the Jews of Palestine. The agricultural school Mikveh Israel, still in existence, was founded by the Alliance Israelite Universelle which purchased for this purpose a large tract of land outside of Jaffa. In 1875 some Palestine Jews took the first step to improve the position of Palestine Jewry by resettlement on land. A group of Jews from Jerusalem purchased some land north of Jaffa and named the site Petach Tikvah.*

In the second half of the nineteenth century outstanding Jews in Central and Eastern Europe came up with many ideas about establishing agricultural colonies in Palestine and settle them with European Jews. The Rumanian Jews had founded two agricultural settlements in Palestine in 1882: one, named later Zikhron Jacob, at Samaria, south of Mt. Carmel: the other, called Rosh Pina, on the road from Tiberias to Lake Huleh. Russian Jews, under the influence of the so-called Biluim, established one colony at Rishon Letzion,

---

* Petach Tikvah—Door of Hope

and another in Petach Tikvah, which had been temporarily abandoned by the Jerusalem Jews. The Polish Jews founded a colony in 1883 north of Rosh Pina.

The colonists met in the beginning with many reverses. They were not accustomed to the Palestinian climate, they suffered from lack of financial resources, they encountered much hostility from the local populace and the Turkish Government, and they lacked farming experience. Baron Edmund de Rothschild of the French branch of the famous Jewish banking family came to the colonists' rescue and took them under his supervision. In 1899 supervision of the Jewish colonies passed from Rothschild to the Jewish Colonization Association. Within a few years after it had come into existence the Zionist Organization began to take an active interest in the colonization program in Palestine.

In 1914, the year of the outbreak of the First World War, there were some 12,000 Jews settled on land in Palestine and working about 100,000 acres. The total Jewish population in Palestine in 1914 numbered about 100,000. In the first half of the nineteenth century the Jewish population in Palestine numbered 10,000 to about 200,000 non-Jews. In 1914 there were 100,000 Jews to 700,000 non-Jews. There was a fundamental difference between the immigration of Jews to Palestine in the second half of the nineteenth century and all other previous immigrations to Palestine. While in former times Jews went to Palestine because they believed that a special virtue or reward is attached to, or derived from, living or dying in the Holy Land, the driving power of the Return which began in the second half of the nineteenth century was the desire to rebuild the Jewish National Homeland.

6. CONCLUSION

In taking leave of this subject two things need to be emphasized. First, when the Jewish National Homeland was destroyed by the Romans, and the Jewish people dispersed all over the world, Palestine was not left without Jews. A small group remained in the Holy Land and clung doggedly to the country and was being reinforced from time to time by immigration from the outside. Thus a Jewish community was in existence in Palestine through all the centuries of the Great Dispersion, dwelling amidst the ruins and desolations of the country, but holding on—a link between the past and the future—until the exile would come to an end, and those dispersed abroad would return. The second thing is this: when the modern Return had brought Jews to Palestine in large numbers and the work of reconstruction of the National Homeland had begun, in the space of 50-60 years the Jews repaired much of the damage which foreign invaders had inflicted on the Holy Land during an era of some twelve hundred years.

Notes to Chapter 1

[1] Emil Schürer, *A History Of The Jewish People In The Time Of Jesus Christ* (T. & T. Clark: Edinburgh, 1900), First Division, vol. 2, p. 253.

[2] H. H. Milman, *The History Of The Jews* (A. C. Armstrong & Son: New York, 1885), vol. 2, pp. 388.9.

[3] Ibid., P. 443.

[4] James Parkes, *A History Of Palestine* (Victor Gollancz: London, 1949), p. 54. Used by permission of Oxford University Press (New York).

[5] Ibid., p. 136.

[6] Ibid., p. 154.

[7] Ibid., p. 221.

[8] Ibid., p. 201.

[9] Ibid., p. 13.

[10] Frederick C. Grant, *The Economic Background Of The Gospels* (Oxford University Press: London, 1926), p. 55. Used by permission.

[11] Walter Clay Lowdermilk, *Palestine, Land of Promise,* (Harper & Bros.: New York, 1944), p. 62. Used by permission.

[12] Lamartine, I., pp. 268, 308-9; quoted in a footnote by Jacob De Haas, *History Of Palestine* (The Macmillan Company: New York, 1934), p. 407.

[13] Dean Stanley, *Sinai And Palestine,* pp. 136, 183; quoted in a footnote by Jacob De Haas, Op. Cit., p. 407.

[14] Jacob De Haas, Op. Cit., p. 16.

[15] Walter Clay Lowdermilk, Op. Cit., p. 78.

[16] Ibid., pp. 74-5.

[17] James Parkes, Op. Cit., p. 96.

[18] Jacob De Haas, Op. Cit., p. 122.

[19] James Parkes, Op. Cit., p. 122.

[20] Ibid., p. 146.

[21] Ibid., p. 261.

[22] Ibid., p. 263.

[23] Ibid., p. 264.

PART TWO

Israel's Resurrection

"Yet for all that, when they are in the land of their enemies, I will not spurn them, neither will I abhor them so as to destroy them utterly and break my covenant with them; for I am the LORD their God. But I will for their sake remember the covenant with their forefathers, whom I brought forth out of the land of Egypt in the sight of the nations, that I might be their God: I am the LORD" (Leviticus 26: 45).

"Comfort, comfort my people, says your God. Speak tenderly to Jerusalem, and proclaim unto her that her affliction is ended, that her guilt is paid off, that she has received from the LORD's hand double for all her sins. A voice of one calling: In the wilderness prepare the way of the LORD, make smooth in the desert a road for our God. Every valley shall be lifted up, and every mountain and hill shall be made low; the uneven ground shall become level, and the rough places a plain. And the glory of the LORD shall be revealed, and all flesh shall see it together, for the mouth of the LORD has spoken" (Isaiah 40: 1-5).

"For Zion's sake I shall not be silent, and for Jerusalem's sake I shall not rest, till her righteousness breaks forth like morning brightness, and her salvation like a blazing torch. And nations will see your righteousness, and all kings your glory; and men will call you by a new name, which the mouth of the LORD will determine. And you will be an adorning coronet in the hand of the LORD, and a royal diadem in the hand of your God. You will no more be called 'Forsaken', and your land will no more be called 'Desolate'; but you shall be called 'My delight is in her', and your land, 'Married'; for the LORD delights in you, and your land shall be married. For as a young man marries a virgin, so shall your sons marry you, and as the bridegroom rejoices over the bride, so shall your God rejoice over you" (Isaiah 62: 1-5).

"Who has heard such a thing? Who has seen such things? Shall a land be born in one day? Shall a nation be brought forth in one moment? For as soon as Zion was in labor she brought forth her sons. Shall I bring to the birth and not cause to bring forth? says the LORD; shall I, who cause to bring forth, shut the womb? says your God"* (Isaiah 66: 8-10).

"The hand of the LORD was upon me, and he brought me out by the Spirit of the LORD, and set me down in the midst of the valley; it was full of bones. And he led me round among them; and behold, there were very many upon the valley; and lo, they were very dry. And he said to me, 'Son of man, can these bones live?' And I answered, 'O Lord God, thou knowest.' Again he said to me, 'Prophesy to these bones and say to them, O dry bones, hear the word of the LORD. Thus says the Lord God to these bones: Behold, I will cause breath to enter you, and you shall live. And I will lay sinews upon you, and will cause flesh to come upon you, and cover you with skin, and put breath in you, and you shall live; and you shall know that I am the LORD.'

So I prophesied as I was commanded; and as I prophesied, there was a noise, and behold, a rattling; and the bones came together, bone to its bone. And as I looked, there were sinews on them, and flesh came upon them, and skin had covered them; but there was no breath in them. Then he said to me, 'Prophesy to the breath, prophesy, son of man, and say to the breath, Thus says the Lord God: Come from the four winds, O breath, and breathe upon these slain, that they may live.' So I prophesied as he commanded me, and the breath came into them, and they lived, and stood upon their feet, an exceedingly great host.

Then he said to me, 'Son of man, these bones are the whole house of Israel; behold, they say, 'Our bones are dried up, and our hope is lost; we are clean cut off.' Therefore prophesy, and say to them, Thus says the Lord God: Behold, I will open your graves, and raise you from your graves, O my people; and I will bring you home into the land of Israel. And you shall know that I am the LORD, when I open your graves, and raise you from your graves, O my people. And I will put my Spirit within you, and you shall live, and I will place you in your own land; then you shall know that I, the LORD, have spoken, and I have done it, says the LORD.

. . . Behold, I will take the people of Israel from the nations among which they have gone, and will gather them from all sides,

---

* The above passage speaks of the precipitate speed and certainty which will mark Israel's rebirth when the hour of her national deliverance will strike.

and bring them to their own land . . . They shall dwell in the land where your fathers dwelt that I gave to my servant Jacob; they and their children and their children's children shall dwell there for ever; and David my servant shall be their prince for ever. I will make a covenant of peace with them; it shall be an everlasting covenant with them; and I will bless them and multiply them, and will set my sanctuary in the midst of them for evermore. My dwelling place shall be with them; and I will be their God, and they shall be my people. Then the nations will know that I the LORD sanctify Israel, when my sanctuary is in the midst of them forevermore" (Ezekiel 37: 1-14, 21, 25-28).

"Now as they were eating, Jesus took bread, and blessed, and broke it, and gave it to the disciples and said, 'Take, eat; this is my body.' And he took a cup, and when he had given thanks he gave it to them, saying, 'Drink of it, all of you. For this is my blood of the covenant, which is poured out for many for the forgiveness of sins. I tell you I shall not drink again of this fruit of the vine until that day when I drink it new with you in my Father's kingdom' " (Matthew 26: 26-29).

"You are those who have continued with me in my trials. As my Father appointed a kingdom for me, so do I appoint for you. That you may eat and drink at my table in my kingdom, and sit on thrones judging the twelve tribes of Israel" (Luke 22: 28-30).

CHAPTER 2

THE ARABS

CHAPTER 2

THE ARABS

No one can approach the problem which the Middle East poses in the contemporary world without a knowledge of the Arabs who occupy the largest part of the Middle East. Prior to the advent of Islam the name "Arab" referred to the people who inhabited the Arabian Peninsula. The earliest mention of Arabs is to be found in the book of Isaiah (eighth century B.C.) where we read: " . . . no Arab will pitch his tent there" (Isaiah 13:20). Another Biblical reference to Arabs is contained in the book of Jeremiah: " . . . like an Arab in the wilderness" (Jeremiah 3:2). The first mention of the existence of Arabs recorded in extra-Biblical sources is that found in Assyrian documents of 854 B.C., representing the Arabs as camel-herding Bedouins.[1] Historically speaking, the Arabs have been identified with the desert in the last twenty-eight hundred years.

Following the advent of Islam in the seventh century the Arabs conquered, in a short time, large areas in the Middle East and in the Mediterranean region, imposing their newly found religion, language, and culture upon the conquered peoples. From then on the word "Arab" identified all those whose native tongue is Arabic, who feel as Arabs, or who speak of themselves as Arabs.

I. THE ARAB CHARACTER

When historians describe the character of Arabs, they have in mind chiefly the Bedouin or nomadic Arabs and those on whom they imposed their way of life. Ibn Khaldun, one of the great early Arab historians (A.D. 1332-1406), represents the Arabs as a people of a savage nature who plunder and wipe out the civilization of the lands which they conquer. They enjoy savagery because they want freedom from authority and from subservience to leadership.[2]

While certain essential character traits are common to all Arab peoples, Arabs inhabiting different areas of the Middle East display certain features which are peculiar to one particular region. Already in the days of the Arab historian Maqrizi (A.D. 1364-1442) there were Iraqui Arabs, Syrian Arabs, Egyptian Arabs, Yemenite Arabs, etc.[3]

II. THE INFLUENCE OF THE DESERT ENVIRONMENT

The sharp contrasts which mark the Arabs' desert habitat have left deep imprints in the Arab soul and culture. A people "formed in such an environment, although ordinarily calm and apathetic, is subject to sudden and violent outbursts of passions, to momentary but irresistible upsurges of energy, to alternatives of chivalrous generosity and savage ferocity. At the same time rapacious and hospitable, greedy and generous, deserving of both blame and admiration, the Arabs exhibit a disconcerting mixture of the most contrasting tendencies. The extremes meet and mix in them, or follow each other abruptly: there are no transitions, no degrees, no nuances in feelings and ideas."[4]

III. ISLAM'S CONTRIBUTION TO ARAB CULTURE

While in the Biblical faith man is represented as being responsible for choosing, of his own free will, between good and evil (see, e.g., Deuteronomy 30:19), in the religion of Islam a person's life is sharply circumscribed and is determined by God from the beginning to the end. There is nothing left for man but "to go through the course of events which have been written down for him in God's Book to the smallest detail. Not even in everyday life can a man do anything either to hasten or otherwise influence events . . . it does not pay and is not even possible to try to do anything to procure an advantage. . . . [Man] himself can do nothing either for or against it. In small things as in great, man is absolutely subject to fate . . . , even his deeds and the way in which he acts are decided beforehand. The logical consequence of such a view is that man has no free will, and further is not personally responsible for his morality and his deeds."[5]

His Islamic orientation makes the Arab attribute "the ills of his society, his mistakes and failures either to fate, to the devil, or to imperialism. Whenever he is blamed for his passivity or corruption, the answer to the accusation is that he is forced by an uncontrollable factor about which he can do nothing. This refusal to assume responsibility in the issues of his life and environment increases the Arab's weakness and encourages his surrender, as if fate were found to act against him and not for him."[6]

Social services are terribly inadequate in the Muslim Middle East. Illiteracy, disease, and squalor, along with abject poverty, are the things which strike the visitor to these parts. Bilharziasis and ankylostomiasis are widespread in Egypt; malaria and trachoma, with its high toll of blindness, in other Middle East countries. A serious obstacle in the eradication of these evils is the general attitude of the

Muslim population. "All disease, they believe, comes from Allah, and if He, in His inscrutable wisdom, desires restoration to health, scientific treatment in a hospital will make no difference."[7]

"A child born crippled limps through life; a child made blind by trachoma is a victim of Allah's will, not man's. And who was to say that Allah chose wrongly in singling out this child? In this gateway [i.e., Cairo] to the Middle East, I realized I had plunged back through the centuries to an almost unbelievable way of life. . . . It was truly pointed out to us that as far as the Middle East was concerned, the French and American Revolutions might never have taken place. The doctrine of human rights and personal liberty— the concept that man has dignity as a human being and the latent power to lift himself from the mire of animal existence—had not penetrated the citadels of Islamic authoritarianism."[8] These are the words of the distinguished member appointed by President Truman to the Anglo-American Committee of Inquiry sent to Palestine prior to the United Nations decision to authorize the creation of a Jewish State in Palestine.

In an authoritative work on the Arab personality the author says this: "In general the Arab mind, dominated by Islam, has been bent more on preserving than innovating, on maintaining than improving, on containing than initiating. In this atmosphere, whatever individual spirit of research and inquiry existed in the great age of medieval Arab culture became gradually stifled; by the fifteenth century, Arab intellectual curiosity was fast asleep. It was to remain inert until awakened four centuries later by an importunate West knocking on its doors."[9]

According to Wilfred Cantwell Smith, "the burning of Cairo [on January 26, 1952], the assassination of Prime Ministers, the intimidating of Christians, the vehemence and hatred in their literature— all this is to be understood in terms of a people who have lost their way, whose heritage has proven unequal to modernity, whose leaders have been dishonest, whose ideals have failed. In this aspect, the new Islamic upsurge [of the Muslim Brothers] is a force not to solve problems but to intoxicate those who cannot longer abide the failure to solve them."[10]

IV. ARAB DISUNION

One of the most puzzling phenomena about the Arabs is the lack of unity among the various Arab nations, notwithstanding the fact that they speak the same language and have predominantly the same religion and culture. Competent authorities are convinced that the true explanation for this is to be found in the Arab character and Arab history prior to the rise of Islam among the Arabs. Driven by the zeal of their newly acquired religion of Islam, as well as by lust for power and wealth, the Arabs poured out of their deserts and within a century overran vast spaces in the Middle East, extending their rule to Spain and reaching as far as the southern border of France. But the Arabs governed this large empire not more than a century. Beginning with the second half of the eighth century, rule of the empire passed out of the hands of the Arabs and into those of other Muslim peoples. This state of affairs was brought about when the old feuds between Arab tribes began to reassert themselves. Assassinations; civil wars between the southern and northern Arab confederacies; and wars between tribes, villages, and even families marked the Arab period of the new Muslim empire. These rivalries and internecine strifes have continued to the present day.[11]

C. F. Volney, who traveled widely in the Arab world in the eighteenth century, describes the effects of these bloody feuds on conditions in Syria and Palestine in the following words: "This discord, which has prevailed throughout the country from the earliest times of the Arabs, causes a perpetual civil war. . . . The mutual devastations of the contending parties render the appearance of this part of Syria more wrecked than that of any other."[12]

A Yemenite noble says this about his countrymen: "The people of Yemen and Asir are still savage; not one of them would trust his brother. They live in perpetual fear and anxiety. . . . They are like wild beasts which fear everything and everybody that may come near them. As to the Yemen . . . all our people are armed, all fight, and all kill for the least thing. We are very jealous for our rights. . . . If in this village two houses should suddenly engage in a fight, the entire population would split into two parties and join in the fight. War could break out in the village. When it subsides, and only then, would the people ask what the cause of the fighting was. They fight first, and then inquire as to the cause of the fight. This is our way of life in Yemen. We fight our own relatives. The brother would fight his own brother, the son his own father. . . ."[13]

"Civil disobedience, taking the form of armed resistance to the government, is a possibility that is always close to the surface in Arab countries. . . . The view that the world is an inimical place where a man must be ready and able to defend himself and his family by force of arms, even against his next door neighbor, is shared by the majority of the population in every Arab country. . . . Arab disunity is a manifestation of a tendency that has been part of the Arab personality since pre-Islamic days. At every level discord has always been present, either actually or potentially. At the slightest provocation the fighting propensity surfaces, a quarrel ensues and easily degenerates into physical violence. . . . Conflict proneness is an outstanding characteristic of the Arab mind."[14]

V.   ARAB STAGNATION

The October 1956 issue of the *Atlantic Monthly* issued a supplement entitled *Perspective of the Arab World* containing a collection of articles written by eminent Arabist scholars. The chronology with which this supplement concludes has fifty-four entries. Of these, twenty-seven entries cover a period of 758 years from A.D. 500–1258. During the major part of this period the Middle East, conquered by the Arabs, had still been exposed, directly or indirectly, to European civilization of which it was an inseparable part prior to the Arab conquests. Only one single entry in the above mentioned chronology deals with the 540 years period between A.D. 1258–1798; the period during which the Middle East was tightly sealed off from European influence. In 1798 the Napoleonic invasion opened up the Middle East once again to European civilization from which it was severed by the Arab conquests. This period of 158 years from 1798–1956 is covered in the above cited chronology by twenty-six entries. These figures are an impressive testimony of the depth of stagnation which settled upon the Middle East in the wake of the Arab conquest following the rise of Islam. The Arab scholar Hitti states that prior to the invasion of Egypt by Napoleon "the people of the Arab world were generally leading a self-contained, traditional, conventional life, achieving no progress and unmindful of the progress of the world outside. Change did not interest them. This abrupt contact with the West gave them the first knock that helped to awaken them from their medieval slumber."[15]

Atiyah, another Arab scholar, declares that until the Napoleonic invasion of Egypt the Arabs had become ossified socially and intellectually. "They had gradually lost the ability to think their way into fresh fields of endeavour and discovery. . . ."[16]

Faris and Husayn state that "until the closing years of the eighteenth century the Arab world was in a state of near stagnation, ingrown, content with its prevailing conditions, resigned to its fate, and blissfully ignorant of the events unfolding around it. Then the West descended upon the Arab world as a conqueror, bringing its culture and science, its missionaries, moral values, and concepts, its mercantile goods and commodities, and political, economic, and military domination." According to these authors the roots of Arab stagnation "go far back into the history of the Arab people," and they maintain that one of the great contributing factors of Arab stagnation is the low position in which the Arabs keep their women.[17]

In a book entitled *These Are the Chains*, the Arab author attributes much of the low Arab status to the religion of Islam. "Ignorance," he says, "based on religious doctrine has tied our people with knot upon knot. . . ." It is "the low state of Islam in every field of human endeavor" which "carries over into the depressed situation of the individual Muslim as compared to the individual Christian in whichever country the two groups are living side by side."[18]

Farrukh, another Arab observer, attributes Arab backwardness to the institutions of learning in Arab lands "which carry the name of seats of learning, but whose original purpose was to keep sound and profitable learning away from the Arabs, and to offer us only theoretical and elaborate subjects such as could not profit us even if they occupied the whole people. . . . At the same time we were cut off from the more important and profitable sciences and arts on which civilization and society turn—and such were studied in Europe by those attending even elementary schools."[19]

Munif Razzaz, who at one time was secretary-general of the Ba'ath Party in Syria, says that beginning with the tenth century Islamic society "became stagnant, tranquil, self-satisfied . . . the spirit of innovation was stifled." He then goes on to say that if not for the impact of Western civilization this state of affairs would have lasted indefinitely.[20]

Notes to Chapter 2

1 Raphael Patai, *The Arab Mind* (Charles Scribner's Sons: New York, 1973), p. 12. I am indebted for much of the information in this chapter to this authoritative work on the Arabs.

2 Ibn Khaldun, *Muqaddima* (Introduction to History); translated from Arabic by Franz Rosenthal (Pantheon Books: New York, 1958), vol. 1, pp. 299, 302, 303, 305.

3 Taqi al-Din Ahmad al-Maqrizi, *Description topographique et historique de l'Egypte: Memoires publiés par les membres de la mission archéologique française au Caire* (Leroux: Paris 1900), vol. 17, p. 139.

[4] Leon Gauthier, *Introduction a l'etude de la philosophie musulmane* (Leroux: Paris, 1923), pp. 34-6. Reprinted with permission of Presses Universitaires de France (Paris).

[5] Hilma Granquist, *Birth and Childhood Among the Arabs* (Söderstrom and Co.: Helsingfors, 1947), p. 177.

[6] Sania Hamady, *Temperament and Character of the Arabs* (Twayne Publishers: New York, 1960), pp. 187-8. Reprinted with permission of Twayne Publishers, a division of G. K. Hall and Co. (Boston).

[7] S. A. Morrison, *Middle East Survey* (S.C.M. Press: London, 1954), p. 94.

[8] Bartley C. Crum, *Behind the Silken Curtain* (Simon and Schuster: New York, 1947), p. 153.

[9] Raphael Patai, Op. Cit., pp. 154-5.

[10] Wilfred Cantwell Smith, *Islam in Modern History* (The New American Library: New York, 1961), pp. 163-4.

[11] See article by Terrence Smith, entitled "Feud Between Bedouin Clans in Sinai Tests Israelis' Diplomatic Skills,"*New York Times*, May 23, 1975.

[12] C. F. Volney, *Travels Through Syria and Egypt in the Years 1783, 1784 and 1785* (London: 1788), vol. 2, p. 203.

[13] Ameen Faris Rihani, Muluk al-Arab (Bierut, 1953, 3rd edition), vol. 1, p. 117; quoted by Nabih Amin Faris and Mohammed Tawfik Husayn in *The Crescent in Crisis: An Interpretive Study of the Modern World* (University of Kansas Press: Lawrence Kansas, 1955), p. 179. Rihani's book and its publisher could not be found in any of the catalogues.

[14] Raphael Patai, Op. Cit., pp. 220-1, 225, 227.

[15] Philip K. Hitti, *History of the Arabs* (St. Martin's Press: New York, 8th ed., 1964), p. 745.

[16] Edward Atiyah, *The Arabs* (Penguin Books: Baltimore, Md., 1955), p. 73.

[17] Nabih Amin Faris and Mohammed Tawfik Husayn, Op. Cit., pp. 46, 168, 172.

[18] Abdallah ali al-Qasimi, *These Are the Chains* (Cairo, 1946), pp. 12-70; Summarized by von Grunebaum, *Islam: Essays on the Nature and Growth of a Cultural Tradition* (Routledge and Kegan: Boston, Mass., 1964), pp. 217-9.

[19] Omar A. Farrukh, *The Arab Genius in Science and Philosophy* (The American Council of Learned Societies: Washington, D.C., 1954), pp. 155-8.

[20] Munif Razzaz, "Arab Nationalism," article in *The Middle East: A Handbook*, ed. by Michael Adams (Praeger Publishers: New York, 1971), p. 353. Copyright 1971 by Anthony Blond Ltd (London).

CHAPTER 3

PALESTINE UNDER THE MANDATE:

A.   *The Period Of 1917-1939*

I. The Palestine Mandate In Operation

1. The Disturbances of 1920
2. The Churchill White Paper
3. The Disturbances of 1929
4. The Disturbances of 1936-1939
5. The Peel Commission
6. The White Paper of 1939

II. Arab Attacks On Jewish Settlements

CHAPTER 3

PALESTINE UNDER THE MANDATE:

A. The Period of 1917-1939

On November 2, 1917, the British Government issued the Balfour Declaration which promised to world Jewry Britain's assistance in the establishment of a Jewish National Home in Palestine. On July 24, 1922, the League of Nations created the Palestine Mandate with the incorporation into it of the Balfour Declaration. The implementation of the Palestine Mandate was entrusted to England.

I. THE PALESTINE MANDATE IN OPERATION

1. THE DISTURBANCES OF 1920

The chief cause behind these disturbances is said to have been the unsettled situation in Syria where Arab nationalists were struggling with the French for the control of the country. Arab discontent with the way things were shaping up in Syria spilled over into neighboring Palestine. For some weeks before the outbreak there was a discernible tense atmosphere in the country. Marauding bands of Arabs were prowling the hill country in the north. Joseph Trumpeldor, one of the promising leaders in the Jewish Chalutz* movement, was killed with five of his companions when he rushed to the defense of Tel Hai, a young Jewish colony near the Syrian border. On Nebi-Musa day, an Arab festival which in that year coincided with the Jewish Passover and the Christian Easter, large crowds were assembled at the Mosque of Omar in Jerusalem. There they listened to fiery speeches filled with violent incitement. Large processions of Arabs marching from the Mosque through the streets of Jerusalem began attacking Jews with the result that there was some loss of life.

When Weizmann, who had arrived in Palestine shortly before the riots, heard rumors of impending disturbances, he informed the British military authorities about the menacing situation and asked them to take extra precautionary measures. They, however, assured him that there was nothing to these rumors, and that the situation was under control. One of the London *Times* correspondents who was in Pales-

---

* Chalutz—pioneer

tine at the time of the riots, wrote in his account of the happenings that while the Zionists overemphasized the scope and significance of the riots, the military administration was not without blame. The Arabs were encouraged by the pro-Arab and pan-Arab sympathies of some of the British officers, and there was an unwillingness on the part of some of the responsible chiefs to adopt a helpful attitude to the Zionist cause.[1]

2. THE CHURCHILL WHITE PAPER

The Churchill White Paper published in June 1922 was the first British Government interpretation of the meaning of the Balfour Declaration. The British Government was preparing to submit the Palestine Mandate to the League of Nations for its approval. An Arab delegation came to England seeking to influence public opinion against the Mandate. The British Parliament debated the Balfour Declaration. A motion to repeal it was made and it won in the House of Lords by a substantial majority. But it was heavily defeated in the House of Commons. In the meantime discussions were carried on between the Colonial Office and the London Zionist Executive about matters connected with the final text of the Mandate to be submitted to the League of Nations. The main points of the Churchill Memorandum which came to be known as the Churchill White Paper were communicated first to the London Zionist group before its official publication. Weizmann relates in his memoirs that it was made clear to the London Zionist Executive "that confirmation of the Mandate would be conditional on our acceptance of the policy as interpreted in the White Paper".[2] The Zionist Executive signified its approval following which it was made public.

The White Paper of 1922 was the first official attempt on the part of the British Government to state what the Balfour Declaration meant and what it did not mean. It was aimed at both the Arab and the Jewish sections of the population. It declared that "the tension which has prevailed from time to time in Palestine is mainly due to apprehensions, which are entertained both by sections of the Arab and by sections of the Jewish population. These apprehensions, so far as the Arabs are concerned, are partly based upon exaggerated interpretations of the meaning of the Declaration favoring the establishment of a Jewish National Home in Palestine, made on behalf of His Majesty's Government on November 2, 1917. Unauthorized statements have been made to the effect that the purpose in view is to create a wholly Jewish Palestine. Phrases have been used such as that

Palestine is to become 'as Jewish as England is English'. His Majesty's Government regard any such expectation as impracticable and have no such aim in view. Nor have they at any time contemplated, as appears to be feared by the Arab Delegation, the disappearance or the subordination of the Arabic population, language or culture in Palestine. They would draw attention to the fact that the terms of the Declaration referred to do not contemplate that Palestine as a whole should be converted into a Jewish National Home, but that such a Home should be founded in Palestine.[3]

"So far as the Jewish population of Palestine is concerned, it appears that some among them are apprehensive that His Majesty's Government may depart from the policy embodied in the Declaration of 1917. It is necessary, therefore, once more to affirm that these fears are unfounded, and that that Declaration, reaffirmed by the Conference of the Principal Allied Powers at San Remo and again in the treaty of Sevres, is not susceptible of change".[4] In another passage the White Paper reassured the Jewish community in Palestine that the Jews are in Palestine "as of right and not on sufferance . . . For the fulfilment of this policy [of the Balfour Declaration] it is necessary that the Jewish community in Palestine should be able to increase its numbers by immigration".[5]

The importance of the White Paper of 1922 in the history of the Palestine Mandate is derived from the following considerations:

1) It has detached Transjordan from Mandate Palestine thus removing large stretches of land from the Jewish colonization program. Had this not been done, and had Great Britain taken the lead in the creation of adequate irrigation schemes, there would have been enough land for both Jews and Arabs.

2) The White Paper of 1922 discloses the beginning of a tendency of the British Government to use ambiguous language when dealing with Palestine. A Jewish National Home is to be established in Palestine, but Palestine as a whole is not to be converted into a Jewish National Home. It is this sort of language which left nobody satisfied and created a great deal of confusion.

3) That this White Paper did not intend to preclude the eventual creation of a Jewish State in Palestine was affirmed by its author, Mr. Churchill himself, when testifying before the Palestine Royal Commission.[6]

3. THE DISTURBANCES OF 1929

In so far as it reflected the age-long yearnings of the Jewish people for the restoration of the Jewish National Homeland in Palestine the Zionist Organization was a national Jewish movement. As a political party, however, its membership represented only a segment of world Jewry. Therefore, the League of Nations Mandate for Palestine contained a provision for the creation of a Jewish Agency which should be representative of all Jews willing to participate in the work of rebuilding the Jewish National Home.

Accordingly, shortly after the Palestine Mandate had been confirmed by the League of Nations negotiations were begun between the World Zionist Organization and the various Jewish parties and groupings with a view to setting up the Jewish Agency for Palestine. These discussions were rather protracted. In the end, all differences were composed and an agreement was reached. On August 11th, 1929, the first constituent meeting of the Jewish Agency opened in Zurich, Switzerland. All sections of the world Jewish community, from the various countries having Jewish populations, were represented at that meeting. "The Jewish Agency brought together as distinguished a group of Jews as we have witnessed in our time; all classes and fields of achievement were represented, from Leon Blum, the great socialist leader, to Marshall and Warburg on the right; from Lord Melchett, one of England's leading industrialists, to Albert Einstein the scientist and Chaim Nachman Bialik the poet".[7] A new milestone was reached in the history of the reconstruction of the Jewish Homeland. In the Jewish Agency the Jews of the world, representing a variety of political, economic and social concepts, banded together to lend a helping hand in the rebuilding of Palestine.

On August 23, 1929, riots broke out in Palestine. Coming only twelve days following the first meeting of the Jewish Agency, it was evident that these riots were the Arab answer to the creation of the Jewish Agency. The immediate cause was the Wailing Wall incident. The evil spirit behind the disturbances of 1929, as well as of many others, was the infamous Mufti of Jerusalem, President of the Supreme Moslem Council. To precipitate the riots appeals were made to the religious fanaticism of the Arab masses. Jewish hospitals and synagogues were attacked, 133 Jews killed, and 339 wounded, and six Jewish colonies were destroyed. The Jews retaliated and about 116 Arabs were killed.

On September 14, 1929, a Commission of Inquiry was appointed with Sir Walter Shaw as chairman "to inquire into the immediate causes of the recent outbreak and to make recommendation as to the steps necessary to avoid recurrence".[8]

The Shaw Report was published in April 1930. It stated that the cause of the riot is to be found in the Arab feeling of hostility to the Jews, stemming from a fear that Jewish immigration and land purchases will eventually result in the displacement of the Arabs and their passing under the domination of the Jews.[9] The Report also stated that the Arab attack was "neither provoked, premeditated, nor directed against the British Administration".[10] It tended to exonerate the Mufti from planning or inciting the riots. It found no fault in the manner in which the Administration handled the situation before reinforcements arrived from Malta and Egypt.

Among its most important recommendations designed to prevent future disturbances the Shaw Commission suggested that the Government define its policy with reference to that part of the Mandate which speaks of safeguarding the rights of non-Jewish communities; review the matter of regulation and control of Jewish immigration; explore the subject of land cultivation and settlement possibilities; in the meantime, eviction of Arab peasant cultivators should be halted; the Government should define its policy with reference to Article 4 of the Palestine Mandate dealing with the status of the Jewish Agency.[11]

In accordance with League of Nations regulations covering the subject of Mandated Territories England, as the Mandatory for Palestine, was required to report annually to the League Council through the Permanent Mandates Commission on the state of Palestine.[12] In agreement with the above, England forwarded to the Permanent Mandates Commission a report covering the 1929 riots, the Shaw findings and recommendations. The Permanent Mandates Commission met in an extraordinary session in June 1930 to study the British Government's memorandum. In August 1930 the Permanent Mandates Commission published the results of its study of the British memorandum. It contained a rejection of the view of the Shaw Report that the outbreak was unexpected or unpremeditated, and that it was not aimed at the British authorities. It declared that had a little foresight been exercised the disturbances might have been avoided. It stated that the inaction of the Mandatory was the chief cause of the disturbances. It accused the Mandatory of not maintaining adequate forces to provide "the essential condition for development of the Jewish National Home, security for persons and property".[13]

In compliance with some of the recommendations of the Shaw Report the British Government announced in May 1930 the appointment of Sir John Hope Simpson to inquire into the subject of land settlement, development and immigration. In October 1930 the Government published the Simpson Report together with a Government Statement of Policy in the form of a White Paper. This Statement of Policy is also known as the Passfield White Paper, so called because Lord Passfield was the Colonial Secretary. The chief points of the Passfield White Paper were as follows: 1) Larger security forces were to be maintained in Palestine; 2) steps were to be taken to establish some form of self-government in the country; 3) drastic changes were to be made in the matter of Jewish immigration and land purchases. If it is realized that the development of the National Home depended on the right of the Jews to settle in Palestine and their right to buy land there, it will be seen that the Passfield White Paper aimed a crippling blow at the very foundation of the Jewish National Home.

The White paper of 1930 provoked a storm of protests from Jews and non-Jews. Weizmann resigned as President of the Jewish Agency, letters of resignation were also sent to Lord Passfield from Lord Melchett who was chairman of the Council of the Agency, and from Felix Warburg as chairman of the Jewish Agency Administrative Committee. On the non-Jewish side, Stanley Baldwin, Sir Austin Chamberlain, Leopold Amery, General Smuts, Sir John Simon, and Lord Hailsham attacked the White Paper and declared it incompatible with the terms of the Palestine Mandate.

Apparently surprised by the force of the opposition to its policy, the Government announced on November 14, 1930, that it had decided to invite the Jewish Agency to consult with the Government on its Palestine Policy. On February 13, 1931, Prime Minister Ramsay McDonald read in the House of Commons a letter which he had addressed to Dr. Weizmann in which the White Paper policy was for all practical purposes reversed.

Thus ended the first decade in the development of the Jewish National Home under the Palestine Mandate. We shall conclude this discussion with the following words from Weizmann's autobiography: "The riots were the strongest effort made up till that time by the Arab leaders to frighten us, by mob action, from continuing with our work in Palestine. They failed. And if the riots were intended, whatever their effect on our nerves, to overthrow the structure of the National Home, they came too late. We had built too solidly and too well. Similarly, the Passfield White Paper may be regarded as the most concerted effort—until the White Paper of 1939—on the part of a British Government to retract the promise made to the Jewish people in the Balfour Declaration. That attack, too, was successfully repulsed".[14]

4. THE DISTURBANCES OF 1936-1939

The events which had their beginning in 1936 were of far-reaching consequences for the development of the Jewish National Homeland. These events, which extended, off and on, over three years, culminated in the White Paper of 1939 which marked another important milestone in the reconstruction of the Jewish Homeland.

The deep hostility on the part of the Palestinian Arab politicians to the idea of a Jewish National Homeland in Palestine was the basic cause of the 1936-1939 riots. This feeling of animosity was intensified by the accelerated tempo of the economic development of Jewish Palestine and the steep jump in the number of immigrants almost immediately following Hitler's rise to power in Germany. Some forty thousand German Jews entered Palestine in 1934, and sixty-two thousand in 1935. The ratio of the Jewish to the Arab population in Palestine was thus slowly but surely increasing and the Arabs could see that the day is not too far off when the Jews in Palestine will cease being a minority of the population.

The timing of the disturbances was closely related to the deteriorating world situation in the nineteen thirties. The rise of Hitler Germany, the Italian invasion of Ethiopia, the destruction of the Spanish Republican regime with the aid of Germany and Italy, and the absorption and remilitarization of the Rhine province by Germany—all these were part of a grand strategy of the Axis powers to weaken and undermine the position of the great democracies. The democracies, on the other hand, were pursuing a policy of appeasement which was to reach its full fruition in 1938-1939. Britain's feeble reaction to Mussolini's designs in the Mediterranean area, the similar attitude of France to Hitler's designs on the European continent, the almost universal desire within the democracies to avert war at any cost, the decided weakening of the moral fiber of the democratic nations—all these created the impression of the dawn of a new era, in which the world was to be dominated by the young and virile dictatorships, and of the approaching demise of the "decadent" democracies. To the discerning observer there was no question on whose side lay the sympathy of the Arab world, pervaded as it was by an autocratic and feudalistic spirit. The sure way for them to gain their objective was to use force. In this the Palestine Arabs were encouraged, in the first place, by the vacillating attitude of the Palestine Administration which, even after it had become evident that the Arabs had thrown the country into an open revolt, was reluctant to adopt strong military measures or even to admit, in the beginning at least, the assistance rendered to Arab terrorists by outside Arab groups or the Axis powers of Italy and Germany. 'The delay in obtaining reinforcements', writes H. J. Simpson, a British staff officer then serving in Palestine—'the restrictions placed on the actions of the troops from the outset, and the latitude to the other side to obstruct their movement became of secondary importance in view of the freedom of movement allowed to rebel leaders . . . The connection between the Arab leaders in Palestine and the Arab bands raised in Palestine, as well as those brought in from abroad, seems to be established. The civil authorities persisted in maintaining that there was no connection . . . they refused to act vigorously against the Arab leaders'.[15]

The first phase of the 1936-1939 rebellion began in April 1936 and lasted to the middle of 1937. Arab rebellious mood became evident towards the end of 1935. In November 1935 the Palestine Arab leaders united and delivered to the Palestine Administration a memorandum in which, among other things, they demanded an immediate cessation of Jewish immigration and prohibition of transfer of land to the Jews.[16] The signal for the rebellion was given in a hold-up of Jews by Arabs on the road from Nablus to Tulkarm on April 15, 1936. On April 26th the Arab party leaders formed the Arab Higher Committee headed by the notorious Grand Mufti, and this Committee called a general strike. Rebel operations in Palestine were under the leadership of Fawzi Kawakji, a Syrian guerrilla fighter and an old friend of the Jerusalem Mufti. Jews were waylaid, Jewish colonies attacked, crops burned, trees uprooted—a practice in which Arabs have engaged for centuries. In spite of this destruction of Jewish life and property, the Palestine Jews have displayed a remarkable restraint and discipline. This was publicly acknowledged by the Government which even decided to enroll 2800 Jews as supernumerary police.[17]

In the fall of 1936 the rebellion began to show signs of abatement. In October 1936 the general strike collapsed. Three factors contributed to this end. The arrival of military reinforcements in September made possible firm and sustained military action against Arab terrorists. The economic hardships which the strike caused began to generate a mood of restlessness and displeasure among the rank and file of the Arab populace. The approach of the orange export season made the termination of the strike even more urgent. Lastly, there was the political factor in the form of the intervention by the outside Arab states. In August 1936 the Arab Higher Committee accepted the intervention of Iraq. Iraq was brought into the picture by the Palestine Administration which is said to have acted on instructions from London. On October 11th an appeal was made to the Palestine Arabs by four Arab states, Iraq, Saudi Arabia, Transjordan and Yemen, urging them to put an end to bloodshed and assuring them of England's good intentions and resolve to do them justice. On October 12th the strike was called off, and the first phase of the 1936-1939 rebellion came to an end.[18]

The second phase began in the second half of 1937 following the publication of the Peel Commission Report. The beginning of this phase was marked by the murder of Mr. Andrews, acting District Commissioner for Galilee, and of his public escort. The following month the Arab Higher Committee and National Committees were dissolved, five prominent members of the Arab Higher Committee were prosecuted and deported to the Seychelles, and the Jerusalem Mufti was removed from his position as President of the Supreme Muslim Council, thus depriving him of access to the funds of that Council amounting at that time to about 60,000 pounds annually. The deported Mufti subsequently left for Lebanon.

The Arab terror in Palestine continued, however, and was directed from the outside by the outlawed Arab Higher Committee. Arab violence in this phase of the revolt was directed not only against Jews and British, but also against those Arabs in Palestine who were for conciliation and peace. Some Arab notables petitioned their district Commissioner for permission to bear arms for self-protection against Arab terrorists, while in November 1937 the Jewish and Arab members of the Jerusalem Municipal Council issued a joint appeal to stop the disorders.

In 1939, the revolt began to show signs of inner disintegration. Dissension broke out between the Arab Higher Committee operating from Damascus and the rebel leaders in Palestine who accused Committee members of allocating to themselves money designated for the continuation of the revolt. One of these gang leaders was said to have declared in Transjordan that since he could no longer obtain money from the Committee he had no further interest in the rebellion. He threatened, however, to return to Palestine and extort their money for his own benefit.[19]

At the same time the military forces were gradually gaining the upper hand in the struggle. The various parts of the country had to be reoccupied. By the end of 1938 all Palestine was under military control. While the rebellion was thus crushed and its main force spent in 1938, it actually did not die out completely until September 1939 when World War Two began.

5. THE PEEL COMMISSION

On July 29, 1937, the British Government made public the appointment of a Royal Commission whose chairman was Lord Peel, and whose terms of reference were: "To ascertain the underlying causes of the disturbances which broke out in Palestine in the middle of April; to inquire into the manner in which the Mandate for Palestine is being implemented in relation to the obligations of the Mandatory towards the Arabs and the Jews respectively; and to ascertain whether, upon a proper construction of the terms of the Mandate, either the Arabs or the Jews have any legitimate grievances on account of the way in which the Mandate has been, or is being, implemented; and if the Commission is satisfied that any such grievances are well founded, to make recommendations for their removal and for the prevention of their recurrence."[20]

The Commission arrived in Palestine on November 15th and spent about two months interviewing various groups and studying the various aspects of the Arab-Jewish problem and the workings of the Mandate. The Arabs boycotted the Commission's sessions until almost the end of the Commission's stay when they appeared to state their case.

Six months later, in July 1937, the Peel Report was published attached to a White Paper in which the British Government stated its policy with reference to the recommendations embodied in the Report. Among the pertinent factors underlying the 1936 disturbances the Commission listed the following:

1) "The desire of the Arabs for national independence and their hatred and fear of the Jewish National Home." This attitude of the Palestinian Arabs was encouraged by the political status of the Arabs in countries outside of Palestine. Some of these have already achieved, others were in the process of achieving national independence. 2) "The pressure on Palestine exerted by world Jewry in view of the sufferings and anxieties of the Jews in Central and Eastern Europe. The increase in this pressure from the beginning of 1933 onwards, and the consequent high figures of Jewish immigration had gravely accentuated Arab fears of Jewish domination over Palestine." 3) "The general uncertainty, accentuated by the ambiguity of certain phrases in the Mandate, as to the ultimate intentions of the Mandatory Power. This uncertainty had (a) stimulated the Jewish desire to expand and consolidate their position in Palestine as quickly as might be, and (b) made it possible for the Arabs to interpret the conciliatory policy of the Palestine Government and the sympathetic attitude of some of its officials as proof that the British determination to implement the Balfour Declaration was not wholehearted".[21]

The recommendations which the Peel Commission offered were of a two-fold character. The first group of recommendations were of a palliative nature designed to treat the symptoms instead of the basic difficulty producing the symptoms. The measures suggested to take care of the immediate need were those concerned with the matter of Jewish land purchase and Jewish immigration. The Commission denied that Jewish land purchases had caused displacement of the Arabs; it nevertheless recommended drastic restrictions of the Jewish right to purchase Arab land. While the Commission conceded that the Arabs had reaped great benefits from Jewish immigration, it advised sharp curtailment of Jewish immigration. From the Jewish point of view the worst feature of the recommendation dealing with immigration was the novel idea that Jewish immigration should not only, as hitherto, be regulated by the country's economic absorptive capacity, but also by political considerations. In the future, Jewish immigration to Palestine should be subject to a 'political high level', and should not exceed 12,000 per year for the next five years.

But these measures, the Commission confessed, will not solve the basic difficulty. It has reached the conclusion that the Palestine problem can be solved only by partitioning the country into a Jewish State, an Arab State, and a neutral enclave embracing the Holy Places of Jerusalem and Bethlehem, which should remain under British Mandate.[22]

The twentieth Zionist Congress, meeting at Zurich from August 3rd to 17th, 1937, took up the Partition proposal, and while the idea was distasteful to many delegates, the steadily worsening conditions of the Jews in Central and Eastern Europe prevented the Congress from rejecting the plan out of hand. It empowered the Executive "to enter into negotiations with a view to ascertaining the precise terms of His Majesty's Government for the proposed establishment of a Jewish State".[23] The Jewish Agency which met in session at the close of the Zionist Congress accepted a similar resolution but directed its Executive to request the British Government to call a conference of Jews and Arabs with a view to 'exploring the possibilities of a peaceful settlement between Jews and Arabs in and for an undivided Palestine on the basis of the Balfour Declaration and the Mandate'.[24]

The Arab Higher Committee, the Arab National Conference, and the Iraq government rejected the partition proposal. The All-India Moslem League condemned the Peel Report.

The Permanent Mandates Commission preparing its report for action by the League of Nations Council significantly remarked that "the present Mandate became almost unworkable once it was publicly declared to be so by a British Royal Commission".[25] At its session on Steptember 16, 1937, the League of Nations Council authorized the British Government to explore the subject of partition but declared that "the Mandate must remain in force 'until such time as it may be otherwise decided' ".[26]

Accordingly, the British Government appointed a Partition Commission headed by Sir John Woodhead with instructions to proceed to Palestine to mark out the partition boundaries. The Report of the Partition Commission was published in October 1938 in which three plans were suggested: one—the original Peel Commission plan, and two—modifications of that plan. The Partition Commission Report expressed its dissatisfaction with all three plans.

Whether or not the British Government was wholehearted behind the Peel Partition proposals, by the time the Woodhead Partition Report was published the British Government rejected the whole idea of partitioning Palestine. A number of factors induced the Government to change its position. Among the most important of these was the skepticism in some quarters about the practicability of the partition scheme, the opposition of the Arabs, and the rapidly deteriorating international situation. Accordingly, the Government issued a new Statement of policy in which it rejected the partition idea. It now resolved to seek help from the outside Arab states in arriving at a solution of the Palestine problem.[27]

6. THE WHITE PAPER OF 1939

In December of 1938 the British Government announced its decision to call a tripartite conference of Jews, Arabs and representatives of the British Government to confer on the subject of Palestine. The Jews were represented by the Jewish Agency, and a number of leading Jews from Great Britain, Palestine, the United States, France, Germany, Belgium, Eastern Europe and South Africa. Besides the Palestine Arabs, the Arab delegation consisted also of representatives of Egypt, Iraq, Saudi Arabia, Yemen and Transjordan. The conference was held in St. James Palace and lasted from February to March 1939. As the Palestine Arabs refused to sit at the same table with the Jews, the actual conference consisted of two parts, that between the Arabs and the British, and between the British and the Jewish Delegation.

It was obvious to the Jews assembled there that the conference was not going to produce a solution for Palestine satisfactory to both Arabs and Jews. But the British Government had prepared a solution of which the Jewish delegation inadvertently became aware at the close of the conference. The contents of the British plan for Palestine which was meant for distribution to the Arab delegates only was by a clerical error addressed to Dr. Weizmann. It contained a number of proposals which were in due time published and became known as the White Paper of 1939. An Arab Palestine State was to be set up in ten years. Jewish immigration to Palestine was to be drastically reduced, only 75,000 to be admitted to Palestine in the next five years, with the complete cessation of all immigration after that except with Arab consent. Jewish right to purchase Arab land in Palestine was to be sharply curtailed. For this purpose a new Land Ordinance was published in February 1940 which divided Palestine into three zones: Zone A, comprising 6415 square miles, or 63.2% of the total area of Western Palestine. In this zone Jews were "prohibited from acquiring land, water, buildings, trees, or any interest or right over land, water, buildings or trees by purchase, lease, mortgage, charge or any other disposition".[28] Zone B, comprising 3225 square miles, or 31.8% of the total area. In this zone a Jew had to receive from the High Commissioner written permission before he could acquire any property. The High Commissioner was to use his discretion whether to give or refuse such permission. Zone C, comprising 5% of the total area of Palestine where a Jew was to have unrestricted right to acquire property.[29]

As to the projected establishment of the independent Arab State in Palestine at the end of ten years, this State will enter into "such treaty relations with the United Kingdom as will provide satisfactorily for the commercial and strategic requirements of both countries in the future".[30]

To the Jews the White Paper of 1939 was a shocking blow, coming at a time when the Jewish people were facing the darkest hour in their history since the destruction of their Homeland by the Romans. Of course, the Jewish representatives rejected the White Paper as both illegal and a breach of faith on the part of England. The Arabs also rejected it, but this was probably a tactical move, hoping thereby to exact more concessions or perhaps consent to the immediate establishment of the proposed Arab Palestinian State.

Certain prominent spokesmen in the British Parliament condemned the White Paper of May 1939. Herbert Morrison speaking on behalf of the Labor Party said this: "We regard this White Paper and the policy in it as a cynical breach of pledges given to the Jews and the world, including America."[31] Clement Atlee, another Laborite, declared: "The action of the Government [of Mr. Chamberlain] in making themselves the judge of their own case, in taking action contrary to the Permanent Mandates Commission's decision, and in disregarding the Council of the League of Nations, will cause . . . very wide feeling that instead of acting up to their obligations under the Mandate, they are flouting the authority of the League and international law".[32] Winston Churchill said in the same parliamentary debate: "I regret very much that the pledge of the Balfour Declaration, endorsed as it has been by successive governments, and the conditions under which we obtained the Mandate, have both been violated by the government's proposals . . . To whom was the pledge of the Balfour Declaration made? It was not made to the Jews of Palestine, it was not made to those who were actually living in Palestine. It was made to world Jewry and in particular to the Zionist associations".[33]

In the House of Lords the Archbishop of Canterbury, the Primate of the Church of England, stated: "They* shall return in their National Home to that minority status which has been their lot

---

* The Jews

through long centuries in every part of the world . . . Whatever a National Home may have meant . . . it surely cannot have meant that".[34]

At a meeting in June 1939 the Permanent Mandates Commission examined the new British Palestine policy as embodied in the White Paper of May 1939. It was the unanimous opinion of the Commission "that the policy set out in the White Paper was not in accordance with the interpretation which, in agreement with the Mandatory Power and the Council [of the League of Nations], the Commission had always placed upon the Palestine Mandate".[35] The majority of the Commission, including its chairman, M. Orts from Belgium, also "declared that the very terms of the Mandate and the fundamental intentions of its authors ruled out any conclusion that the policy of the White Paper was in conformity with the Mandate".[36]

II. ARAB ATTACKS ON JEWISH SETTLEMENTS

Arab attacks on Jewish settlements occurred sporadically from the very beginning of the Jewish reconstruction program in Palestine towards the nineteenth century. In the days of the British Mandate Arab attacks grew in intensity and extent. There were three waves of Arab disturbances in the 1920-1939 period. The main target of the 1920 riots were the Jewish villages in the northern part of Upper Galilee. Most of the Jewish inhabitants left the area during the riots, but a small group under the leadership of Trumpeldor remained. They held out for two months experiencing great hardships and suffering loss of life. On March 1, 1920, Trumpeldor and five of his companions were killed. The remainder of the small defense force escaped.

The second wave of disturbances began in August 1929. The outbreaks started with an assault on the Jewish quarters in Jerusalem. In the city of Hebron fifty-nine Jews—men, women and children— were murdered. A number of Jewish villages were attacked. Altogether, 108 Jews were killed and 187 wounded. Jewish property amounting to several hundred thousand pounds was destroyed or stolen.

Concerning the third series of Arab disturbances which commenced in 1936 and did not stop entirely until the beginning of the Second World War, the following account is given by the Very Reverend Dr. Norman Maclean, Chaplain to King George VI, formerly moderator of the General Assembly of the Church of Scotland,

and Chaplain of St. Andrews Church in Jerusalem from 1939 to 1940: "When war was declared . . . [the Arab rebellion] came to an inglorious end. There is another reason for this sudden peace that has fluttered down on this so troubled a country, and that is, that the sinews of war have been cut. It is a well-known and established fact that the [Arab] bandits were recruited from the villages when the harvest was past and work had ceased, and each was paid a wage of three pounds a month for the pleasant work of waylaying Jews and killing them. . . The money came from Germany and Italy. Documents were intercepted which proved that the Arab terrorists received 50,000 pounds from [Nazi] Germany and 20,000 pounds from [Fascist] Italy to finance their campaign; and when the war broke out the supply ceased. An effort was made to levy it from the villages, but the . . . [Arab peasants] got weary of paying murderers, and instead of giving money, they began to hand over the murderers to the police. The truth is that the Arabs in the villages have suffered more from the terrorists than did the Jews, for the terrorists killed far more Arabs than they killed Jews. And then there was the problem of arms and ammunition and of land mines. These came from Germany. The war put a stop to that.

The troubles experienced by Jews and Arabs in Palestine, and the losses inflicted on a martyred nation, have been entirely owing to the vacillations, the ever-changing plans, the feebleness of will of the British Government. It was the uncertainty regarding the policy that would be pursued next week, or next month, that was the underlying cause of much of the unrest that afflicted the country. . . There were 3,000 bandits, constituting only 0.3 per cent of the Arab population, yet the British Government felt palsied when confronted with the task of suppressing them. The Jews were being murdered, settlements were being attacked, but it was only late in the day that the Government provided settlers with arms for self-defense, and then not on a sufficient scale".[37]

The fortitude and heroism with which the Jewish settlers met the Arab attacks is depicted by the same writer in the following report: Givat Ada was then an isolated colony in the hills of Ephraim. The settlers were a small group and their colony was continually raided by the Arabs. But they carried on dauntlessly. Like their ancestors after their return from the Babylonian exile, they were engaged in rebuilding the Jewish Homeland with tools in one hand and an instrument for self-defense in the other. "Then the long-dreaded night attack took place. The wife of a man, Moshe Goldberg, whose name was Naomi, was busy in her kitchen, tidying the house before retiring for the night. Her twin daughters, aged eight, were in their beds. The father was at the village meeting. Everything was as peaceful as the stars now beginning to shine overhead, when suddenly there rang out the agonized cries of the two children. They were caught out of their cots by the brigands, and were being carried, struggling and screaming, towards the door. The mother added her cries of terror to those of her children. She threw herself on the kidnappers, scratching their faces, and trying to free her daughters. They thrust her aside with blows that nearly stunned her, and carried the children out into the night. The mother staggered outside, leaving blood-marks on the porch and door. She stumbled after the murderers, crying the names of her daughters, but the effort proved too great. The blows she had received proved fatal. She was found dead under a fig-tree against which she had fallen.

By this time the villagers were aroused, and each man grasped his gun and ran to his appointed post . . . The peaceful scene of a few minutes before became an inferno of yells, of shots and of the cries of the smitten. The bandits, carrying the struggling children, found themselves intercepted. The father had rushed up distracted, with three other settlers now armed and ready to fight. They fired at the gangsters. The Arabs held up the two captive children in the line of fire, but the rescuers were not deterred. The father fired with the rest, for he cried out that he would prefer his daughters to be killed than thus fall into the hands of the enemy. He continually shouted their names, calling out, 'Avishag, Orpah, here is father: come, come! And they struggled as best they could to free themselves, but the bandits held them fast.

Along the street the retreating Arabs, with the two children, made their way, still firing. They were forced to take refuge in a house . . . There they were set upon. The owner of the house and a brother . . . had guns and bullets which they used to such good effect that the two girls were rescued . . .

Instantly a call had been sent out to the nearest settlement for help, and succor came speeding by car . . . The women and children were gathered into the People's House, and the survivors fell back on this, meaning to defend it to the last. There were only thirty families in this settlement, and for forty-five minutes that handful of men withstood the attack. Rescue came at last. A patrol of Jews happened to be near. When the brigands saw the rockets fired by the rescuers as a message that they were near, they fled. The attackers outnumbered the defenders by at least five to one . . ."[38]

The above story, the writer continues, is an example of what was happening all over Palestine where there were Jewish settlements. "What is remarkable is that no Jews ever thought of retreat. The work went on as if peace reigned. When a man was murdered, five men stepped into his place, ready for the same fate, if need be . . . No work ceased; no building stopped; no plough rusted in the furrows. The Jews realized that they could no longer look to a Government that could not vindicate law or punish murder, and took more and more their own defense into their own hands . . .

Even in the worst of times the process of establishing new settlements went on. In July 1938, when the days were at their blackest, word was passed that at daybreak on July 18th the Jews were to go up and make a settlement in the hills of Judea. The settlement was to be a memorial to five of their number who were murdered in the vicinity eight months before . . . The previous evening the workers began to assemble for the march: lorries loaded with hut frames ready to be put up, quarriers, carpenters, mason laborers, road-makers—everything was arranged to the smallest detail. Before dawn, in the light of electric torches, hundreds gathered round the graves of the five martyrs whom they were to commemorate. Then a voice called the five dead men by name and went on: 'Today we are going up to the land which you have dedicated with your blood . . . Daily our comrades fall in different parts of the land. Even at this moment when we go up this mountain, we cannot be certain that we are not erecting a living monument to some other comrade'. Then the command was given: 'Up', and the procession started: the laden lorries led the way; then the buses carrying the artisans; the cars laden with men who would be on watch and guard, and then the pedestrians . . .

Suffice it to say that ere the night fell the settlement in memory of the five who were killed was firmly established. There, amid wild surroundings, the work of reclamation goes on. It is like a lighthouse casting its saving beams over the surge . . . That was the answer of the Jews to their would-be exterminators. They passed a watchword one to another when they heard of a new horror: 'The way to stop the horror is by establishing new settlements; by setting more Jews to plough and dig; more Jews to work.' And so they did unhesitatingly. Nothing could stop them. And when any race are animated by a spirit such as that nothing can possibly stop them."[39]

Notes to Chapter 3

[1] Chaim Weizmann, *Trial and Error* (The Jewish Publication Society of America: Philadelphia, 1949), vol. 1, p. 256. Used by permission of Harper & Row (New York).

[2] Ibid., vol. 2, p. 290.

[3] The Churchill Memorandum, *Palestine, Correspondence* with the *Palestine Arab Delegation* and the *Zionist Organization* (British White Paper, Cmd. 1700), pp. 17-21; see, *Great Britain and Palestine, 1915-1945* (Royal Institute of International Affairs: London, 1946), pp. 155-6.

[4] Ibid., p. 156.

[5] Ibid.

[6] *Palestine Royal Commission Report, 1937,* Chapter II., Paragraph 39; quoted in *The Jewish Plan for Palestine,* p. 303.

[7] Chaim Weizmann, Op. Cit., vol. 2, p. 314.

[8] See, *Great Britain and Palestine, 1915-1945,* p. 45.

[9] Ibid., pp. 45-6.

[10] Ibid., p. 46.

[11] Ibid., pp. 46-7.

[12] Article 22 of the Covenant of the League of Nations, Paragraghs 7 and 9; quoted in *Great Britain and Palestine, 1915-1945,* p. 151.

[13] *League of Nations Document, C.* 355, M. 147, 1930, vi; see, *Great Britain and Palestine, 1915-1945.*

[14] Chaim Weizmann, Op. Cit., vol. 2, p. 335.

[15] H. J. Simson, *British Rule and Rebellion* (W. Blackwood & Sons, Ltd.: London, 1937). Used by permission.

[16] *Great Britain and Palestine, 1915-1945,* p. 86.

[17] Ibid., p. 90.

[18] Ibid., pp. 92, 95-6.

[19] The London *Times,* May 10, 1939; see, *Great Britain and Palestine, 1915-1945,* p. 119.

[20] The London *Times,* July 30, 1936; see, *Great Britain and Palestine, 1915-1945,* pp. 91-2.

[21] The Peel Report; see, *Palestine Royal Commission: Report* 1937 (British Blue Book, Cmd. 5479): see, *Great Britain and Palestine, 1915-1945,* pp. 98-9, 160-164.

[22] Ibid.

[23] Chaim Weizmann, Op. Cit., vol. 2, p. 387.

[24] *New Judea,* August-September 1937, pp. 235-6; quoted in *Great Britain and Palestine, 1915-1945,* p. 106.

[25] *Great Britain and Palestine, 1915-1945,* p. 103. Used by permission.

[26] Ibid., p. 107.

[27] Ibid., p. 111.

[28] *The Jewish Plan for Palestine,* p. 305.

[29] Ibid.

[30] Ibid.

[31] *Hansard Parliamentary Debates,* House of Commons (His Majesty's Stationery Office: London, May 23, 1939), vol. 347, 2142.

[32] *Hansard Parliamentary Debates,* House of Commons (His Majesty's Stationery Office: London, February 28, 1940), vol. 357, 2057.

[33] *Hansard Parliamentary Debates,* House of Commons (His Majesty's Stationery Office: London, May 23, 1939), vol. 347, 2171.

[34] *Hansard Parliamentary Debates,* House of Lords (His Majesty's Stationery Office: London, May 23, 1939), vol. 113, 115.

[35] Permanent Mandates Commission, Minutes of the Thirty-sixth Session, p. 275.

[36] *The Jewish Plan for Palestine,* p. 306.

[37] Norman Maclean, *His Terrible Swift Sword* (Christian Council on Palestine: New York, 1941), pp. 70-72. Copyright by Victor Gollancz; used by permission.

[38] Ibid., pp. 94-96.

[39] Ibid., pp. 98-100.

CHAPTER 4

PALESTINE UNDER THE MANDATE:

B.　The Period of 1939-1948

I.　THE CONTRIBUTION OF JEWISH PALESTINE TO
WORLD WAR TWO

II.　ARAB BEHAVIOR IN WORLD WAR TWO
  1. Egypt
  2. Syria and Lebanon
  3. Iraq
  4. Transjordan
  5. Palestine Arabs
  6. Conclusion

III.　THE COLLAPSE OF THE PALESTINE MANDATE
  1. The Growing Deterioration of British Rule in Palestine
  2. The Termination of the Palestine Mandate and the Rebirth of the State of Israel

CHAPTER 4

PALESTINE UNDER THE MANDATE:

B. *The Period of 1939-1948*

I. THE CONTRIBUTION OF JEWISH PALESTINE TO WORLD WAR TWO[1]

Palestine having been a mandated territory, its population was exempt from conscription. Nevertheless soon after the outbreak of World War Two an appeal for volunteers for national service was issued by the Jewish Agency in cooperation with the National Council of Palestine Jews. In response to this call 85,781 men and 50,262 women registered for war duty. The total number of Palestine Jewry did not exceed half a million. Some 30,000 Palestine Jews volunteered for military service with the armed forces. They served in France, Belgium, Greece, Crete, Italy, North Africa, Syria, and Malta.

The war activities of the home front of Jewish Palestine left an enviable record. Following the collapse of France the British were forced to transfer to Britain most of the ground personnel of the Royal Air Force in Egypt, in anticipation of the expected German invasion of the British Isles. Accordingly, the Jewish Agency was requested to supply, if possible, 1,200 mechanics and specialists for all kinds of jobs. The Agency promptly provided 1,500 men qualified to do the jobs of the evacuated Royal Air Force ground personnel. Jewish industry in Palestine was confronted, as a result of the war, with a series of most difficult problems. Jewish industry had not been geared for the production of the type of goods and items which the armed forces needed. Machines turning out certain peace-time products had to be reconverted in a hurry in order to be able to manufacture items for which they were not designed. To use one illustration, the presses which were normally making cement floor tiles had to be redesigned for the production of anti-tank mine components. When the import of raw materials was cut off, Jewish manufacturers ransacked salvage depots and made good use of the various waste materials.

A wide variety of war items were manufactured. Among these were: barbed wire, fire-extinguishers, bolts and nuts, shipbuilding tools, cranes, air-compressors, machine-gun parts, hydraulic jacks, electric transformers, wire strainers, die-blocks, engine tanks, precision weights for ships, spare parts for automobiles, chains for tanks, anchors, ship's propellors, safes, locks and signal lanterns. Three million units of anti-tank mines, six million two-gallon containers and accumulators for tanks and for the Royal Air Force were made.

Besides producing new products for war use, Jewish industry in Palestine did a great job in repairing machines which had broken down, guns and ships. Haifa was the ship repair center in Palestine. Most of the two thousand workers engaged in ship repairing in Haifa were Jews. Ships were often brought to Haifa for reconditioning because the job could not be done at other nearby ports. A damaged refrigeration ship transporting meat for the Eighth Army was repaired at Haifa in six days, when the naval authorities expected that job to take months. An oil tanker was badly damaged by fire and the repair job was estimated to take nine months. At the port of Haifa the job was completed in two months.

The food processing industry of Jewish Palestine also did much useful service. Large quantities of wheat were milled for the Army and cold-storage facilities supplied. Breads, biscuits, chocolate, yeast, edible fats, citrus fruits, and jams were delivered to the armed forces on various fronts from Eritrea to Syria, and from Africa to Persia.

The textile and rubber and leather industries also made a sizeable contibution to the war effort. Furs for the Royal Air Force pilots, flying vests and fur gloves; camouflage nets, knitted goods, underwear and socks; khaki uniforms, tents and cameras; silk for parachutes, inflatable rubber belts and rubber gloves. Over a million pairs of boots and shoes were manufactured.

Optical instruments for the Navy and Royal Air Force were manufactured and also repaired in the workshops of Professor Goldberg. Professor Goldberg, a German refugee, was formerly technical director of the Zeiss Works at Jena in Germany. Geodetic instruments were also made.

A variety of hospital articles were manufactured in Palestine. Among these were ambulances, field kitchens, glass ampules, medical instruments. Ether which was a difficult item to import from abroad because of its inflammable qualities was also produced in Palestine.

The electro-technical industry produced blackout testing instruments, electro-magnetic mine detectors, crystals for the manufacture of microphones and earphones. Repairs were made of measuring instruments. Testing instruments for electric wires were assembled, emergency generators were also assembled.

The Hadassah-University Medical Center organized training courses in tropical diseases for army officers, army scientists, and doctors. The Laboratory of Pathologic Physiology performed blood examinations for the military hospitals in Palestine, and tested the vitamin content of food articles for the manufacturers and military authorities. Large quantities of anti-typhus vaccine were prepared for troops, refugees and war workers in Russia and the Middle East. Jewish scientists of the University staff were assigned to the various military malaria control units in the Middle East.

The great significance of the achievements of the Palestine Home Front in World War Two lay in this that it became the great supply and service center for the armed forces of the Middle East. Valuable man-power was conserved, critical war items were manufactured, urgent repairs were made and services were supplied, thus saving valuable ship space at a time when Allied ships were constantly attacked by enemy airplanes and submarines. Here is the testimony of the former British Commercial Agent writing in a survey of Palestine's part in World War Two: '. . . I wonder how many people know that every one of the millions of the land mines used in the brilliant campaign which retrieved the situation at Alamein from imminent complete disaster and ended by 'knocking Rommel for six' was manufactured in Palestine. This country filled army contracts to the value of eight million pounds in 1942, and the figure rose to something like eleven million pounds in the following years . . . The list of goods supplied to the army is long and impressive and cannot be quoted here in full, but some extracts from it may be given: 100,000 accumulators, six million dry-battery cells, between eight and nine million yards of electric cables, six million two-gallon containers . . . foodstuffs galore . . . It must be allowed that this is quite an astonishing record for a small country . . .'

II. ARAB BEHAVIOR IN WORLD WAR TWO[2]

As one reviews the World War Two record of the Arab countries one is impressed with the common pattern which characterizes their conduct. The behavior of the Palestinian Arabs falls into the same pattern. As long as the outcome of the Second World War was uncertain the Arab governments pursued a policy of caution. They tried to avoid taking any definite step which would align them on the side of the Allies or give offense to the Axis powers. It was only towards the end of the war, when an Allied victory appeared certain, that they all jumped on the Allied band wagon, and this primarily to be assured of membership in the United Nations organization. In the following brief and sketchy review we shall see where exactly the Arab states stood in the life and death struggle between Democracy and Fascism and Nazism.

1. EGYPT

Both the Egyptian Court and the Parliament pursued a pro-Fascist and anti-British course. Britain was blamed for Egypt's cotton crisis in spite of the fact that Britain purchased the entire cotton crop at a price which the Egyptians had forced up in the bargaining. Had not Britiain agreed to do this not a bale of Egyptian cotton would have been sold. Ironically enough, the British were held responsible for German air bombings of Egyptian territory. British soldiers were often attacked in the streets. A well organized Fifth Column was active in Egypt whose most important function was to transmit war information to the Germans and Italians. In the summer of 1941 it was uncovered that Salih Harb Pasha, the Defense Minister in Ali Maher's cabinet, had passed on to the Italian Military Intelligence the secret plans of Egypt's defenses, as well as British military information which the Egyptian Government received from British authorities. On May 12, 1941, during the anti-British coup in Iraq, Al-Masri, Egypt's Chief of Staff, made an attempt to reach the Axis lines in an airplane. He was arrested when he made a forced landing on Egyptian soil. Salim Radwan, an officer of the Royal Egyptian Air Force, and his friend Mohammad Abu as Saud, flew to Rommel's headquarters in an Egyptian airplane on July 7, 1942, delivering to him important war information.

The successive Egyptian governments, from that of Ali Maher to Mustafa Mahas, had repeatedly stated that they would declare war as soon as any German or Italian forces invaded Egyptian territory. But they refrained from doing this even when the forces of the Axis powers had penetrated deep into Egyptian territory. It was not until February 1945 that Premier Ahmed Maher Pasha declared war on the Axis. Immediately following his announcement to the Egyptian Chamber of Egypt's war declaration Ahmed Maher was shot dead while he was on his way to repeat the announcement in the adjoining Senate.

2. SYRIA AND LEBANON

After the fall of France Syria and Lebanon were ruled by the Vichy French Regime. Sympathy for and collaboration with the Axis powers was pretty general in these two countries. There was only one political group which was loyal to the Allied cause. The leader of this group was Dr. Abd ur-Rahman Shahbandar. In 1940 Dr. Shahbandar was assassinated by pro-Nazi Syrians and his party went out of existence.

When the British army entered Syria Arab leaders offered their full cooperation to Vichy French General Dentz. As late as 1943-44 it was discovered that espionage on behalf of Nazi Germany was carried on at the American University of Beirut by Syrian, Lebanese, and Palestinian Arab students.

3. IRAQ

At the outbreak of World War Two the pro-Nazi elements in Iraq prevented that country from fulfilling its treaty obligations to its British ally. The Kailani uprising against Britain was the work of many representative elements of the Iraqi people, as shown by a collection of documents published in Iraq under the name of Al-Wathba. These documents showed that the leaders of the uprising had the support of officials, tribal chiefs, workers, and Bedouins. The heads of the Moslem religion backed the revolt and called upon the faithful to rise up and destroy the British. Muhammed al-Khatib, Director of the Supreme Moslem Theological Seminary in Karbala, published a 'fatwa' in which it was declared that it was the duty of the Iraqi people to join the fight.* The Chief Preacher of Baghdad appealed to the Moslem world for help in the fighting**.

The rebel Government of Rashid Ali re-established diplomatic relations with Nazi Germany. A treaty was signed according to which Germany was given rights to the Mosul oil fields, and the right to use the railways and the airports. Germany, on her part, promised to provide military help to Iraq***.

The Iraq insurrection against the Allied cause aroused great enthusiasm in the Arab world. Congratulations were sent to the insurgent regime by King Farouk as well as Egypt's recognition of the

---

* Al-Bilad of May 6, 1941
** Shakir al-Badri; see, Al-Bilad of May 27, 1941
*** British Broadcasting Co. on June 17, 1941; Al-Thaghr of June 18, 1941

rebel government. Congratulatory messages were also addressed to the Iraqi regime by Hashim Atasi, President of the Syrian Republic from 1936 to 1939 and one of the leaders of the "National Block"; also from Riad-es-Solh, Lebanese Premier in 1943-44 and member of the Lebanese delegation to the United Nations in 1946. Messages of encouragement were also sent by the chief of the Bedu tribes in Al-Jazira; from Hasan Mahmud Amin Huseini, who was then religious head of the Lebanese Shi-ites; Muhammad Tawfiq Khalid, who was the Sunnite mufti in the Lebanon; from Ihsan al-Jabri, one of the prominent leaders of the "National Block".

4. TRANSJORDAN

Nazi propaganda had been carried on in Transjordan for months preceding the Iraq revolt. As a result of this some detachments of the Transjordan Frontier Force mutineed when ordered to help the British put down the Iraqi revolt. About five hundred men of the Transjordan Frontier Force either resigned or were dismissed. The Bedu tribes in the desert between Iraq and Transjordan made frequent raids on the workers employed on the oil pipe-lines and on several occasions the pipe-line was cut in several places.

5. PALESTINE ARABS

The behavior of the Palestine Arabs in World War Two conformed to the general pattern of that of the Arabs in the other countries of the Middle East. Very few Palestinian Arabs enlisted in the armed forces. It is said that at least half of those who did enlist in Palestine either deserted later or were discharged because they were found unfit for the service. A number of the leaders of the Palestine Arabs resided in Axis or neutral countries where they collaborated with the Axis powers.

6. CONCLUSION

While Europe was ravaged by war, and European nations suffered severe privations, the Arab countries were scarcely affected by military operations, and the Arab peoples derived enormous benefits from the war. The Allies constructed airports, roads, and railway lines. They often purchased Arab products for which they had no immediate use, in order to bolster Arab economy and keep Arab peoples contented. They supplied Arab countries with goods and foodstuffs at a time when their own people at home experienced all sorts of shortages. Thousands of Arab people found employment at unusually high wages. In addition to these huge profits direct subsidies were made in some cases. Thus Saudi-Arabia was compensated by Britain for the financial loss suffered on account of the suspension of Moslem pilgrimages. In spite of all these extraordinary benefits which came to the Arabs during the war their sympathies lay with the enemies of the Allies. Their war record is one of obstructionism, treason and collaboration with the enemy.

III. The Collapse Of The Palestine Mandate

1. the growing deterioration of british rule in palestine

The magnificent part which the Palestine Jews had played in World War Two should not be taken as indicating that they accepted the state of affairs brought about and envisaged by the White Paper of 1939. They threw themselves wholeheartedly into the war on the side of the democracies, first, because Nazi Germany was the arch-enemy of the Jewish people, and, second, because world Jewry was part of the democratic West ideologically. As long as they were facing a common foe the Jews of Palestine had to disregard their controversy with Britain. But as soon as the danger of invasion receded by the defeat of Mussolini's African forces and Rommel's German legions relations between the Palestine Jews and the British Administration in Palestine entered an era of growing hostility.

The so-called "Jewish Terror" which prevailed in Palestine from the end of the Second World War until the establishment of the State of Israel in 1948 must be viewed in the context of the Jewish catastrophe in Europe and the part which the White Paper of 1939 had contributed to this catastrophe. The Jews in and out of Palestine never doubted the illegality of the White Paper of 1939. The Permanent Mandates Commission to whom England was responsible for the administering of the Mandate regarded the White Paper as violating the letter and spirit of the Mandate. The Anglo-American Committee on Palestine supported this view.

Accordingly, the denial to the Jews of the right to purchase land in Palestine was to the Jews tantamount to the worst racial laws in Nazi Germany, applied in the very country where they were supposed to reconstruct their National Homeland. Bad as the land purchasing laws were, the immigration laws put in force by the 1939 White Paper were even worse. Before the Balkan countries were occupied by the Germans in World War Two many Jews fleeing before the Nazis found their way to the Balkan states hoping to get across to Palestine by way of Turkey and Syria. Turkey was perfectly willing to let these unfortunate Jews pass through as long as Britain would permit them to enter Palestine. But it was just then that the British bolted the gates of Palestine. It was only when the Nazis invaded the Balkan countries thus cutting off the only avenue of escape for the Jewish refugees that the British opened the doors of Palestine. Just before the outbreak of the Second World War the Colonial Secretary of the British Government was requested to grant permission to bring into Palestine 20,000 Jewish children from Poland and 10,000 from the Balkan countries. But permission was refused and these thousands of children perished at the hands of the Nazis.[3] In the sight of the Jews, and of all decent people, the British were responsible for the death of many tens of thousands of Jews who could have been saved.

This deplorable behavior of the British in Palestine convinced the Jews that the British presence in Palestine had no further legal or moral basis, and that the British were in Palestine merely to serve their own interests. This line of reasoning led some groups among the Palestine Jews to the belief that there is nothing left to them but to meet force with force.

As the full extent of the Jewish tragedy in Europe was becoming better known in America the Palestine problem moved up to the forefront of world events. At a Zionist Conference held in New York in May 1942 the Biltmore Program was adopted. It called for un-limited immigration into Palestine; that the Jewish Agency for Palestine be given full authority in matters of immigration and up-building of Palestine; the establishment of a Jewish Commonwealth in Palestine; the creation of a Jewish Army.[4] In 1943 and again in 1944 resolutions were introduced into the United States Congress on behalf of Palestine. The 1944 resolution urged that the Government of the United States use its good offices to reopen Palestine for the free entry of Jews and for the establishment in Palestine of a free and democratic Jewish Commonwealth.[5]

Following the defeat of the Nazi armies the Allied occupation authorities immediately became confronted with the problem of the shattered remnants of European Jewry. Earl Harrison had made a personal study of refugee conditions in Europe and in the fall of 1945 he reported to President Truman in which he declared that Palestine is the only place where these Jewish survivors could be resettled. President Truman appealed to Prime Minister Atlee for the immedi-ate admission of 100,000 Jewish refugees into Palestine.

At this juncture it is necessary to state that in July 1945 the British Labor Party had won the General Election and had formed the new Government with Clement Atlee as its Prime Minister and Ernest Bevin as the Foreign Secretary. To appreciate the part which the Labor Government played in the final phase of the Palestine Mandate we ought to realize that, according to Harold Laski, the theoretician of British socialism, the Labor Party for some thirty years had been passing pro-Zionist resolutions at its Party conferences.[6] In December 1944 the Labor Party had adopted the following Palestine plank: "There is surely neither hope nor meaning in a Jewish National Home unless we are prepared to let the Jews, if they wish, enter this tiny land in such numbers as to become a majority. There was a strong case for this before the war, and there is an irresistible case for it now, after the unspeakable atrocities of the cold-blooded calculated German-Nazi plan to kill all the Jews of Europe."[7] "Let the Arabs be encouraged to move out as the Jews move in . . .The Arabs have many wide territories of their own: they should not seek to exclude the Jews from this small area of Palestine which is less than the size of Wales."[8] It is quite probable, as was pointed out by one member of the Anglo-American Committee of Inquiry, that the Labor Party adopted such an outspokenly pro-Zionist stand because it really had not expected to win the election.[9] Be as it may, within several months from its accession to power the Labor Government repudiated the pledges of the Labor Party given so repeatedly to the Jewish people.

To President Truman's appeal for the immediate admission into Palestine of 100,000 Jews Bevin responded with a proposal for the appointment of an Anglo-American Committee of Inquiry to examine the whole problem of European and Palestine Jews. President Truman accepted the proposition, and a Committee was appointed consisting of six British and six American members. The Committee was instructed to investigate the whole situation and make recommendations to take care of the immediate need and to suggest a permanent solution. The Committee was allowed 120 days in which to complete its task.[10]

The Committee held sessions in Washington, London, Egypt, Palestine, and some of the surrounding Arab countries. In addition, various members of the Committee visited several European countries, including the extermination and displaced persons camps. They found that in spite of the annihilation of the majority of Europe's

Jews antisemitism in Central and Eastern Europe was still strong. They also learned, much to their amazement, that the vast majority of the Jewish survivors in Europe desired to leave Europe and wanted to go to Palestine. Even America held no attraction to them. Apparently, as a result of the awful calamity which had befallen the Jewish people, they lost all faith in the basic decency of the Gentile world, and wanted to reconstruct their broken lives among their own people.

The Report of the Anglo-American Committee was completed and signed on Good Friday of April 1946 after four months of investigative work. The Report contained the following recommendations: 1) Immediate admission to Palestine of 100,000 Jewish refugees from Europe; 2) Revocation of the restrictive land and immigration laws of the White Paper of 1939; 3) The government of Palestine should revert to the basis of the Mandate pending the establishment of a trusteeship under the United Nations.[11]

President Truman accepted the recommendation about the 100,000 refugees but was silent with reference to the other recommendations. Mr. Atlee declared in the House of Commons that the admission of the refugees into Palestine is only part of the Report and that the Report must be dealt with in its entirety. Furthermore, he added, that the disarming of all private armies must take place before any large-scale immigration into Palestine. In other words, the British Government rejected the recommendations of the Anglo-American Committee which the British were instrumental in creating. It should be remembered that the Anglo-American Committee had not mentioned a word about disbanding of private armies, by which the Government really aimed to disarm the Jews and leave them defenseless. The Committee felt that if the underlying cause of the troubles in Palestine will have been removed the regime of violence will die a natural death, and not before. We should also emphasize that the British Government had turned down the Committee Report in spite of Mr. Bevin's promise to the Committee that he would accept its recommendations if arrived at unanimously. The Committee Report was achieved unanimously, but Mr. Bevin broke his word of promise and refused to accept the Committee's recommendations.

In contrast to this attitude of the British Government one should mention the courageous and honorable position which President Truman had taken in a letter to King Ibn Saud of Arabia. This, in spite of the pressure on behalf of the Arab cause which American oil interests in Arabia were said to have exerted on the American Government. In his letter the President declared: 'The government and people of the United States have given support to the concept of a Jewish national home in Palestine since the termination of the First World War, which resulted in the freeing of a large area of the Near East, including Palestine, and the establishment of a number of independent states which are now members of the United Nations.

"The United States, which contributed its blood and resources to the winning of that war, could not divest itself of a certain responsibility for the manner in which the freed territories were disposed of, or for the fate of the peoples liberated at the time. It took the position, to which it still adheres, that these peoples should be prepared for self-government and also that a national home for the Jewish people should be established in Palestine. I am happy to note that most of the liberated peoples are now citizens of independent countries."[12]

The President then stated that the Jewish National Homeland had not yet attained its full development, and he added that it is "only natural, therefore, that this government should favor at this time the entry into Palestine of considerable numbers of displaced Jews not only to find shelter there but also to contribute their talents and energies to the upbuilding of the Jewish national home."[13]

2. THE TERMINATION OF THE PALESTINE MANDATE AND THE REBIRTH OF THE STATE OF ISRAEL

In the meantime the situation in Palestine continued to deteriorate. In the spring of 1947 Britain decided to refer the whole Palestine problem to the United Nations. The United Nations created the United Nations Special Committee on Palestine, known in its abbreviated form as UNSCOP. This Committee proceeded to Palestine in the summer of 1947 and examined the whole situation there. It brought back a report in which it recommended the partition of Palestine into a Jewish and Arab State. The problem of partition was then studied by the United Nations Ad Hoc Committee on Palestine at Lake Success in October and November. On November 29, 1947, at a meeting of the General Assembly of the United Nations, by a majority vote of thirty-three to thirteen, the following resolution favoring partition was approved: 'The Mandate for Palestine shall terminate as soon as possible, but in any case not later than August first, 1948 . . . Independent Arab and Jewish States, and the specific international regime for the City of Jerusalem . . . shall come into existence in Palestine two months after the evacuation of the armed forces of the Mandatory Power has been completed, but in any case no later than October first, 1948.'[14]

In the months following the United Nations Partition Resolution, a move was set on foot to nullify the United Nations November decision. When the Security Council of the United Nations met late in February 1948 there was evidence that even the United States was veering from its November position. Weizmann relates in his memoirs that when he had arrived in Washington on March 18 the tide against the November Resolution was irresistible. "The President"—he writes—"was sympathetic personally, and still indicated a firm resolve to press forward with partition. I doubt, however, whether he was himself aware of the extent to which his own policy and purpose had been balked by subordinates in the State Department."[15]

British conduct in Palestine in this interim period was unbecoming of a great power. She was obstructive all the way. We shall quote the following passage from Weizmann's book: "The Mandatory Power refused the United Nations Committee* entry into Palestine, refused to permit the organization of a Jewish militia to take over defense, refused to comply with the Assembly's recommendation to open a port of immigration, refused to hand over any of the Government services to an incoming Jewish successor; it expelled Palestine from the sterling bloc, dismantled the equipment of administration without handing any of it over, and simultaneously allowed the Government services to disintegrate. But while Palestine was closed to the Committee of the United Nations, its frontiers were open to the invasion of irregular Arab forces, which came across the Allenby Bridge on the Jordan, an easily guarded point."[16]

On March 19, 1948 the United States representative in the Security Council announced the United States' reversal of its policy with regards to the November 29 Partition Resolution. He recommended that a special session of the United Nations be called to consider the matter of a trusteeship for Palestine. In the meantime the implementation of partition should be suspended, and a truce should be arranged in Palestine. In mid-April the United Nations

---

* The Committee appointed by the United Nations to proceed to Palestine and to begin the implementation of the November 29 Partition Resolution.

General Assembly reconvened. By that time the fighting in Palestine between the Palestinian Jews and the Arab forces had taken a good turn for the Jews. In the United Nations many delegates, including those from Australia, New Zealand and Eastern Europe, came to the defense of the Jews and demanded that the United Nations abide by its November Partition Resolution. On May 13 Weizmann addressed a letter to President Truman asking him for American recognition of the Government of the newly constituted State of Israel. "The word, I think,"—he wrote—"will regard it as especially appropriate that the greatest living democracy should be the first to welcome the newest into the family of nations."[17]

On May 14, 1948 Professor Jessup, speaking for the American delegation at the United Nations General Assembly, rose and read the following statement from the White House: "This Government has been informed that a Jewish State has been proclaimed in Palestine, and recognition has been requested by the Provisional Government itself. The United States recognizes the Provisional Government as the de facto authority of the new State of Israel."[18]

Notes to Chapter 4

[1] The material in this section is, unless otherwise indicated, based on the information gleaned from the *Contemporary Jewish Record* (New York), August 1942; and from *The Jewish Case*, published in 1947 by the Jewish Agency for Palestine in Jerusalem.

[2] The material in this section is, unless otherwise indicated, based on the information gleaned from *Palestine*, October 1946, published by the American Zionist Emergency Council in New York City; from *The Jewish Case*, published in 1947 by the Jewish Agency for Palestine; and from *Great Britain and Egypt 1914-1951* (Royal Institute of International Affairs: New York, 1952).

[3] *The Jewish Plan For Palestine* (The Jewish Agency For Palestine: Jerusalem, 1947), p. 309.

[4] *New York Times,* May 11, 1942; quoted in *Great Britain and Palestine 1915-1945* (Royal Institute of International Affairs: New York, 1946), p. 134.

[5] *Manchester Guardian,* February 8, 1944; see, *Great Britain and Palestine 1915-1945*, p. 135.

[6] Bartley C. Crum, *Behind The Silken Curtain* (Simon and Schuster: New York, 1947), pp. 54-5. Used by permission.

[7] Ibid., pp. 50-1.

[8] Ibid., p. 55.

[9] Ibid.

[10] For the terms of references see, Richard Crossman, *Palestine Mission* (Harper & Brothers: New York, 1947), p. 206.

[11] Bartley C. Crum, Op. Cit., p. 281.

[12] Ibid., p. 293.

[13] Ibid.

[14] Chaim Weizmann, *Trial and Error* (The Jewish Publication Society Of America: Philadelphia, 1949), vol. 2, p. 459.

[15] Ibid., p. 472.

[16] Ibid., p. 470.

[17] Ibid., p. 478.

[18] Ibid.

CHAPTER 5

THE ORIGINS AND BACKGROUND OF THE BALFOUR DECLARATION

I. THE MORAL BASIS OF THE MANDATE

II. THE PROMULGATION OF THE MANDATE

III. THE POLITICAL FACTOR

IV. THE RELIGIOUS FACTOR

CHAPTER 5

THE ORIGINS AND BACKGROUND OF THE BALFOUR DECLARATION

I. THE MORAL BASIS OF THE MANDATE

The Palestine Mandate, initiated by Great Britain and confirmed by the League of Nations and the United States of America, conceded to world Jewry the right to establish a Jewish National Home in Palestine. Since at the time of the promulgation of the Mandate Palestine was inhabited by a population the vast majority of whom was non-Jewish the question arises what was the moral basis of the Palestine Mandate.

The answer to this question is manifold. In the first place the age-long hostility of the world to the Jews, accentuated by the resurgence of antisemitism in the era preceding the First World War, called for a solution of the Jewish problem on a world-wide level. The reawakening of Jewish nationalism in the second half of the nineteenth century was related to the simultaneous development of the nation-state concept in Western thought. In the light of this concept a nation without a country of its own was an abnormal phenomenon. "In the twentieth century a people without nationhood is a people without virility."[1] The principle of national self-determination, which became one of the war aims of the Allies in the First World War and was incorporated in President Wilson's Fourteen Points, was a recognition of the nation-state concept. The Balfour Declaration which was the basis of the Palestine Mandate was an attempt to solve the problem of Jewish homelessness in the spirit of the principle of national self-determination. "We are adjured"—Lord Cecil declared on December 2, 1917—"to respect the principle of self-determination. . .The British Empire was the first organization to teach that principle to the world and one of the great causes for which we are in this war [First World War] is to secure to all peoples the right to govern themselves and to work out their own destiny. One of the great steps—in my judgement, in some ways the greatest step—we have taken in carrying out this principle is the recognition of Zionism."[2]

But why was Palestine singled out as the country in which to apply to the Jewish people the principle of national self-determination? The

74

answer to this lies in the general recognition of the historical association which through the centuries existed between the Jewish people and Palestine. Palestine is the land where the Jews became a nation. It is the land where they wrote the Bible and where they created spiritual values which have become the spiritual heritage of the civilized world. "The history of Jewish Palestine" . . .—the Royal Commission of 1937 declared—"had been enacted for the most part in a country about the size of Wales: but it constitutes one of the great chapters in the story of mankind. By two primary achievements . . . the gift of Hebraism in ancient Palestine to the modern world must rank with the gifts of ancient Greece and Rome. Christians, moreover, cannot forget that Jesus was a Jew who lived on Jewish soil and founded His gospel on a basis of Jewish life and thought."[3]

It is the hope of a return to Palestine which kept the Jews alive as a nation in the long and bitter years of their dispersion. 'It is our belief in a mystical force, our conviction of a return to the land of Israel, which has kept us alive'—[4] Weizmann declared before the Anglo-American Committee of Inquiry on Palestine. "Jewry was forcibly dispersed and the Jewish religion and culture, which enabled the Jews to survive for centuries as a people without a country, are based on belief in the return to Zion."[5]

The above considerations outweighed the fact that at the time of the framing of the Balfour Declaration the Arabs formed the majority of the inhabitants in Palestine. Furthermore, only under the Jews had Palestine been a distinct, independent, political state. "In the twelve centuries and more that had passed since the Arab conquest Palestine had virtually dropped out of history"—[6] these are the words of the Palestine Royal Commission Report. Speaking in the House of Lords on June 27, 1923, Lord Milner, who represented himself as "a strong supporter for pro-Arab policy," stated that "Palestine can never be regarded as a country on the same footing as the other Arab countries. You cannot ignore all history and tradition in the matter . . . and the future of Palestine cannot possibly be left to be determined by the temporary impressions and feelings of the Arab majority in the country of the present day."[7]

II. The Promulgation Of The Mandate

The events which culminated in the promulgation of the Palestine Mandate go back to the year 1906. In that year Chaim Weizmann, who had been associated with the Chemistry Department of the University of Manchester, was introduced to Balfour, then a member of the British Government. During the conversation Balfour wanted to know the reason why the Zionist Organization had turned down the British Government's offer of the Uganda district of East Africa as a place for Jewish colonization. Weiszmann's reply impressed Balfour with the strength of the Jewish attachment and devotion to Palestine. Weizmann, on the other hand, became convinced, as a result of this meeting with Balfour, of the great possibility of enlisting British sympathetic interest in a Jewish Homeland in Palestine.[8]

Eight years later, on December 3, 1914, C. P. Scott, the distinguished and able editor of the *Manchester Guardian*, a great friend of the Weizmann family and of the Zionist movement, arranged for Weizmann an interview with Lloyd George, then the Chancellor of the Exchequer of the British Government. Lloyd George showed a keen interest in the progress of Jewish colonization work in Palestine and he advised Weizmann to bring the matter of Palestine to the attention of Balfour, and of Herbert H. Asquith who was then Prime Minister. Acting upon Lloyd George's suggestion Weizmann went to see Balfour who was then First Lord of the Admiralty. Balfour, who had remembered Weizmann since his first visit in 1906, greeted him with the words: 'Well, you haven't changed much since we met,' and, continuing in the same breath, he said: 'you know, I was thinking of that conversation of ours, and I believe that when the guns stop firing you may get your Jerusalem.'[9] This brief interview which had taken place in Balfour's office was followed up a few days later with a meeting in Balfour's home lasting several hours.

For the next three years discussions of the Palestine question were carried on in the British press and between Weizmann and the various British cabinet members. On June 13, 1917, Weizmann wrote to Sir Ronald Graham, senior official in the Foreign Office, in which he said: 'It appears desirable from every point of view that the British Government should give expression of its sympathy and support of the Zionist claims on Palestine. In fact, it need only confirm the view which eminent and representative members of the Government have many times expressed to us, and which have formed the basis of our negotiations throughout the long period of almost three years.'[10] A few days later Weizmann, together with Sir Ronald Graham and Lord Rothschild, went to see Balfour. Weizmann suggested in this conversation that the time had come for the British Government to issue an official statement of British policy concerning Palestine. This Balfour promised to do and he asked Weizmann to submit to him the text of a declaration which he, in turn, could present to the War cabinet. The original draft of this declaration was worked out by the Zionists in England and handed to Mr. Balfour by Lord Rothschild on July 18, 1917. Due to strenuous objections of some very influential British assimilationist Jews who had no sympathy with the Jewish national movement the original draft underwent important changes which made the declaration less favorable to the Zionist cause. On October 16, 1917, President Wilson sent his approval of the principles enunciated in the final draft of the declaration. On November 2, 1917, Mr. Balfour, who was then Foreign Secretary of the Government of which Lloyd George was Prime Minister, sent, at Weizmann's suggestion, a letter to Lord Rothschild in which he said: "Dear Lord Rothschild, I have much pleasure in conveying to you on behalf of His Majesty's Government the following declaration of sympathy with Jewish Zionist aspirations, which has been submitted to and approved by the Cabinet."[11] Then followed the text of the declaration: "His Majesty's Government view with favor the establishment in Palestine of a National Home for the Jewish people, and will use their best endeavors to facilitate the achievement of this object, it being clearly understood that nothing shall be done which may prejudice the civil and religious rights of the existing non-Jewish communities in Palestine or the rights and political status enjoyed by Jews in any other country."[12] This letter ended with the following sentence "I should be grateful if you would bring this declaration to the knowledge of the Zionist Federation."[13]

This statement of British official policy, known since then as the Balfour Declaration, was, as already mentioned, approved by President Wilson, and soon after it received official endorsement by the following nations: Yugoslavia on December 27, 1917; France on February 9, 1918; Italy on May 9, 1918; China on December 14, 1918.[14]

"The field in which the Jewish National Home was to be established was understood, at the time of the Balfour Declaration, to be the whole of historic Palestine,"[15] which included Transjordan. As to the meaning of the Balfour Declaration we have the testimony of Lloyd George, who held the office of Prime Minister at the time of the framing and publication of the Declaration. His testimony as given to the Palestine Royal Commission in 1937 is in part as follows: "The idea was . . . that a Jewish state was not to be set up immediately by the Peace Treaty . . . It was contemplated that . . . if the Jews had meanwhile responded to the opportunity . . . and had become a definite majority of the inhabitants, then Palestine would thus become a Jewish Commonwealth."[16]

The Balfour Declaration was in due course of time presented at the Peace Conference of San Remo in 1920. After considerable discussion the Conference confirmed the Declaration and entrusted Britain with the fulfillment of the terms of the Mandate. The next international body to deal with the Palestine problem was the League of Nations. On Saturday, July 24, 1922, on the last day of the League Council meeting, held in London, the Palestine Mandate was ratified with an unanimous vote. Thus the Palestine Mandate giving the Jews of the world the right to establish a Jewish National Home in Palestine was the unanimous decision of Great Britain, America, and fifty-one nations as represented in the League of Nations. After citing the full text of the Balfour Declaration in the preamble, the League of Nations Mandate for Palestine made the following significant addition: "Whereas recognition has thereby been given to the historical connection of the Jewish People with Palestine and to the grounds for reconstituting their National Home in that county . . ." Not "constituting" as worded in the Balfour Declaration but "reconstituting."[17]

III. THE POLITICAL FACTOR

There were two factors which prepared the way for the promulgation of the Balfour Declaration. One of these was the immediate political factor which grew out of the exigencies of the First World War. The second was the religious or spiritual factor which existed long before the First World War.

The state of the war in the months preceding the publication of the Balfour Declaration is described in the following brief excerpts. The first of these may be considered the official version and is given by David Lloyd George, who was Prime Minister when the Balfour Declaration was issued. "In 1917," he states, "the issue of the War was still very much in doubt. [The Germans] had smashed the Rumanians. The Russian Army was completely demoralized by its numerous defeats. The French Army was exhausted and temporarily unequal to striking a great blow. The Italians had sustained a shattering defeat at Caporetto."[18]

A more sombre account of the same situation is given by the Chaplain-in-Ordinary to King George VI from whom we already quoted in a previous chapter: "The Prime Minister and the Foreign Secretary* knew that Britain was in a position well-nigh desperate; and that the failure of their Allies had brought them to the brink of ruin. What was the position? The Russian Army was hopelessly demoralized and Russia was on the eve of laying down her arms. The French Army, owing to bad leadership, was in a condition perilously near mutiny. The submarines were sinking war shipping at an alarming rate that threatened famine. The Italians had been overwhelmed by disaster at Caporetto. No American divisions were yet ready for the trenches."[19]

It was this extremity of the Allies in the First World War which became the opportunity for which the Jewish people had been waiting for some 19 centuries. Soon after the War broke out, in October 1914, Weizmann wrote the following letter to Schmarya Levin, an American Zionist in New York: 'As soon as the situation is somewhat cleared up we could talk plainly to England and to France with regard to the abnormal situation of the Jews, having combatants in all armies, fighting everywhere, and being nowhere recognized . . . Now is the time when the peoples of Great Britain, France, and America will understand us . . . The moral force of our claims will prove irresistible; the political considerations will be favorable . . . But we must be ready for the moment when it comes.'[20]

That moment came in 1917 when the War was at its most perilous phase. Lloyd George, at that time Minister of Ammunitions, happened one day to mention to C. P. Scott, Editor of the *Manchester Guardian*, the scarcity of acetone, a chemical essential to the British Navy. Scott told Lloyd George of a brilliant scientist in the chemistry department of Manchester University who might find the answer to this problem. The man Scott had in mind was Weizmann.

Lloyd George summoned Weizmann to London, and placed before him the matter of the shortage of acetone. 'If,' Lloyd George said, 'we are to have the munitions which will enable us to win the War, we must have acetone. Can you help us?' Weizmann said that he will see what could be done. 'The need is imperative,' Lloyd George said, 'how soon will you be in a position to provide the need?' 'As soon as the final experiment is successful,' was Weizmann's reply.

---

* Balfour

After several months of much experimental work in England and in Canada one of the most crucial problems of the War was solved.[21]

This work for the British Government brought Weizmann in frequent contact with members of the British Government, and afforded him the opportunity to call to their attention the centuries-old Jewish longing for the restoration of their nationhood in Palestine. Upon the successful completion of the acetone assignment the British Government asked Weizmann what kind of reward he wished for his services. Weizmann's reply was that there was only one kind of reward he desired: a National Home in Palestine for his Jewish people.[22]

As mentioned in the beginning of this chapter, Weizmann had been introduced to Lloyd George for the first time in December 1914. At that meeting Lloyd George displayed a keen interest in the subject of the return of the Jews to Palestine. But from the very beginning this question was fraught with many possible complications. It had international, racial, and religious facets, each of which was capable of tipping the scale heavily in one or the opposite direction. Britain's Allies had to be consulted. There were the Arabs whom the British were seeking to stir up against the Turks. How would the Vatican react to the formation of a Jewish Palestine? Under the Arabs much of Palestine was a desert waste. Could such a place be fit for settlement by European Jews?

Weizmann and his fellow Zionists were urging Britain to assume a Protectorate of Palestine. In the beginning the British displayed a reluctance to assume such a responsibility in the Middle East. They suggested that the Zionist leaders present this proposition to France or to America. They proposed a joint administration of Palestine by several powers, by France and England, or by America and England. In a letter to his friend, Mr. C. P. Scott, written on November 12, 1914, Weizmann said: 'Don't you think that the choice for the Jewish people is now within the limits of discussion at least? I realize that we cannot claim anything, we are much too atomized for it, but we can reasonably say that should Palestine fall within the sphere of British influence, and should Britain encourage a Jewish settlement there, as a British dependency, we could have in 25-30 years about a million Jews out there, perhaps more; they would develop the country, bring back civilization to it, and form a very effective guard of the Suez Canal.'[23]

In another communication to the same editor of the *Manchester Guardian* written in March 1915, Weizman said: 'The British Cabinet is not only sympathetic towards the Palestinian aspirations of the Jews, but would like to see them realized. I understand that Great Britain would be willing even to be the initiator of a proposal to that effect at the Peace Conference. But . . . Great Britain would not like to be involved in any responsibilities. In other words, they would leave the organization of the Jewish Commonwealth as an independent political unit entirely to the care of the Jews. At the same time there is a view prevalent that it is not desirable that Palestine should belong to any Great Power.

'These two views are in contradiction. If Great Britain does not wish anybody else to have Palestine she will have to watch it and stop any penetration by another Power . . . Watching is a much less efficient preventative than an actual Protectorate. I therefore thought that a middle course could be adopted, viz: the Jews to take over the country, the whole burden of organization falls on them, but for the next ten or fifteen years they work under temporary British Protectorate.'[24]

The Russian Revolution in the early months of 1917, the collapse of the Eastern front, and the bad state of the War on the Western front combined to put pressure on England to come to a definite decision with regards to Palestine. In the period of the First World War half of the world's Jews lived in Tsarist Russia and the United States of America. The majority of American Jews were of East European origin. To the Jews Tsarist Russia meant oppression and discrimination. Only four years before the outbreak of the First World War, in 1910, a pogrom was staged in Odessa on the Black Sea where Jews were attacked, beaten, and killed. During the period of the 1905 revolution some 400 Jews were killed in the same city of Odessa. Two years earlier a massacre of Jews took place in Kishinev. No wonder that during the first part of the War the millions of East European and American Jews sympathized with the cause of Germany.

It was in those gloomy days of 1917, while America was making preparations for entry into the War, that two situations called for urgent action on the part of the Allies. One of these was to deny to the Germans access to the Russian food supplies, and to make it difficult for them to shift their armies from the Russian front to the West. The second one was to strengthen the Allied cause in America. The British Government gained the conviction that the attainment of both these objectives would be facilitated if world Jewry's sympathies could be won over to the Allied cause. In addition, the Allies could also count on Jewish financial help at a time when the gold reserves and marketable securities of the Allied countries were approaching exhaustion.[25]

It was under these circumstances that when Balfour in his capacity as Foreign Secretary presented his Declaration to the members of the Government for a vote, he said, 'that, from a purely diplomatic and political point of view, it is desirable that some declaration favorable to the aspirations of the Jewish nationalists should now be made. The vast majority of Jews in Russia and America, as, indeed, all over the world, now appeared to be favorable to Zionism. If we could make a declaration favorable to such an idea, we should be able to carry on extremely useful propaganda both in Russia and in America.'[26]

"The Zionist leaders," declared Lloyd George, "gave us definite promise that, if the Allies committed themselves to giving facilities for the establishment of a National Home for the Jews in Palestine, they would do their best to rally to the Allied cause Jewish sentiment and support throughout the world. They kept their word in the letter and the spirit . . ."[27] German efforts to benefit from the harvests of the Ukraine and the Don basin were frustrated, and the Germans were forced to keep in Russia hundreds of thousands of their troops. While these results cannot be attributed entirely to Jewish activities, "we have good reason to believe," Lloyd George said, "that Jewish propaganda in Russia had a great deal to do with the difficulties created for the Germans in Southern Russia after the peace of Brest-Litovsk."[28]

Through Sir Mark Sykes and Colonel Lawrence*, both of whom were deeply interested in promoting the welfare of the Arab peoples, while at the same time they were sympathetic to the cause of a Jewish Palestine, the British decision concerning a Jewish Palestine was transmitted to King Hussein of Arabia and his son Feisal. Hussein was then the acknowledged leader of the Arab peoples.[29] "The Arab leaders," says Lloyd George, "did not offer any objection to the declaration so long as the rights of the Arabs in Palestine were respected. Pledges were given to the non-Jewish population of Palestine who constituted the great majority of its inhabitants, as well as to

---

* "Lawrence of Arabia"

the Jews . . . There was a two-fold understanding given to them, that the establishment of a Jewish National Home would not in any way, firstly, affect the civil or religious rights of the general population of Palestine; secondly, would not diminish the general prosperity of that population. Those were the only pledges we gave to the Arabs."[30]

IV. The Religious Factor

While the Balfour Declaration had the full support of Britain's French and Italian Allies, it would have never seen the light of the day had Zionist leaders been led to deal with the French or Italian Governments instead of with the British Government. Lloyd George informs us that while the selection of the particular time for the publication of the Balfour Declaration was determined by political and diplomatic considerations, the British attitude to the Zionist idea rested on different grounds. "Men like Mr. Balfour, Lord Milner, Lord Robert Cecil, and myself," Lloyd George declares, "were in whole-hearted sympathy with the Zionist ideal. The same thing applied to all the leaders of public opinion in our country and in the Dominions, Liberal, Conservative, and Labor."[31]

Weizmann who was born and raised in Eastern Europe where he had witnessed a paganized and Jew-hating form of Christianity, discovered in the 40 years of his dealings with British leaders that the secret of British sympathy with the idea of a Jewish National Home in Palestine was the English people's profound reverence for the Bible. "Men like Balfour, Churchill, Lloyd George," he says, "were deeply religious, and believed in the Bible, . . . to them the return of the Jewish people to Palestine was a reality, so that the Zionists represented to them a great tradition for which they had enormous respect . . . The same spirit animated men like Smuts* and Milner . . . Those British statesmen of the old school, I have said, were genuinely religious. They understood as a reality the concept of the [Jewish Return]. It appealed to their tradition and their faith. Some of them were completely baffled by the opposition to our plan on the part of the assimilated Jews . . . Lord Milner was a great friend of Claude Montefiore, the spiritual leader of the anti-Zionists; but on this point he would not be influenced. Milner understood profoundly that the Jews alone were capable of rebuilding Palestine, and of giving it a place in the modern family of nations. He said publicly: 'If the Arabs

---

* Field Marshal Smuts of South Africa

think that Palestine will become an Arab country, they are very much mistaken'. "[32]

British attachment to the Bible has its origin in the Puritan period. "No greater moral change has ever passed over a nation than passed over England during the years which parted the middle of the reign of Elizabeth from the meeting of the Long Parliament. England became the people of a book, and that book was the Bible . . . It was read in churches and read at home, and everywhere its words, as they fell on ears which custom had not deadened, kindled a startling enthusiasm . . . Elizabeth might silence or tune the pulpits; but it was impossible for her to silence or tune the great preachers of justice, and mercy, and truth, who spoke from the book which she again had opened for her people . . . Its effect was simply amazing. The whole temper of the nation felt the change. A new conception of life and of man superseded the old. A new moral and religious impulse spread through every class."[33]

Balfour acquired his interest in the Jewish people from his mother, Lady Blanche Balfour, the sister of Lord Salisbury. She "embodied all that was best in the tradition of Victorian piety. She waited and looked eagerly for the second Advent [of Christ] . . . Sitting in the Whittingehame pew in his parish church, young Balfour heard the pure evangelical doctrine of his day with fire: 'The Jew first must return to Zion and then will come the final consummation.' When Balfour met Dr. Chaim Weizmann in Manchester in 1906, he realized that his mother's faith was not a dream, that the new Jerusalem had firm foundations on earth."[34]

When Balfour visited America in 1917 and broached the subject of the Jewish National Home to President Wilson, he found the President's interest in the Zionist cause no less intense than his own. "For Woodrow Wilson was also brought up in the same great tradition: he had imbibed from his father in his youth what Balfour had learned from his mother. The son of a Presbyterian minister, he had nothing to learn from the worshipper in Whittingehame parish church. President Wilson was in the end as enthusiastic a believer in Zionism as Lord Balfour. He stated the Zionist idea thus: 'I am persuaded that the Allied nations, with the fullest concurrence of our Government and our people, are agreed that in Palestine shall be laid the foundations of a Jewish commonwealth.'[35]

Upon Balfour's return from the United States the stage was set for presenting to the members of the Cabinet the Government Statement on Palestine. Fierce opposition was offered by Edwin Montagu, Secretary for India, a Jew and a spokesman of a group of wealthy British assimilationist Jews who feared that a reborn Jewish nation in Palestine might somehow prejudice their sheltered position in their native England.

A heated discussion ensued and Balfour defended energetically the Zionist position. "It was then the Prime Minister, David Lloyd George, caught fire from Balfour's winged arguments. And when the Welshman kindled, the heavens were aglow. He also was brought up in the same great tradition. As a boy he often heard the same arguments and the same doctrines which Woodrow Wilson heard from his father and Balfour from his mother. His uncle, the Baptist cobbler, could speak thereon as one inspired.

"Zionism claims many noble Jews as its originators," continues the Very Reverend Norman Maclean, "but few realize that the three men who made the policy possible were Christians—an American Presbyterian, a Scottish Presbyterian, and a Welsh Baptist. These were the men who lifted it up from the oratory of assemblies which had no power, and from the efforts of struggling groups of early settlers, to the Council Chambers of Governments which controlled half the world, and which secured for it the sanction of the League of Nations and of all the Governments therein represented."[36]

In her pamphlet on the Balfour Declaration, Balfour's niece states that the Jewish desire to recapture national normalcy appeared to the British as a perfectly natural urge. But, she continues, "understanding of the deeper and more spiritual aspects of Zionism comes to them from another source. There is no better guide to Jewish nationalism than the Old Testament. Knowledge of the Bible and reverence for its teachings have permeated the British character and British political life for centuries, and markedly so in the British attitude towards the Jews. It influenced the Puritans when they admitted them back to this country some four hundred years ago. It influenced Lloyd George and Balfour when a British Government acknowledged the historic claim of Jewry to the Promised Land. It influenced leaders of thought in the intervening period, notably in the great and pious Victorian Age. Lord Shaftesbury, the statesman and social reformer, found time to devise a scheme for bringing the Jews back to Palestine under the guarantee of the five Western Powers. This was in 1838, nearly sixty years before the Zionists at their First Congress formulated their 'Basle Program' . . . Lord Shaftesbury had laid his plans before Lord Palmerston, then Foreign Secretary, and received a promise of consideration. 'But (he wrote in his diary) though the motive be kind, it is not sound. I am forced to argue politically, financially, commercially; these considerations strike him* home; he weeps not like his Master over Jerusalem**, nor prays that now at last she may put on her beautiful garments.' "[37]

In her biography of her distinguished uncle Mrs. Dugdale thus describes the religious side of Balfour's personality: "None who shared his daily life ever doubted the importance in his eyes of the things that are unseen and eternal . . . He was confirmed in the Church of England while he was at Eton, and was ever afterwards a communicant in that Church, as well as in the Church of Scotland . . . Communion was held quarterly at the Parish Church at Whittingehame, and he always attended it when he was at home. At Whittingehame every Sunday evening family prayers were read by him. They consisted of the Lord's Prayer, the General Confession, and prayers from the Anglican liturgy, including often the Collect for Sunday, and a chapter from the Bible, which he always chose himself; Isaiah, or the Psalms, or St. Paul's Epistles were perhaps drawn upon most."[38]

"Balfour's interest in the Jews and their history was lifelong," his niece relates. "It originated in the Old Testament training of his mother, and his Scottish upbringing. As he grew up, his intellectual admiration and sympathy for certain aspects of Jewish philosophy and culture grew also, and the problem of the Jews in the modern world seemed to him of immense importance. He always talked eagerly on this, and I remember in childhood imbibing from him the idea that Christian religion and civilization owes to Judaism an immeasurable debt, shamefully ill repaid."[39]

"During his last illness," she tells us, "recalling in conversation some of the great events which he had helped to shape, and some of the great movements which he had watched developing during his eighty years of life, he said that perhaps nothing that he had done or tried to do, would prove of more permanent value to the world than his support for the Jewish national cause."[40]

When the Balfour Declaration was made public by the British Government on November 2, 1917, there was great rejoicing among

---

* Lord Palmerston
** This has reference to Christ's weeping over Jerusalem shortly before His Crucifixion.

Jews and Christians. "For the Jews," the Very Reverend Norman Maclean says, "this was the greatest event since Titus destroyed Jerusalem, for their restoration as a nation and their deliverance from brutality and terror were now bound up with the greatest Empire on earth, whose word was as good as its bond. No wonder Jewry went delirious with joy and no wonder a great multitude of earnest Christians rejoiced with them, for they saw in that Declaration the fulfillment of the conditions which must precede the final triumph of righteousness—the coming again of the Lord."[41]

Notes to Chapter 5

[1] Richard Crossman, *Palestine Mission,* (Harper and Brothers: New York, 1947), p. 72. Reprinted by permission of A. D. Peters & Co.

[2] Quoted in *The Jewish Plan For Palestine,* (The Jewish Agency For Palestine: Jerusalem, 1947), p. 109.

[3] *Palestine Royal Commission Report, 1937,* Chapter I., paragraph 7, pp. 4-5; quoted in *The Jewish Plan For Palestine,* p. 105.

[4] Bartley C. Crum, *Behind The Silken Curtain,* (Simon and Schuster: New York, 1947), p. 169.

[5] Richard Crossman, Op. Cit., p. 70.

[6] *Palestine Royal Commission Report, 1937,* Chapter I., paragraph 11, p. 6; see, *The Jewish Plan For Palestine,* p. 105.

[7] *Hansard Parliamentary Debates,* House of Lords (His Majesty's Stationery Office: London, June 27, 1923), vol. 54, 669.

[8] Chaim Weizmann, *Trial and Error,* (The Jewish Publication Society Of America: Philadelphia, 1949), vol. 1, pp. 109-111.

[9] Ibid., vol. 1, p. 152.

[10] Ibid., vol. 1, p. 203.

[11] *The Jewish Plan For Palestine,* p. 301.

[12] Chaim Weizmann, Op. Cit., vol. 1, p. 208.

[13] *The Jewish Plan For Palestine,* p. 301.

[14] Ibid.

[15] *Palestine Royal Commission Report, 1937,* Chapter II., paragraph 42; see, *The Jewish Plan For Palestine,* p. 301.

[16] *Palestine Royal Commission Report, 1937,* Chapter II., paragraph 20; see, *The Jewish Plan For Palestine,* p. 301.

[17] *Great Britain and Palestine, 1915-1945,* (Royal Institute of International Affairs: London, 1946), p. 151.

[18] David Lloyd George, *The Truth About The Peace Treaties* (Victor Gollancz Ltd.: London, 1938), vol. 2, p. 1119. Published as *Memoirs Of The Peace Conference,* New Haven, Conn., 1939. Used by permission of Howard Fertig, Inc., New York, 1970, and Beaverbrook Newspaper, Ltd., London.

[19] Norman Maclean, *His Terrible Swift Sword*, (Christian Council On Palestine: New York, 1941), p. 33.

[20] Quoted by Blanche E. C. Dugdale, *Arthur James Balfour*, (G. P. Putnam's Sons: New York, 1937), vol. 1, p. 161. Used by permission.

[21] Norman Maclean, Op. Cit., p. 38.

[22] Ibid.

[23] Quoted by Mrs. Edgar Dugdale, *The Balfour Declaration: Origins and Background*, (The Jewish Agency For Palestine: London, 1940), p. 23. Used by permission.

[24] Ibid., p. 24.

[25] David Lloyd George, Op. Cit., vol. 2, p. 1122.

[26] Ibid., pp. 1136-7.

[27] Ibid., p. 1139.

[28] Ibid., p. 1140.

[29] Ibid.

[30] Ibid., p. 1142.

[31] Ibid., p. 1122.

[32] Chaim Weizmann, Op. Cit., vol. 1, pp. 157, 178-9.

[33] John Richard Green, *A Short History Of The English People*, (The Colonial Press: New York, 1899), vol. 2, pp. 139, 141. Used by permission of E. P. Dutton & Co., Inc.

[34] Norman Maclean, Op. Cit., pp. 30-1.

[35] Ibid., p. 31.

[36] Ibid., p. 32.

[37] Mrs. Edgar Dugdale, *The Balfour Declaration: Origins and Background*, p. 9.

[38] Blanche E. C. Dugdale, *Arthur James Balfour*, vol. 1, p. 30.

[39] Ibid., p. 324.

[40] Mrs. Edgar Dugdale, *The Balfour Declaration: Origins and Background*, p. 5.

[41] Norman Maclean, Op. Cit., p. 26.

CHAPTER 6

THE NULLIFICATION OF THE BALFOUR DECLARATION

I. THE POLITICO-ECONOMIC FACTOR

II. THE MORAL FACTOR

    1. The Immediate Effects of the White Paper of May 1939

    2. England's Spiritual Decadence

III. GOD'S OVERRULING PROVIDENCE

CHAPTER 6

THE NULLIFICATION OF THE
BALFOUR DECLARATION

Introduction

Two sets of circumstances combined to induce Britain to assume the Palestine Mandate. We discussed these in the preceding chapter. Similarly two sets of circumstances moved Britain to nullify the aims of the Palestine Mandate. A discussion of these is the subject of this chapter.

I. THE POLITICO-ECONOMIC FACTOR

In the preceding chapter mention was made that before the British Government came to a definite decision in favor of a Jewish National Home in Palestine, it manifested a reluctance to assume the responsibility associated with the administration of a Palestine Mandate. A number of reasons may have dictated a policy of caution. But the chief reason behind Britain's hesitancy to assume a purely British protectorate over Palestine must have been the lack of a strong material incentive. Realizing this, the Zionists were striving to supply this deficiency by an attempt to convince British leaders that Palestine would guard the interests of the British empire, especially with respect to the Suez Canal.[1] In ten to fifteen years after the publication of the Balfour Declaration certain conditions developed which made this Jewish foresight terribly relevant. In one of Daniel's visions the Mediterranean area is depicted as the focus of great political upheavals during certain periods of the Times of the Gentiles, (Daniel 7:2).[2] During the centuries of the Jewish Dispersion, when the Mediterranean region was cut off from Europe by Mohammedan occupation, the Mediterranean world was in a state of political, economic and cultural stagnation. In the years since the promulgation of the Balfour Declaration the Mediterranean area has experienced a reawakening and has once again become, not a center, but the center of international disturbances, a veritable keg of dynamite.

Two factors produced this changed state of affairs. One of these has to do with the presence of vast oil deposits in this area. During the 19th century Turkey's financial position was in such a precarious condition that only foreign financial loans were keeping her from bankruptcy. This condition existed at a time when an enormous oil wealth lay concealed underground within the confines of the Turkish empire. Within a few years following the liberation of Palestine from Turkish rule and the framing of the Palestine Mandate fabulously rich oil deposits have been located in the territories of the former Turkish empire. It is estimated that the Middle East has larger oil reserves than any other single part of the world, and about half of the world's known oil reserves.[3]

Britain and the United States have been the largest oil concession holders in the Middle East. The British Government has a controlling voice in the British-held concessions, while American oil interests are privately owned. While America has large oil deposits within her own boundaries and can draw also on oil reserves from other oil producing countries on the American Continent, Great Britain and Western Europe depend on Middle East oil to supply their industrial needs. Palestine assumed its strategic importance in this oil picture in the beginning of the 1930's. In 1934 the Iraq Petroleum Company opened a pipeline from Kirkuk, in Iraq, to Haifa. In that year also the British completed the construction of a modern deep-sea harbor in Haifa. The length of this pipeline from Kirkuk to its Haifa terminal is 620 miles with a branch line 540 miles long running to Tripoli, in Syria. These piplines had each a daily capacity of 45,000 barrels of oil. In addition, the Anglo-Iranian Oil Company and the Anglo-Saxon Petroleum Company constructed in Haifa a large refinery which began to operate a few months after the outbreak of the Second World War with a daily production of over 80,000 barrels of oil. Prior to the Arab-Jewish War in 1948 these companies had planned to enlarge Haifa's oil refining facilities which would have made of Haifa the largest refinery in the Middle East after Abadan in Persia. With the continued expansion of the oil producing facilities of the vast Arabian oil fields plans were being made to develop another oil handling port in the Gaza district of Palestine, a hundred miles south of Haifa. The importance of Palestine as an oil handling center consisted in this that the Kirkuk-Haifa pipeline reduced transportation costs considerably by eliminating 3,300 miles of sea-route and the toll, which in 1947 amounted to 18 cents per barrel, payable in passing through the Suez Canal.[4]

To the above we should add that except for the oil concessions in Iran* no oil concession in the Persian Gulf area was acquired before

* Persia

1925 and most of them were leased in the 1930's.[5] It is therefore no mere coincidence that from 1930 on British policy in the Middle East was bent on appeasing the Arabs and nullifying the aim of the Palestine Mandate.

The second factor which served to move Palestine to the forefront of British imperial policy was of a strategic and military nature. Italy's expansionist designs in the Mediterranean area and the mounting aggressive pressure of Nazi Germany made Britain cast about for potential allies. Next to France and the countries bordering on the English Channel the Near East was of the utmost strategic importance to the security of Britain. From there she received the oil supplies to run her industry at home and to operate her ships at sea; in the Near East was the highly strategic Suez Canal, and through the Near East ran the most direct path to India and Britain's Far East Dominions and other possessions.

To protect this highly vulnerable and vitally important Near East region Britain must have allies. Hence British foreign policy in the Near East during the 1930's concentrated on gaining the friendship of the Arab nations and concluding with them mutual assistance pacts for the defence of the Near East in the case of war. To appease the Arabs the Palestine Mandate had to be scrapped. In the overall picture of the security of the British Empire, of what significance was the Jewish National Homeland in Palestine? In the appeasement scheme of Chamberlain no small nation counted for very much. Was not little Czechoslovakia, one of the finest democracies in Central Europe with a gallant army and valuable munition works, thrown to the Nazi wolves in the hope of keeping these wolves away from the doors of the great powers? What better treatment could the Jewish people expect? Wherein the White Paper of 1930 failed, Chamberlain's White Paper of 1939 succeeded. The British Government nullified the Palestine Mandate. But World War II proved the utter futility of Chamberlain's appeasement policy both in Europe and the Near East, as it was based, literally and figuratively, on the shifting sands of the Middle East deserts.

When the Second World War ended Russia emerged as one of the two greatest world powers. Her geographical proximity to the Near and Middle East and her re-entry into Middle East politics made her a potential threat to British Middle East interests. The aim and end of British Middle East policy following World War Two were essentially the same as in the 1930's just preceding World War Two: to safeguard communications with Australia and New Zealand and the Far Eastern areas of the British Commonwealth; to maintain owner-ship, and control over the British air-fields around the Persian Gulf.[6] The political realignment of the world at the end of World War Two, and the growing violence of Egyptian nationalism clamoring for the evacuation of British troops from the Suez Canal region, made the retention of Palestine an urgent military necessity for Britain. In the view of the British Chiefs of Staff the port of Haifa, second only to Alexandria as a naval base, was excellently suited to take the place of Alexandria should Britain be forced to leave Alexandria; and the northern part of the Negev—the southern desert region of Palestine—could replace the military base of the Suez Canal.[7] Thus Palestine loomed as the keystone in Britain's strategy for the protection of the oil-fields of the Near East and the safeguarding of the life-line of the British Empire; while Palestine's geographic proximity to Egypt would have made the defense of the Suez Canal relatively easy.

To implement these plans of the British Chiefs of Staff, Bevin, Foreign Secretary in the post-World War Two Labor Government, decided to continue the Chamberlain's 1939 White Paper policy of nullification of the Palestine Mandate. British plans for the Middle East were to be based on the continued appeasement of the Arab states as potential allies in the case of an armed conflict with Russia. This, in spite of the sad experience with the Arab states in World War Two. Well-informed observers have repeatedly stated that in the pursuance of her post-World War Two Middle East policy England had the support of the extensive American oil interests in the Near East and, unofficially at least, of the American Chiefs of Staff and State Department. "It was well known in Britain", declares Cross-man, a Labor Party member of the British Parliament and a former member of the Anglo-American Committee of Inquiry on Palestine, "that the American oil interests and the American Chiefs of Staff were at least as anti-Zionist as the Foreign Office. Mr. Bevin has always hoped that they would be strong enough to swing the admin-istration behind his 'realistic' policy for dealing with Zionism. That this hope was not fantastic was later proved by the [Truman] administration's about-face on partition."[8]*

When the State of Israel smashed the invading Arab armies the British Middle East policy of 1945-6 collapsed as fully as did the

---

* The partition of Palestine which the United Nations had voted in November 1947.

Chamberlain 1939 policy of which it was a continuation. And yet it need not have been so. Who should have known better than the British of the low value of Arab military power. In his book *Palestine Mission* Crossman says: "All . . . [Arab States] are economically and militarily feeble and would be quire unable to fight a modern war without the active assistance of a great power."[9] "An Arab expert in Cairo told me that the Haganah* was the most powerful military force in the Middle East, apart from the British Army, and has completely transformed the balance of power."[10]

In an article on the necessity to insure an uninterrupted flow of oil from the Middle East, written obviously under the impact of the outcome of the 1967 war between Israel and the Arabs, the writer, a vice-president of the Standard Oil Company (New Jersey), makes among other things the following statement: "The United States imports only 3 to 4 per cent of its oil supply from the area. But this in no way implies that Middle East oil is unimportant to the interests of the United States. Our friends and allies throughout the free world depend on Middle East oil. If those nations were to be cut off from their Middle East sources of supply, their economies would be very gravely affected. This would have severe repercussions on the American economy, not to mention the damage to political stability and military security within the free world . . . The oil resources of the Middle East are so important to the interests of everybody concerned that supplies will have to be continued. The free world needs these supplies if its future requirements are to be met; and the Middle East depends on the existence of free world markets . . . In the past, economic realities have ultimately prevailed over political considerations, and there is reason to expect that they will in the future. We need the Middle East, and the Middle East needs us."[11]

That the above is an unsatisfactory evaluation of the Middle East situation is evident to any student of history. The political instability of the Arab Middle East stems from a variety of circumstances having nothing to do with Israel's return to the Middle East. In the first place, every geographic region which witnesses the rapid rise of independent nations experiences political turmoil until these new nations attain political maturity. This was the case with the emergence of the new European nations in the Middle Ages. It is so now in Africa and Asia. The political unrest in the Arab Middle East is

---

* Jewish defense force in existence before the establishment of the State of Israel.

compounded by a multiplicity of circumstances peculiar to this region, such as the presence in its midst of vast oil reserves and the Suez Canal international highway, and the rivalry between the West and communist Russia.

Geopolitically Israel is an insignificant factor in the Middle East. She occupies a notch in the Middle East. Her little country is poor in natural resources, and much of it is desert. The Jewish population in Israel numbers at the present about 2½ million. How could she possibly be a threat to the tens of millions of the Arab world?

But opposition to Israel has been taken advantage of by various competing and contesting parties to advance their interest. Russia has been using hatred of Israel to incite the Arabs against the West. The self-appointed and unscrupulous Arab politicians have used hostility to Israel to keep the Arab masses in line and to divert their attention from the real cause of their exploitation and poverty.

As to the oil supplies in the Arab territories the West has located the oil fields and developed them. It is the West which supplies the customers for the oil. Russia has no need for the Arab oil, she has her own oil fields. "Ibn Saud, as well as other Arab potentates," Bartley C. Crum said, "were more dependent upon the revenues from American and British oil concessions than we were dependent upon them. They needed our capital, our industry, our experience, and our commercial protection. . . As for the bogey of Ibn Saud and the others withdrawing their oil concessions to offer them to the Soviet, this seemed to me altogether untenable. There is too great a gap between the economic socialism of Russia and the economic feudalism of Saudi Arabia and Iraq. It seemed highly unlikely to me that Ibn Saud and the other Arab rulers would be able to maintain their privileged status if they permitted Russian economic expansion into their countries."[12]

As to the statement by the vice-president of the Standard Oil Company that "economic realities have ultimately prevailed over political considerations, and there is reason to expect that they will in the future", this is not the way this writer reads history. The people that came over on the Mayflower were moved by a determination to set up on the American Continent a political state in accordance with their religious concepts. The Jews who were motivated by economics did not go to Palestine. The Pioneers who left their European homes in the last quarter of the 19th century and went to Palestine were driven by one desire: to put an end to the tragedy of Jewish national homelessness. They went back to Palestine to re-establish a Jewish State. They were motivated by political, not economic, considerations. Why did the Jews pick Palestine to establish there their National Homeland? The answer is, because the Jewish people originated there. The name "Jew" identifies a person or people whose origin is traced directly to the Judaean Kingdom. The name "Arab" designates a person or a people that belongs to the Arabian Peninsula, whether by virtue of race or language.

In the beginning of his article on the Middle East crisis the vice-president of the Standard Oil Company says this: "As an oilman, I tend to think first of its oil; but the area has an historic importance that goes back many centuries before the discovery of oil. The Middle East was the birthplace of our very civilization. Three great religions originated in the area." The three great religions are, of course, Judaism, Christianity and Islam. At the very beginning of its national existence Israel was enjoined not to give priority to economic considerations. As they were standing at the borders of the Promised Land, ready at God's command to enter and take possession of it, Moses sought to impress upon the Israelites one of the enduring lessons of their forty years experiences in the Wilderness, namely, "that man does not live by bread alone, but that man lives by everything that proceeds out of the mouth of the LORD" (Deuteronomy 8:3). The survival of the Jewish people, one of the great marvels of history, is proof of the truth of the above statement.

Centuries later Jesus Christ said to His Jewish people: "Therefore do not be anxious, saying, 'What shall we eat?' or 'What shall we drink:' or 'What shall we wear:' For the heathen seek all these things; and your heavenly Father knows that you need them all. But seek first his kingdom and his righteousness, and all these things shall be yours as well" (Matthew 6: 31-33). Before He commenced His Messianic ministry Jesus Christ went into the Wilderness, there to be tried and tested as Israel had been in the long ago. As He meditated on the nature of the work which He came to do, the Tempter suggested to Him that the easy way to achieve His goal is to build His Kingdom on a materialistic foundation. "If you are the Son of God," he said to Him, "command these stones to become loaves of bread" (Matthew 4:3). Had Christ succumbed to Satan's temptation He might have been acclaimed by Israel and placed on a throne instead of on a cross. But He could not have fulfilled the intent and purpose of the Law of Moses (Matthew 5: 17-18), nor could He have founded the New Covenant promised by Jeremiah (Jeremiah 31: 31-34; 31: 30-33 Hebrews). The world would not have had a Savior who died for its sins. Mankind would never have known a God who "so loved the world that He gave His only begotten Son, that whoever believes in Him should not perish, but have eternal life" (John 3:16). Consequently, Christ rejected Satan's advice and He said to the Tempter: "It is written, 'Man shall not live by bread alone, but by every word that proceeds from the mouth of God'" (Matthew 4:4).

II. THE MORAL FACTOR

The moral, or rather immoral, aspect of Britain's nullification of the Palestine Mandate found full expression in the publication of the so-called White Paper of May 1939. Its main points were presented in a previous chapter. It forbade settlement by Jews in nine-tenths of Mandate Palestine. 75,000 Jewish immigrants were to be admitted into Palestine in the space of five years. After 1944, Jewish immigration would continue only with Arab acquiescence, which meant that for all practical purposes, Jewish immigration to Palestine after 1944 would be terminated, and the Jews in Palestine would be reduced to a status of a permanent minority. An Arab State would be set up in Palestine within ten years after the promulgation of the White Paper.

1. THE IMMEDIATE EFFECTS OF THE PAPER OF MAY 1939

The Second World War began soon after the issuing of the White Paper of 1939. Many Jews from Central and Eastern Europe managed to escape by way of the Balkan countries before these countries were overrun by the Nazis. Their aim was to reach the shores of Palestine. The British Government shut the doors of the Promised Land in their face. Thousands of these Jews could have been saved. Among these refugees fleeing from Nazi-occupied countries were the intellectual leaders of Europe: professors and doctors of world-wide fame, men at whose feet Westerners considered it a privilege to sit and learn.

The ships which they hired to make their escape were derelicts long out of service. The fares which they were compelled to pay were exorbitant. As many as could be crowded into these ships were permitted to embark. There were no sanitary provisions. Food was scarce and often unedible. There were no sleeping accommodations. Words fail to describe the horrible conditions which prevailed on these coffin-ships which sailed the seas, with every port shut against them, for no country would admit them.

When refused entry at the ports of Palestine the passengers on one of these ships, moved by despair, shut the officers in their quarters and in the dark of the night drove the ships on the beaches. Not knowing what to do with this wretched human cargo the Palestinian authorities appealed to the Government in London for instructions. The reply from London was that since the current immigration quota for Jews was already exhausted no more Jews could be admitted into the country. The Very Reverend Norman Maclean, who was chaplain of St. Andrew's Church in Jerusalem at that particular period, had the opportunity to gain first-hand information concerning these stranded coffin-ships. Commenting on the heartless behavior of the Chamberlain Government, he says in his stirring book, *His Terrible Swift Sword*: "It was manifest that the finer feelings of the human heart had already been blunted. Yet this position was scarcely conceivable; that a condition of things should at last be reached when men would debate whether shipwrecked women and children should be saved from the devouring sea . . . A handful of Christians* seemed suddenly to remember words of their Master: 'I was a stranger and you took me not in.' One of these Christians felt as if he were suddenly touched by a hand stretched from the Great Unseen, and he turned to his companion, as they gazed on the stranded ship and its so dreadful a throng gazing hungrily towards the land; and he recited in a low and awed voice: 'Then shall He say also unto them on the left hand, Depart from me, accursed ones, into the eternal fire which has been prepared for the devil and his angels; for I was a refugee and you took me not in; naked and you did not clothe me; sick and in a coffin-ship and you did not visit me' ".[13]

What the local Palestinian officials could not do, the Medical Health Officer succeeded in doing. The ship had been carrying these unfortunate refugees for three months, and rats, the carriers of the plague, were everywhere. A message was cabled to London that unless immediate action is taken the plague might break out and spread to inhabitants of Tel Aviv on whose sand beaches the ship was stranded. Then, not until then, permission to land was granted.

"It has often been remarked", continues the Very Reverend Maclean, "that when Empires enter on their decline the degeneration

---

* Who were watching the scene from the beaches.

begins at the top and takes a long time to reach the man behind the plough or behind the spear. . . When the policemen, who had formed the cordon guarding the shore, saw these starved and destitute people staggering to land, they were moved to the very depths of human compassion. They snatched the babies out of their mother's arms and carried them; they lifted the children on their shoulders; . . . they put all the money they had in their pockets into the trembling hands of ragged men and women! They saw before them their own parents, their own grandparents, reduced to this. Tears were in their eyes, but their voices rang out good cheer and welcome. . .

"In a few days the companies who thus landed at last on the shore of their National Home found themselves behind barbed wire— detained in camps. . . Their kindred were anxious to teach them new crafts. They were not allowed. The quota had been exceeded. Homes were open to them. They were not allowed. . . There was work waiting to be done; they must not do it. They had committed an unforgivable crime; when they ought to have accepted their fate and have submitted to slavery and death, they had the hardihood to escape. Illegality such as that must be curbed."[14]

2. ENGLAND'S SPIRITUAL DECADENCE

How could England deny to these sons and daughters of woe access to the only refuge which seemed left, the land which Balfour, Lloyd George and Woodrow Wilson had intended to be their asylum? How could such treatment be meted out by a Government of a country which all over the world had been a champion of the oppressed and the support of the free? How could a Government which represented an Empire composed of a multitude of nationalities, races and religions, held together by an ideal of liberty and equality, apply discriminatory landholding and immigration laws to the people of Palestine?

These are some of the questions the Very Reverend Norman Maclean was asking when he wrote his book. The answer is, in the first place, appeasement and political expediency. The 3,000 Arab gangsters, who drew their pay from Hitler and Mussolini and who filled Palestine with their crimes, had to be appeased. By this time, on the eve of World War Two, Chamberlain and his Colonial Secretary should have known that appeasement was ineffective. Ethiopia was swallowed up by Mussolini, but Mussolini was not appeased. Manchuria was taken over by Japan, yet Japan was not appeased. Czechoslovakia was sold down the river, but Hitler was not appeased. Not only did appeasement not bring "peace in our time", it paved the way for the Second World War.

But appeasement, as an international policy, proved not only a miserable and disastrous failure; it was dishonorable and immoral. As far as the Palestine Mandate was concerned, the framers of the appeasement policy knew that no scheme could be pushed through the House of Commons which was an open repudiation of the Balfour Declaration. Hence the new policy had to be presented in such a form which would suggest that it constitutes a fulfillment of the Balfour Declaration, while in reality it represented a subversion of it. Reverend Maclean declares that this was nothing but the technique of the big lie which the Nazis had pursued so successfully.

This new policy with relation to Palestine was based on a reinterpretation of the Balfour Declaration. To grasp its full significance, we need to have, once more, before us the text of this Declaration. It was addressed by Balfour to Lord Rothschild, as one of the leaders of the British Zionists, and it was prefaced with the following sentence:

"I have much pleasure in conveying to you, on behalf of his Majesty's Government, the following declaration of sympathy with the Jewish Zionist aspirations, which has been submitted to and approved by the Cabinet.

His Majesty's Government view with favor the establishment in Palestine of a National Home for the Jewish people, and will use their best endeavors to facilitate the achievement of this object, it being clearly understood that nothing shall be done which may prejudice the civil and religious rights of the existing non-Jewish communities in Palestine or the rights and political status enjoyed by Jews in any other country".

The qualifying clause, "it being clearly understood that nothing shall be done which may prejudice the civil and religious rights of the existing non-Jewish communities" had as its purpose the protection of the civil and religious privileges of the various religious communities, such as Christian and Mohammedan communities. The word "Arabs" is not even mentioned in the Declaration.

The reinterpretation of the Balfour Declaration by the Chamberlain Government consisted in the sudden discovery that the main objective of the Declaration was the qualifying clause, "it being clearly understood that nothing shall be done which may prejudice the civil and religious rights of the existing non-Jewish communities". Upon this premise the chief aim of the Balfour Declaration was the establishment in Palestine of an Arab State. But if this reinterpretation is correct, then how could it be reconciled with the opening words addressed by Balfour to Lord Rothschild: "I have much pleasure in conveying to you, on behalf of His Majesty's Government, the following declaration of sympathy with the Jewish Zionist aspirations"; how could it be reconciled with the main thrust of the text of the Declaration, "His Majesty's Government view with favor the establishment in Palestine of a National Home for the Jewish people, and will use their best endeavor to facilitate the achievement of this object"?

But this dishonorable approach designed to make it appear that the Chamberlain Government is actually carrying out the intent of the Balfour Declaration did not have smooth sailing. This, because among the members in Parliament, as well as among the people back home, there were still many Christians who in 1939 believed, no less fervently than the Christians in 1917, that the Balfour Declaration was a Divinely-ordained means of bringing about a restoration of the Jews to their Land in accordance with Biblical promises. The position of that segment of British Christians was spelled out by Sir John Haslam of Lancashire where Puritanism "that saved the soul of England is still alive and still a force".[15] Sir John was one of the speakers in the House of Commons on July 20, 1939, during a debate centered around the refusal of the Permanent Mandates Commission of the League of Nations to acknowledge that the British Government White Paper of May 1939 represents a true interpretation of the Balfour Declaration and of the Palestine Mandate entrusted to Britain by the League of Nations.

Sir John began his address with a reference to a statement by the speaker who preceded him, who said that the Bible must be kept out of consideration in dealing with the Palestine Mandate. "The hon. Member", Sir John declared, "said that we must take no notice of the Bible. I propose to take particular notice of that Book. It has been my guide, philosopher and friend in this world, and I am hoping it will be until I reach the next. The law of this country insists that the Archbishop of Canterbury, before he puts the crown on the head of the King, before he can make him King of this country, shall say: 'Those are the oracles of God. This is the most precious thing this world offers'. Is it surprising that after that some of us appreciate the doctrines and the tenets contained in that Book? That is the law of this country, and whatever the hon. Member may say I am prepared, and always shall be, to take notice of the tenets contained in that Book . . .

"[The late] Lord Balfour", Sir John continued, "saw clearly that materialism was not the only object in life of either individuals or nations . . . Lord Balfour saw the Jews scattered over all the countries of the world. He knew many of them had an ideal, a longing, an ambition, a soul-stirring desire. Those ideals and desires were then and are now centered in Palestine, the Promised Land. Solomon said, 'Where there is no vision the people perish', and the Jews then and the Jews today dream of Palestine. It is in their sleeping dreams and in their waking thoughts, and I refuse to blame them for it. Lord Balfour, the man who knew, revered and endeavored to follow out the teachings contained in that Book which the hon. Member said we must take no notice of, said there was a new day dawning for the Jews—to use his own words from his famous Declaration: 'The coming of a new era in the life of a deathless people'. He said there was a new prospect of life for an unconquerable and everlasting race whom no tyranny or persecution could ever vanquish or destroy.

"At the time [Balfour] was Foreign Secretary [he said]: '. . . I hope [the Arabs] will remember that while this Assembly and all those it represents throughout the world desire Great Britain to establish this Home for the Jewish people, it was the Great Powers, and especially Great Britain who freed [the Arabs] from the tyranny of their brutal conquerors:

"[Balfour] goes on to say that the Arab race has received great benefits from this country and ought to be grateful, and the present Colonial Secretary* insinuated that they were grateful. I have never seen much sign of it; and I have seen from the Jews quite as high an appreciation of the blessings they have received from the British people as ever I have seen from the Arab people themselves . . . [Lord Balfour] said to the Jews speaking at a meeting in the City of London at which Lord Rothschild was in the chair: 'If we fail you you cannot succeed. I feel assured we shall never fail you'.

"I ask myself, are we failing them today? We have given a pledge to the Jews . . .

---

* Mr. Malcolm MacDonald

"Ten years after Lord Balfour had issued his famous proclamation he spoke again and repeatedly in the House of Lords. Those who doubt should read his speech in the House of Lords on 21st July, 1922, five years after, and on the tenth anniversary of his famous Declaration. . . He said that Palestine was in every sense of the word to be regarded as a home for the Jewish people . . .

"The Jews regard Palestine as their native land, whether they were actually born there or not. Millions of them who have never been to Palestine at all regard that country as their home, just as millions of people of the British race who have never set foot in this country regard this country as their home.

"As long as I can remember, Palestine has been known as the Promised Land. Promised to whom? It was promised to the Jews by Lord God Almighty. Almost every book of the Old Testament and many of the New Testament repeat that promise. . . I hope that all hon. Members know Deuteronomy, one of the greatest Books in the greatest series of Books ever bound together. I have pointed out to hon. Members what the law of the land says about this great Book . . . After I left this House [of Commons] this morning at a quarter to eight, and after sitting all night, I was looking at the Bible, and I turned to this [Thirty-fourth] chapter. In the first verse I read:

'And the LORD showed him'—Moses—'all the land of Gilead, unto Dan. All Naphtali and the land of Ephraim, and Manasseh, and all the land of Judah, unto the utmost sea.

And the south, and the plain of the valley of Jericho, the city of palm trees, unto Zoar.

And the LORD said unto him, This is the land which I swore unto Abraham, unto Isaac, and unto Jacob, saying, I will give it unto thy seed: I have caused thee to see it with thine eyes, but thou shalt not go over thither'.

"I could give innumerable examples to this Committee . . . I will content myself with one further quotation. It is from Amos, chapter 9, verse 14, and it is very apt to the present discussion. It is as follows:

'And I will bring again the captivity of my people Israel, and they shall build the waste cities'—notice that—'and inhabit them' —and how can they inhabit them if they cannot enter the country— 'and they shall plant vineyards, and drink the wine thereof; they shall also make gardens, and eat the fruit of them. And I will plant them upon their land, and they shall no more be pulled up out of their land which I have given them, saith the LORD thy God.'

This was written 700 or 800 years before Christ, but it is being fulfilled today. Who are we to attempt to frustrate that promise made by the God of all the earth? Rather it is that this generation, this nation and this House of Commons should assist in fulfilling that promise. Other promises have been made, and I could give innumerable examples, but I have satisfied myself just with these. Every hon. Member who has spoken today has borne testimony to the fact that the land is no longer desolate. Before the Jews attempted to return there, in response to our pledge, it was desolate, without man or beast. Now, instead of the thorn has come up the fir tree, instead of the briar has come up the myrtle tree; the wilderness and the solitary places are glad, and the desert is rejoicing and blossoming as the rose.* This is happening under our very eyes, and I think it ill becomes this House to attempt, and I refuse to have anything to do with attempting, to stop that process.

I will add one more quotation. I know of three translations of the Psalm 15, but I think the best of them, and indeed, the best of all the translations of all the Psalms, is that of Miles Coverdale, which is to be found in our historic Prayer Book—the book that is the law of the land so far as the Church of England is concerned— from which daily we read Psalm 67 in opening the proceedings of this House. Psalm 15 says:

'LORD, who shall dwell in thy tabernacle: or who shall rest upon thy holy hill? Even he, that leadeth an uncorrupt life: and doeth the thing that is right, and speaketh the truth from his heart.' I am trying to speak the truth from my heart today. It goes on to say:

'He that sweareth unto his neighbor and disappointeth him not: though it were to his own hindrance.

Whoso doeth these things: shall never fall.'

That psalm has come to be known as the Gentleman's Psalm. We claim to be a Christian nation; at least we can all claim to be gentlemen. I would repeat:

'Whoso doeth these things shall never fall.'[16]

In reporting Sir John's speech, Reverend Maclean says that "a great hush fell on the House of Commons as the words of Holy Writ

---

* The words in this sentence are found in Isaiah 55:13 and 35:1.

rang through the Chamber, filling it with awe . . . And the old Puritan from Lancashire sat down. He had shown Englishmen and Scotsmen their true selves. No doubt they were living on the religious capital bequeathed by their ancestors. They were consuming it and not adding to it."[17]

"We claim to be a Christian nation; at least we can all claim to be gentlemen". Can a nation which goes back on its word, which subverts its promises, call itself Christian? Can some one give up God and remain a gentleman? Not the kind of gentleman referred to in the "Gentleman's Psalm" in which one's right conduct and his nearness to God are inseparable.

The following somber words addressed to England in the beginning of World War Two are equally applicable to all of present day Western Civilization.

"What is it we are in danger of"? Is it the passing of the Empire—that great confederation of nations whose common bond is freedom and not fetters? . . . Is it the loss of material resources without which life cannot be sustained? Something of far greater value than these lies on the issue; something that will not be settled by the smashing of armies or the sinking of fleets. It is the fate of our souls that is at stake. For already it is apparent that darkness is upon us. Is the twilight falling because the justice, the truth, and the mercy which are the fruit of religion cannot be sustained when religion has passed away? Is it not manifest that the fruit of faith cannot survive the faith? . . .[18]

"The time has passed when an appeal to the soul can sweep into action the will of a civilized and mechanized generation such as this. Freudians and Behaviorists, and a motley throng grotesquely named, have seen to that. Where the materialists had sown, strange broods now reaped the harvest. Any theory would find its quota of believers, but on one condition only—that it ruled out a personal God. This is the only possible explanation why a Gladstone no longer thrills a whole nation with the vision of righteousness, why a Wilberforce no longer cries aloud*, why a Wesley no longer awes the multitude by summoning them to the Great White Throne. No appeal can be made to the soul of a generation who are convinced that they have none".[19]

---

* Wilberforce, one of a group of English Christians who in the 18th century thundered against slavery.

III. GOD'S OVERRULING PROVIDENCE

In 1875 Benjamin Disraeli, a Christian Jew, also known as Lord Beaconsfield, then Prime Minister of Great Britain, acquired for England 170,000 shares of the Suez Canal. Altogether there were 400,000 such shares, and most of the balance were owned by French interests. The Suez Canal was originated, planned and financed by a French group, and constructed by a French engineer. The Egyptian ruler, the Khedive Ismail, owned 170,000 Suez shares. Because of his extravagance he frequently got himself in financial difficulties. In November 1875 he decided to sell his Suez shares. When Disraeli became aware of the Khedive's decision to sell his shares he saw at once the great advantage which England would reap from the ownership of these shares. Since, however, Parliament was not then in session, he could not obtain the needed funds. He had only several days to decide. The Jewish banking house of the Rothschilds came to his rescue by loaning to the British Government four million pounds which was the price of the 170,000 shares.

The acquisition of the Suez shares was a brilliant move on the part of Disraeli, both financially and politically. It is said that in the first fifty years since the purchase the original sum was repaid in interest and dividends about eight times over.[20] Politically, the Suez Canal became an important element in Britain's foreign policy and it gave England a new interest and standing in Egypt. The purchase of the Suez Canal shares showed that Disraeli fully appreciated the importance of the Suez Canal as a sea route to India, at that time an important British possession.

In the second half of the 19th century Russia displayed a growing ambition to take over the Balkan lands which at that time had been under Turkish rule. Russia had for a long time been dreaming of the occupation of Constantinople, the capital of Turkey, placing her in possession of the Straits linking the Sea of Marmara with the Agean, with penetration into the Mediterranean.

In 1875 the revolt of the Bosnians on the Balkan peninsula appeared to give to Russia the long-sought opportunity to realize her expansionist aims. In 1876 the Bulgars and Serbs followed the example of the Bosnians by rising in rebellion against Turkish rule. Confronted with a widespread insurrection the Sultan of Turkey, Abdul Hamid, suppressed the uprising, especially that of the Bulgars, with utmost ferocity. In April 1877 Russia invaded the Balkans under the pretext of liberating the Balkan Christians from Turkish cruelty. But Disraeli was not deceived. He understood perfectly well that Russia was aiming at the occupation of Constantinople and the penetration into the Mediterranean. The war lasted about nine months and the Turks put up stiff resistance. Russia lost about 100,000 men. But in the end the Turks were overwhelmed by the sheer weight of numbers. In March 1878 the Treaty of San Stefano was concluded which imposed severe terms on Turkey.

England and Austria declared that the Treaty of San Stefano was unacceptable to them. Accordingly, a call went out for a conference of European Powers for the purpose of revising the terms of the San Stefano Treaty. Berlin, the capital of Prussia, was selected as the conference site. In the meantime Disraeli put in force certain war measures designed to impress the Russians with the gravity with which England viewed the newly created situation. A British fleet sailed to the Sea of Marmara, and Indian troops landed at the Mediterranean island of Malta.

Exhausted by the war with Turkey, Russia sought by all means to avoid a confrontation with England. She therefore consented at the Berlin Congress to drastic revision of the San Stefano Treaty. In accordance with this revision Bosnia-Herzegovina was given to Austria, Russian power in the Balkans was considerably reduced, and the island of Cyprus was given to England to be used as a naval base from which the British fleet was in an excellent position to discourage any hostile military moves against Constantinople and the Straits.

Thus England's Jewish Prime Minister not only secured for England a controlling interest in the Suez Canal, but at the Berlin Congress he also succeeded in preventing Russia from gaining a foothold in the Mediterranean which would enable her some day to pose a threat to the Suez Canal.

The British delegation at the Berlin Congress was composed of Disraeli, the Prime Minister, Lord Salisbury, the Foreign Secretary, and Lord Odo Russell, Britain's Berlin ambassador. Lord Salisbury took with him as his secretary his young nephew, Arthur James Balfour.[21] Fifty years later Chaim Weizmann, in an attempt to overcome British reluctance to assume a Protectorate over a Jewish Palestine, sought to impress Mr. Balfour and the other members of the British Government with the fact that such a British Protectorate would be a safe-guard to the Suez Canal.[22]

In their determination to nullify the aims of the Balfour Declaration Chamberlain and Bevin were motivated by a desire for immediate gains, with disastrous lasting consequences. Under the dual Anglo-French administration the Suez Canal was used by many nations engaged in the furtherance of world commerce. Relying on Russia's support Nasser seized in 1956 control of the Suez Canal. In the first eleven years since this seizure the Suez Canal was closed by him twice; the second closure took place in the June 1967 war with Israel, and at this writing the Suez Canal has remained closed for almost two years.

Moreover, the stationing at this time of a squadron of Russian warships in the Mediterranean—the fulfillment of an old aspiration of Russian imperialism—in the vicinity of the Suez Canal,[23] serves as an assurance that the Middle East turmoil will be kept boiling, and the waters of the Mediterranean, the Biblical Great Sea, will for some time remain in a troubled state.

The White Paper of the Chamberlain Government designed to set at naught the aims of the Balfour Declaration was issued in May 1939. About three months later World War Two began. One of the writers whom we quoted on several occasions in this work, looked upon World War Two as the terrible swift sword of Divine Judgment. It was in the first place a judgment on the people of Germany who in the days following World War One were wont to blame all their woes on the Versailles Treaty, notwithstanding the fact that Germany bore as much—if not more—responsibility for World War One as any of the warring nations of Europe; World War Two was a judgment on the German people who hailed Hitler as their savior because he put millions of unemployed Germans back to work, even though the jobs which Hitler created consisted chiefly of fashioning instruments of war in preparation for world conquest; World War Two was a judgment on the people of Germany who, with few exceptions maintained silence when their Government exterminated millions of innocent Jews and non-Jews; finally, the loss by Germany of its position as a first-rate world power, the tearing away by Russia of the eastern part of Germany with the subjection of its people to communism, is a further Divine judgment on a Germany whose Government helped in 1917 plant communism on Russian soil in the hopes that this will hasten the disintegration of Russia,[24] and in 1939 concluded an alliance with Russian communism in order to have a free hand in the conquest of Europe.

The Second World War was a judgment on France which in the years between the two World Wars failed to use her formidable military resources to prevent Hitler from violating one clause after another of the Versailles Treaty, thus encouraging him to proceed from one aggressive act to another; finally, the war was a judgment on France which stood silently by when Hitler subjugated Czechoslovakia with whom France had had a defensive alliance.

Last, but not least, the Second World War was a judgment on Chamberlain's England which was willing to gain security for herself at the expense of smaller and weaker nations; which thought that you can have peace without fighting for it, that you can build peace on a foundation of unrighteousness, which, in reality, is peace with dishonor.

May the experiences of the years between the two World Wars serve as a somber lesson for our generation, confronted as we are by one of history's greatest tyrannies. To communism, coexistence with the West and with other non-communist countries means conquest by subversion from within of one country after another—until it has gained world supremacy. We, in this generation, are faced with a choice of being willing to extinguish small fires which the communists ignite here and there, or of doing nothing and wait until the communists have brought upon this world another era of darkness, or precipitated a nuclear war with world-wide devastation. Whether we like it or not, in this evil world in which we now live, if we want peace, we must be willing and ready to defend it. For eternal vigilance has always been the price of liberty and of a worthwhile decent existence.

As to the State of Israel, its existence constitutes one of the most amazing proofs of the trustworthiness of God's Word, and a Divine warning to all of Israel's would-be destroyers, past, present and future. "Thus says the LORD, who gives the sun for light by day and the fixed order of the moon and the stars for light by night, who stirs up the sea so that its waves roar—the LORD of hosts is his name: 'If this fixed order departs from before me, says the LORD, then shall the descendants of Israel cease from being a nation before me for ever'" (Jeremiah 31: 35-36; 31: 34-35 Heb.) The State of Israel came into being in spite of everything which the Chamberlains and the Bevins had done to prevent it. It stands, on one hand, as a Divine rebuke to their policies which were nothing but pure opportunism, living from hand to mouth, and devoid of moral principles;[25] on the other hand, as a tribute to the statesmanship, wisdom, vision and farsightedness of that noble band of British leaders of the World War One period, who belonged to a generation of Christians that revered the Bible as the Word of God and faithfully adhered to the principles enunciated in the "Gentleman's Psalm" a portion of which we shall cite again as a fit conclusion of this chapter.

> "LORD, who shall dwell in thy tabernacle,
>   or who shall rest upon thy holy hill?
> Even he, that leadeth an uncorrupt life,
>   and doeth the thing that is right,
>   and speaketh the truth from his heart.
>
> He that sweareth unto his neighbor
>   and disappointed him not, though
>   it were to his own hurt.
>
> He who doeth these things shall never
>   fall." (Psalm 15: 1-2, 4-5).

Notes to Chapter 6

[1] Chaim Weizmann, *Trial and Error* (The Jewish Publication Society of America: Philadelphia, 1949), Vol. 1, p. 192.

[2] A discussion of this subject is found in the last part of this book.

[3] *The Middle East* (Royal Institute International Affairs: London & New York, 1954), Appendix IV.

[4] Ernest Aschner, *"Oil, Palestine, And The Powers"*, article printed in *Commentary* (New York), May, 1947.

[5] *The Middle East* (Royal Institute of International Affairs: London & New York, 1954), Appendix IV.

[6] R. H. S. Crossman, *"The Role Britain Hopes To Play"*, article printed in *Commentary* (New York), June 1948. Used by permission.

[7] Idem.

[8] Idem.

[9] Richard Crossman, *Palestine Mission* (Harper & Brothers: New York, 1947), p. 109.

[10] Ibid., pp. 157-8.

[11] George T. Piercy, *"The Middle East Crisis In Perspective"*, article in *The Lamp* (New York), Spring 1968. Used by permission.

[12] Bartley C. Crum, *Behind The Silken Curtain*, p. 249.

[13] Norman Maclean, *His Terrible Swift Sword* (Christian Council on Palestine: New York, 1941), pp. 18, 20. The Biblical words cited are a paraphrase

of a passage in the New Testament in which Christ describes His judgment of the nations upon His return to earth. (Matthew 25: 31-46).

[14] Ibid., pp. 21, 22-23.

[15] Ibid., p. 62.

[16] *Hansard Parliamentary Debates* (His Majesty's Stationery Office: London, July 20, 1939), pp. 848-855.

[17] Norman Maclean, Op. Cit., pp. 64, 68.

[18] Ibid., p. 24.

[19] Ibid., p. 20.

[20] R. C. K. Ensor, *England* (Oxford University Press: London, 1952), p. 38.

[21] Ibid., Note 3, p. 49.

[22] Chaim Weizmann, Op. Cit., Vol. 1, p. 192.

[23] See article *"Russia Flexes New Flexibility"*, in the *Economist* (London); reprinted in the *Sun* (Baltimore) May 26, 1968.

[24] See *"German Political Intervention in Russia during World War I"*, article by George Katkov, in *Revolutionary Russia*, ed. by Richard Pipes (Harvard University Press: Cambridge, Mass., 1968), pp. 63-96.

[25] Chaim Weizmann, Op. Cit., Vol. 1, p. 178.

CHAPTER 7

THE BREAKDOWN OF THE PALESTINE
MANDATE

I. THE JEWISH CONTRIBUTION TO THE BREAKDOWN OF THE MANDATE

    1. The Negative Factor

    2. The Positive Factor

II. THE ARAB CONTRIBUTION TO THE BREAKDOWN OF THE MANDATE

    1. Arab Leaders in World War One favored the Restoration of the Jews in Palestine.

    2. The Reason for Subsequent Arab Opposition to a Jewish Palestine.

CHAPTER 7

I. The Jewish Contribution To The Breakdown Of The Mandate

1. THE NEGATIVE FACTOR

The Jewish share in the breakdown of the Palestine Mandate is of a two-fold character. On one hand, the Jews failed in the first decade of the Mandate to proceed with the speed which the urgency of the occasion demanded. On the other hand, by the very success of their accomplishments they aroused the opposition of all those forces which believed that the Jewish activities in Palestine are menacing the status quo of the Middle East. Emerging from the San Remo Peace Conference which confirmed the Balfour Declaration and decided to give the Mandate to Great Britain, Lloyd George, then British Prime Minister, made the following prophetic statement to Chaim Weizmann: 'You have no time to waste. Today the world is like the Baltic before a frost. For the moment it is still in motion. But if it gets set, you will have to batter your heads against the ice blocks and wait for a second thaw'.[1]

There were a number of circumstances which prevented the Jews from following up Lloyd George's advice. One of the most grievous losses which the cause of Zionism sustained following the First World War was the separation of the Russian Jews from world Jewry. Love for Zion was more intense and more deeply rooted among the Jews of Russia than among the Jews in any other country of the world. Political Zionist activity was illegal in Tzarist Russia. During the brief reign of Kerenski's democratic regime following the overthrow of the Romanov dynasty Russian Jews raised three hundred million rubles for the Zionist cause to make it possible for Russian Jews to emigrate to Palestine. This money, however, was confiscated by the Bolsheviks who had turned Kerenski out and taken over the government in Russia. The Russian communists stopped Jewish emigration to Palestine and outlawed all Zionist activity. Thus Russian Jewry was cut off from world Jewry and, consequently, lost to the Zionist cause.

The loss of Russian Jewry made Polish Jewry the largest center of Zionist activity in the post-World War One era. But there were a number of circumstances which made it impossible for Polish Jewry to play its full part in the work of reconstruction of the Jewish National Homeland. In the first place, due to changed conditions following World War One, but, especially, because of the antisemitic policy of the Polish regime, the Jews of Poland became and remained impoverished. Second, the orthodox Jews of Poland, forming a large percentage of Polish Jewry, were not wholeheartedly on the side of Political Zionism. This, in the first place, because of the prevailing orthodox belief that Jews should not proceed with the rebuilding of the Holy Land until Messiah comes; then, also, the secularism of many Zionist leaders, and the religious indifference or even irreligious attitude of some of the Zionist pioneers, did not help to allay Orthodox apprehensions. The Jewish working class of Poland was another numerically large group. Following World War One the vast majority of Jewish labor in Poland was under the guidance of the Jewish socialist party, called the Bund, which was anti-Zionist in its ideology. Polish Jewry had also its share of assimilationists who, as the assimilationists in other countries, believed that the solution of the Jewish problem lay in the total submerging of the Jews in the midst of the non-Jewish population.

In spite of the serious dislocations caused by the First World War European Jews in general clung doggedly to the belief that somehow world conditions will become stabilized, and the Jewish position in Europe will improve. The European Jews were simply incapable of foreseeing or visualizing the great catastrophe which was to overtake them in less than a quarter of a century. This will account for the preoccupation of many Jewish leaders at the Peace Conferences following the First World War with the matter of securing minority rights for the Jews in the countries of their residence. This will also explain the readiness with which American Jewry allocated huge sums of money for relief for the European Jewish communities. "It was heartbreaking"—says Weizmann—"to see them pour millions into a bottomless pit, when some of the money could have been directed to the Jewish Homeland and used for the permanent settlement of those very Jews who in Europe never had a real chance."[2]

Many of the well-to-do Jews in America and other lands were opposed to the idea of a Jewish State in Palestine for fear of being accused of dual loyalties by their non-Jewish fellow-countrymen. It took seven years of bickerings, persuasions and negotiations before these well-to-do Jews, who preferred to call themselves non-Zionists, consented to form with the Zionists the Jewish Agency for Palestine. In the meantime the task of rebuilding the National Homeland suffered from shortage of money, money needed to buy land, to clear and rehabilitate the soil, to eliminate the malaria-breeding swamps, to purchase farm equipment. For many years the main financial support for the work in Palestine came mostly from poor Jews.[3] Thus much precious time was lost, and great opportunities were wasted.

Then the fury of Nazism struck and changed radically the whole picture. Within a few years the large centers of European Jewry were wiped out, and European Jews—whose ancestors had settled in parts of Europe two thousand years ago—were pulled out by their roots, with no hope or chance of ever being replanted in the soil of the European continent. A sense of homelessness swept over the Jewish people everywhere, even in countries outside of Nazi Europe. Among the Jews imprisoned in the Nazi concentration camps there were former socialists, assimilationists, orthodox, atheists, and those representing other ideologies. While awaiting death at the hands of their tormentors they found ample time to do some soul searching. With a contrite heart many confessed their ideological sins of pre-World War Two days, sins of believing themselves secure in Europe, sins of propagating the idea that the Jewish problem can be solved in the socialist, assimilationist, or traditional orthodox way, sins of withholding their support from the Jewish National Homeland. The Nazi torture chambers purged them of their former ideologies, and the vast majority of those who came out alive had one burning desire only: to join their brethren in the Land of Israel.

2. THE POSITIVE FACTOR

Incredible as it may sound, the effect of Jewish accomplishments in Palestine proved to be of such a disturbing character that it had much to do with the disintegration of the Palestine Mandate. The deeply ingrained Arab way of life, the feudal nature of Arab economy, and the British inclination to leave things well alone, all of these felt the challenge provoked by Jewish activities in Palestine.

As to the Arab way of life, the following statements are by two Britishers, both of whom acquired a good knowledge of the Arab people. Major Jarvis, former Governor of the Sinai Peninsula, says that "the Arab is not one of the world's workers, as all forms of manual labor are abhorrent to him and in his opinion it is bad form for a man to soil his hands with a mattock or shovel. The Arab works about ten days out of the three hundred and sixty-five: during the autumn rains he spends five days ploughing a stretch of suitable desert land for his barley crop and yokes to the plough any pair of animals he possesses, i.e., two camels if he is a man of substance, if not, a camel and a donkey, and occasionally a donkey and a goat, and in extreme cases his wife and daughter. His plough is a bent bit of wood with a sharpened point and is precisely the same in every way as the plough used three thousand or more years ago. In the spring he and his family put in another five days harvesting the crop, and, judging by his equanimity, if the barley is a complete failure owing to drought, one can only come to the conclusion that he is on the whole pleased, as the awful necessity of garnering the corn is thereby obviated and moreover he will have no tax to pay—the fact that he will also have to go hungry does not worry him at the time. This is typical of the race, for I have never met any people who live so entirely in the present as they do—the future worries them not a jot, and with them time is not a dimension, it is merely a state of mind . . .

The Arab is sometimes called the Son of the Desert, but . . . this is a misnomer as in most cases he is the Father of the Desert, having created it himself, and the arid waste in which he lives and on which practically nothing will grow is the direct result of his appalling indolence, combined with his simian trait of destroying everything he does not understand. A great part of the country in which he now ekes out his haphazard existence was at one time fairly prosperous and productive and, by failing to repair damage done by wear and tear of weather and by wantonly wrecking conduits and cisterns he was too lazy to use, he has succeeded in creating a sun-scorched, treeless desert which will remain a wilderness so long as he encumbers the land."[4]

"For every indolent race," says the Very Reverend Norman Maclean, "resents bitterly the coming of any change—especially the coming of those who work. The activity of others is felt to be an offense against the life of contemplation in the shade. Sir Flinders Petrie* described to me how his camp at Gaza, his implements and all his camp equipment were destroyed, to the value of hundreds of pounds—all because the surrounding Arabs objected to so much activity in the neighborhood."[5]

---

* Eminent British archaeologist

"Arab patriotism and Arab self-respect had been deeply affronted and would continue to be affronted by the development of the [Jewish] National Home," said Richard Crossman, one of the British members of the Anglo-American Committee of Inquiry; "but if I believed in social progress, I had to admit that the Jews had set going revolutionary forces in the Middle East which, in the long run, would benefit the Arabs."[6]

Walter C. Crum was one of the American members of the Anglo-American Committee of Inquiry. This is what he said: "Here before your eyes is proof that Palestine Jewry is bringing civilization to the Middle East. You did not need to have streets of squalor and a population diseased and beaten by life. From the [British] Colonial Office and the Arab hierarchy you got the impression that such things were destined to be in this part of the world, that such was the way of life in the Middle East and nothing could be done about it. At least one Colonial official had told me, 'Oh, well, they prefer to live that way, you know.' But here the Jews proved it was not necessary to live so."[7]

II. THE ARAB CONTRIBUTION TO THE BREAKDOWN OF THE MANDATE

1. ARAB LEADERS IN WORLD WAR ONE FAVORED THE RESTORATION OF THE JEWS IN PALESTINE.

The reawakening of Arab nationalism coincided with the beginning of Jewish colonizing activities in Palestine in the second half of the 19th century. In the years immediately preceding, and during, the First World War Arab nationalists were dreaming of the creation of a large Arab empire comprising the vast territories now occupied by Iraq, Syria, Lebanon, Jordan, Israel and the Arab peninsula. However, the Allied Powers which were fighting in World War One for the liberation of these territories from Turkish rule made it clear to the Arab nationalist leaders that they do not propose to include Palestine in Arab nationalist schemes. The top Arab leaders made no strenuous objections to this, since they recognized Palestine's unusual position, both on account of its historical association with the Jewish people, and its religious significance for the whole of Christendom. Emir Feisal, the son of King Hussein, the leader of the Arab liberation movement, is reported as having declared on behalf of his father that "Palestine, in consequence of its universal character, be left on one side for the consideration of all parties interested. With this exception he asked for the independence of the Arabic areas enumerated in the memorandum."[8]

This same Feisal, who later became King of Iraq, in his capacity as head of the Arab delegation at the Paris Peace Conference wrote a letter to Mr. Felix Frankfurter, then a member of the American Zionist deputation, a portion from which is reproduced below:

> "Hedjaz Delegation
> Paris
> March 3, 1919

Dear Mr. Frankfurter:

I want to take this opportunity of my first contact with American Zionists, to tell you what I have often been able to say to Dr. Weizmann in Arabia and Europe. We feel that the Arabs and the Jews are cousins in race, suffering similar oppressions at the hands of powers stronger than themselves, and by a happy coincidence have been able to take the first step toward the attainment of their national ideals together.

We Arabs, especially the educated among us, look with the deepest sympathy on the Zionist movement. Our deputation here in Paris is fully acquainted with the proposals submitted by the Zionist Organization to the Peace Conference, and we regard them as moderate and proper. We will do our best, in so far as we are concerned, to help them through; we will wish the Jews a most hearty welcome home.

With the chiefs of your movement, especially with Dr. Weizmann, we have had, and continue to have, the closest relations. He has been a great helper of our cause, and I hope the Arabs may soon be in a position to make the Jews some return for their kindness. We are working together for a reformed and revived Near East, and our two movements complete one another. The Jewish movement is national and not imperialistic. Our movement is national and not imperialistic; and there is room in Syria for us both.[9] Indeed, I think that neither can be a real success without the other . . . I look forward, and my people with me look forward, to a future in which we will help you and you will help us, so that the countries in which we are mutually interested may once again take their place in the community of civilized peoples of the world.

> Yours Sincerely,
> Feisal"[10]

King Hussein himself is reported to have made the following statement. 'At the same time we saw the Jews from foreign countries streaming to Palestine . . . The cause of causes could not escape those who had the gift of a deeper insight; they knew that the country was for its original sons (Abnaihi l'asliyin) a sacred and beloved homeland . . . The return of these exiles (jaliya) to their homeland will prove materially and spiritually an experimental school for their brethren.'[11]

Two months before writing his letter to Mr. Felix Frankfurter Emir Feisal had made the following agreement with Dr. Weizmann: 'In the establishment of the Constitution and Administration of Palestine, all such measures shall be adopted as will afford the fullest guarantees for carrying into effect the British Government's [Balfour] Declaration of November 2nd, 1917. All necessary measures shall be taken to encourage and stimulate immigration of Jews into Palestine on a large scale, and as quickly as possible to settle Jewish immigrants upon the land through closer settlement and intensive cultivation of the soil. In taking such measures the Arab peasant and tenant farmers shall be protected in their rights, and shall be assisted in forwarding their economic development.' To this agreement Feisal attached one condition: 'If the Arabs are established as I have asked in my manifesto of January 4 addressed to the British Secretary of State for Foreign Affairs, I will carry out what is written in this agreement. If changes are made, I cannot be answerable for failure to carry out this agreement.'[12]

Referring to this agreement the Palestine Royal Commission Report of 1937 makes the following significant statement. "The Arabs do not appear to realize in the first place that the present position of the Arab world as a whole is mainly due to the great sacrifices made by the Allied and Associated Powers in the War. . . (But for the Allied victory), it is improbable that the Arab countries, except Palestine, would now have become or be about to become independent States."[13] "There was a time when Arab statesmen were willing to concede little Palestine to the Jews, provided that the rest of Arab Asia were free. That condition was not fulfilled then, but it is on the eve of fulfilment now."[14]

2. THE REASON FOR SUBSEQUENT ARAB OPPOSITION TO A JEWISH
   PALESTINE

Why is it then that when Israel proclaimed its independence in 1948 it was attacked by those very same Arab states which have

won their independence in fulfilment of the promises of the Allies?
The Allies had kept their promises to the Arabs, why have the Arabs
not kept their leaders' promises to the Jews? What is the underlying
cause of Arab hostility to the Jews?

These are some of the questions that must have troubled the
members of the Anglo-American Committee of Inquiry and to which
they were seeking an answer. As they were probing deeper and
deeper into the heart of the matter some of them hit upon certain
basic factors underlying the whole vexing problem of Arab-Israel
relations. They discovered, among other things, that perfectly friendly
relations prevail between Jews and the rank and file of Arabs. "Down
at the Dead Sea, Arabs and Jews worked in harmony . . . In the citrus
industry, for example—one of Palestine's great industries—Jewish
and Arab orange growers cooperate . . . In the rural areas of
Palestine I found the Arabs looking upon the Jews with great respect.
Farmers themselves, they regarded with approval these people who
worked the land so earnestly, who were ready to stay up all night
with a sick lamb, and whose sense of values toward the simple things
of earth—planting, harvesting, irrigating—was like their own."[15] "The
basic truth of Arab-Jewish life in Palestine is that political conflict
on high levels does not affect the relations among the men on the
street. I could find no conflict of interests . . . Yet, despite this lack of
conflict of interests, despite this lack of hatred and animosity in
everyday life, in spite of the signs of neighborly friendship I had
seen myself, apparently a feud does exist on the higher levels."[16]

But who, or what, is behind this high-level opposition to the
Jewish National Homeland? The writer of the lines cited above
states that Mrs. Goldie Meyerson, the American Jewish woman who
for years had been very active in the Palestine labor movement,
testified before the Anglo-American Committee, that in the twenties
Jewish employers and workers had urged upon the Mandatory
Government to set up minimum wage legislation for all workers, both
Jewish and Arab, in Palestine. But the Mandatory Government
refused to do this. The Jews had repeatedly tried to raise the Arab
level to that of the Jewish, but apparently with little success.[17]
It is stated that "much of the difficulty in raising the Arab standard
of living lies in the opposition of the Arab effendi to having Arab
workers reach the same wage levels as the Jewish workers".[18] "The
community of interests of the kings, sheiks, and effendis in the
various Arab lands is unquestionably the main factor behind the

seemingly united front of the Arab states in their fight against Zionism. And in this united front, the Arab masses are unprotected. What we have is a class interest of state rulers, land-owners, and officialdom. To them as distinct from the multitudes of the Arab peoples, Zionism's social and technical innovations are a threat because they mean lifting the masses from their ignorance and serfdom".[19] In another passage the same writer declares that in order to keep the unrest of the rising generation from boiling over and destroying the Arab feudal system the reactionary Arab ruling classes attribute all Arab misfortunes to foreign domination and they identify the Jewish National Homeland with this foreign imperialism, whereas actually Zionism is the only force in the Near East which could help bring release to the exploited and impoverished Arab masses.[20] "It was obvious," this writer and member of the Anglo-American Committee continues, "that there were vested interests militating against a Jewish-Arab understanding. Two distinct groups, each for reasons of its own, are opposed to a Jewish Palestine. The Arab kings and effendis form the first group. British imperialism represents the second—and both, in that 'passive alliance' cited by Dr. Einstein, were now acting as one against the common enemy."[21] "Their basic interest seemed to be the preservation of the status quo . . . In that desire, I concluded reluctantly, they were joined by the British Colonial Office and its staff throughout the Middle East."[22]

There is yet another aspect of Arab antagonism to the Jewish National Homeland which has even wider implications. It often acts as a screen to disguise Arab animosity to the West. Azzam Pasha's* objection to the return of the Jews to Palestine is not because he objects to Jews as Jews, but because the Jews are coming back as Westerners. 'Our Brother', he said, 'has gone to Europe and to the West and come back something else. He has come back a Russified Jew, a Polish Jew, a German Jew, an English Jew. He has come back with a totally different conception of things, Western and not Eastern.'[23]

Many of the other Arab representatives who appeared before the Anglo-American Committee expressed the same sentiment as Azzam Pasha. Their resentment to the Jew often sprang from an intense dislike for the West. "As the roll call of witnesses continued,

---

* Secretary of the Arab League

it was evident that their antipathy was toward Westernism: that was
the encroachment they fought. Was this not perhaps the basic
tragedy of the Middle East? Westernism meant higher standards of
living; it meant reduction in infant mortality, in disease, in poverty;
it meant opening the door to some measure of freedom and happiness
to the forgotten men and women of this area of the world. It was
this, precisely, to which our witnesses objected. Most tragic of all,
as long as they remained representatives of a feudal aristocracy
which draws its power from its privileged position, supported by the
toil of the Arab masses, they had to object. I felt that even on the
highest intellectual levels here there was no confidence in democratic
processes, and, I am afraid, little understanding of them."[24]

Notes to Chapter 7

[1] Quoted by Chaim Weizmann, *Trial and Error* (The Jewish Publication
Society of America: Philadelphia, 1949), vol. 1, p. 260.

[2] Ibid., vol. 2, pp. 304-5.

[3] Ibid., vol. 1, p. 253.

[4] C. S. Jarvis, *Three Deserts* (John Murray: London, 1936) pp. 143, 160.
Used by permission.

[5] Norman Maclean, *His Terrible Swift Sword* (Christian Council On Palestine: New York, 1941), pp. 97-8.

[6] Richard Crossman, *Palestine Mission* (Harper & Brothers: New York,
1947), p. 167.

[7] Bartley C. Crum, *Behind The Silken Curtain* (Simon and Schuster: New
York, 1947), p. 195.

[8] David Lloyd George, *The Truth About The Peace Treaties* (Victor Gal-
lancz Ltd.: London 1938) vol. 2, p. 1042.

[9] Certain Arab spokesmen consider Palestine to be a part of Syria.

[10] Quoted by Chaim Weizmann, Op. Cit., vol. 1, pp. 245-6.

[11] from an article printed in the Arabic newspaper *Al-Qibla* (Mecca), No.
183 of March 23, 1918, attributed to King Hussein by George Antonius, the
great historian of the Arab national awakening (See George Antonius, *The
Arab Awakening*, p. 269); quoted in *The Jewish Plan For Palestine*, p. 107.

[12] Quoted by Chaim Weizmann, Op. Cit., vol. 1, p. 247.

[13] *Palestine Royal Commission Report, 1937*, Chapter 2, paragraph 19, p.
24; see, *The Jewish Plan For Palestine*, pp. 108-9.

[14] *Palestine Royal Commission Report, 1937*, Chapter 23, paragraph 5, p.
395; see, *The Jewish Plan For Palestine*, p. 108.

[15] Bartley C. Crum, Op. Cit., p. 228.

[16] Ibid., p. 229.

17 Ibid., p. 227.
18 Ibid.
19 Ibid., p. 230.
20 Ibid., p. 156.
21 Ibid., p. 230.
22 Ibid., p. 155.
23 Quoted by Richard Crossman, Op. Cit., p. 109.
24 Bartley C. Crum, Op. Cit., p. 152.

CHAPTER 8

THE REUNION BETWEEN THE JEWISH PEOPLE AND THEIR ANCIENT HOMELAND

I. THE GREAT RETURN

1. The First Aliyah
2. The Second Aliyah
3. The Third Aliyah
4. The Fourth Aliyah
5. The Fifth Aliyah
6. The Sixth Aliyah
7. The Seventh Aliyah

II. THE ESTABLISHMENT OF AGRICULTURAL SETTLEMENTS

1. The Kvutza
2. The Moshav Ovdim
3. The Moshav Shitufi
4. The Moshava

THE REUNION BETWEEN THE JEWISH PEOPLE AND THEIR ANCIENT HOMELAND

I. THE GREAT RETURN

Throughout the long centuries of their Dispersion there was an almost constant movement of Jews back to Palestine, both individually and in groups. Most, if not all, of these returnees went back for religious reasons. What distinguished the migrations of the past from the modern Return which commenced some 75 years ago was that the people of the modern Return went to Palestine with a definite aim to rebuild there the ancient National Homeland. Aliyah is the Hebrew name for the various immigration waves of the Jews into Palestine beginning with 1882. There were six such Aliyahs prior to the establishment of the State of Israel and the seventh began right after the proclamation of independence.

1. THE FIRST ALIYAH, 1882-1884, 1890-1891.

The First Aliyah consisted of two influxes, the first of which took place in 1882-1884, and the second in 1890-1891. It was the first of six waves of immigrations to Palestine which gave birth to the modern Jewish agricultural activities in Palestine and culminated in the restoration of the State of Israel. The First Aliyah immigrants came from Russia. The Russian pogroms* of 1881, the renewed anti-Jewish policy of the Russian Government as reflected in the "May Laws" published in May 1882, imposing new political restrictions and disabilities on the Jews of Russia, brought to an abrupt end the era of liberalism of the preceding decade under Tzar Alexander the Second. These new developments caused many Jews in Russia to despair of any hope of a permanent improvement in the position of Jews in Russia. As a result of the changed circumstances there began a mass movement of Russian Jews out of the country. Hundreds of thousands left Russia for the Americas and the liberal countries of Western Europe. A very small portion of this mass exodus made its way to Palestine. The expulsion of the Jews from

---

* Pogrom—massacre of Jews.

Moscow in 1891 provided a fresh impetus to Jewish emigration from Russia and sent more Jews to Palestine thus completing the First Aliyah.

The immigrants of the First Aliyah were mainly middle class men, teachers, students, artisans and tradesmen. Some of these had enough of their own means to enable them to settle in the country, while others were assisted by the Chovevei Zion* organizations which had come into existence about that time. The Jewish population in Palestine just prior to the First Aliyah numbered about 24,000. The First Aliyah brought several thousand Jews into the country.

2. THE SECOND ALIYAH, 1904-1914.

The Second Aliyah began in 1903 and ended in 1914. Taking advantage of the Russo-Japanese war the liberal element in Russia staged an uprising demanding social reforms. Its hands tied by the war, the reactionary Russian Government showed at first a willingness to conciliate the revolutionary movement. But when the war ended the Government turned against the liberal elements and the revolutionary movement was crushed in 1905. In order to channel the bitterness of the masses away from itself the ruling clique of Russia engineered an outbreak of pogroms against the Russian Jews in which many Jews were slaughtered in cold blood.

This turn of events convinced many Russian Jews who had pinned their hopes on a victory of the social-democratic forces that there is no future for them in Russia. Once again they took up the wandering staff and left the country by the thousands. Most of them went to the United States. But a few made their way to Palestine having gained the conviction in their hearts that the Jewish problem will not be solved except by the rebuilding of the Jewish National Homeland in the land of their forefathers. The Second Aliyah consisted largely of Jews from Russia, and the immigrants were students, artisans, office clerks, teachers and small businessmen. During the period of the Second Aliyah 35,000 Jews are said to have entered Palestine.

3. THE THIRD ALIYAH, 1919-1923.

Two historical events combined to produce the Third Aliyah: 1) The Balfour Declaration by which Britain obligated herself to

* Chovevei Zion—Lovers of Zion.

help the Jewish people to establish in Palestine a Jewish National Home; 2) the sufferings of the Eastern European Jews in World War One climaxed by terrible pogroms at the end of the war in which many thousands of Jews were done to death. It was the greatest mass slaughter of Jews in modern times prior to the Hitler era. As a result of these experiences many Jews were led to believe that there is no future for Jews in Eastern Europe. A new wave of emigration began, mostly to the Americas, some to Central and Western Europe, but a certain number of Jews went to Palestine.

As in the two previous Aliyahs, the immigrants of the Third Aliyah came predominantly from Eastern Europe. The distinguishing feature of the Third Aliyah was the fact that many of the immigrants had undergone some training before their departure for Palestine. Under the guidance of the Chalutz* Organization, the candidates for emigration to Palestine were sent to training camps where they were taught farming and certain mechanical trades allied to farming so as to be able to handle and repair farm tools and machines. In these camps the pioneers were also prepared physically and psychologically for the rugged and harsh conditions of life in Palestine. At the end of the prescribed training course only those were selected who were found to be fit material for the work of reconstruction of the Jewish Homeland in Palestine. This, incidentally, was the first time that the prospective emigrant to Palestine had the opportunity to learn before his departure the things he will have to know and do when he arrives in the country. In the period of the Third Aliyah, from 1919 to 1923, some 37,000 Jews entered Palestine. Most of these came without means of their own.[1]

4. THE FOURTH ALIYAH, 1924-1926.

About 50 percent of the immigrants in the Fourth Aliyah came from Poland, 20 percent were from Russia. The emigration from Poland was occasioned by the new nationalist economic policy of the Polish Government which proved detrimental to the economic position of a large segment of the Jewish population. That the tightening of the immigration laws of the United States was a determining factor for the Fourth Aliyah goes without saying. The majority of the immigrants were of the lower middle class, with a small percentage of capitalists, and a sizeable proportion of workers. About 80 percent of the immigrants of the Fourth Aliyah settled in the main urban

---

* Chalutz—Pioneer.

centers of Palestine, i.e. Jerusalem, Haifa and Tel Aviv. 60,000 Jews arrived in Palestine during the Fourth Aliyah.[2]

5. THE FIFTH ALIYAH, 1929-1939.

The outstanding feature of the Fifth Aliyah was the large influx of German-speaking Jews, i. e., Jews from Germany, and German-speaking Jews from Czechoslovakia and Austria. Between 1920 and 1932 only 2000 German Jews entered Palestine. When Nazism began to rule Germany the trickle of German-Jewish immigration to Palestine became a broad stream. Thus in 1933, the year Hitler became leader of Germany, 7510 German Jews arrived in Palestine; in 1934, 9729 Jews left Germany for Palestine, and in 1935, 8460 German Jews went to Palestine. The number of German-speaking Jews that reached Palestine between 1933 and 1939 was 56,663 or 27.7 percent of the total immigration to Palestine during the Fifth Aliyah.[3]

The second important feature of the Fifth Aliyah was the large percentage of capitalists among the immigrants. A "capitalist" according to the definition of the British Mandate Government was one who brought with him L.P.*1000.[4] It is said that never before has there been such an influx of capital into Palestine. This may be seen from the fact that between 1921 and 1931 Jewish investments in Palestine amounted to 20 million Palestinian pounds, while in the 4 years between 1932 and 1935 Jews invested in Palestine 31 million Palestinian pounds.[5] The German Jews made up about 40 percent of the capitalists who entered Palestine with the Fifth Aliyah.

A goodly number of German Jews were physicians, scientists, engineers, and well trained technicians. They came at a time when the rapid growth of industry and commerce and the expanding economy of the country were in great need of people with technical knowledge and experts in the various scientific fields. In spite of the high culture and the many technical skills which the German Jewish immigrants brought with them, about 25 percent of them became farmers. The total number of Jews who emigrated to Palestine in the Fifth Aliyah reached around 227,129.[6]

An important development which took place in the Fifth Aliyah era was the setting up of an organization, the Youth Aliyah Bureau,

---

* L.P.—Palestinian pound of sterling. A Palestinian pound was worth four dollars U.S.A. currency at pre-World War Two exchange rate.

which was assigned the task of transferring Jewish children from Germany to Palestine. This Bureau was put in charge of an American Jewish woman, Henrietta Szold, who had been active in Zionist affairs for many years. These youngsters were selected from youth movements, sent to camps where they received several weeks' preparation, and then moved to Palestine. Upon their arrival in the country they were placed in agricultural settlements, youth villages, and other institutions, where they received two years' training. They divided their time equally between the class-room and the workshop or the farm.

This immigration of Jewish youth to Palestine was later extended to other countries as well; in the years between 1934 and 1950 the Youth Aliyah Organization brought over to Palestine 45,000 Jewish children from 57 countries and transformed them into productive and useful members of the Jewish Community in Palestine.[7]

6. THE SIXTH ALIYAH, 1940-1945.

The British White Paper Law put into effect in 1939 placed severe restrictions on Jewish immigration into Palestine. This Law, together with the fact that a large part of Europe was occupied by Nazi Germany, made the departure of Jews for Palestine in World War Two days next to impossible. And yet some 52,000 Jews managed to escape and enter Palestine from 1940 to 1945.[8]

7. THE SEVENTH ALIYAH.

The reconstitution of the State of Israel, the first independent Jewish State in over 2,000 years, and the promulgation of the Law of Return which entitles every Jew to settle in Palestine, were the beginning of the Seventh Aliyah. It was the signal for a mighty tide, a mass-movement of Jews from all over the world towards Eretz Israel, the Land of Israel. In the 65 years, from the commencement of the modern Jewish colonization work in Palestine to the founding of the State of Israel in 1948, some 550,000 Jews had entered Palestine.[9] In the first 6½ years of the existence of the State of Israel, 727,088 Jews had entered Palestine.[10]

The following are a few significant factors about the Seventh Aliyah:

(1) The largest group came from Europe, especially from Eastern and Central Europe. Those from Eastern and Central Europe were the ones who had somehow managed to elude the Nazi death

chambers; the second largest group of immigrants came from Africa, especially North Africa.

(2) It was a world-wide ingathering. Every continent and many countries were represented. Whole Jewish communities were moved to the Land of Israel and many countries gave up their whole Jewish population. The Jews of Yemen and Iraq had lived in these countries at least 2000 years.

(3) Most of those from Eastern and Central Europe and North Africa came practically penniless. Those from Nazi occupied European countries were broken in body and spirit; while those from Moslem lands were afflicted with the diseases prevalent in those parts. Moreover, the Oriental Jews, such as the Yemenites, by coming to Israel, were transplanted to an environment whose civilization was hundreds of years superior to the one in the country of their origin.

The following is a list of Jewish immigrants, according to the countries of their origin, who entered the State of Israel between May 15, 1948, and December 31, 1954. While in the years subsequent to that date immigration of Jews to Israel fluctuated, it has continued to this day.

IMMIGRANTS BY COUNTRIES OF ORIGIN[11]

(May 15, 1948—December 31, 1954)

ASIA

Turkey	35,055
Iraq	125,896
Iran	27,534
Yemen	45,738
India	4,354
Other countries	12,790
Total	251,367

AFRICA

Tunisia, Algeria, Morocco	67,226
Libya	32,552
South Africa	683
Other countries	19,630
Total	120,091

EUROPE

Soviet Russia	8,277
Poland	107,393
Rumania	121,715
Bulgaria	38,226
Yugoslavia	7,764
Greece	2,309
Germany and Austria	11,335
Czechoslovakia	18,880
Hungary	14,796
United Kingdom	2,157
Holland	1,325
France	3,342
Italy	1,385
Other countries	2,049
Total	340,953

AMERICA AND OCEANIA

United States	1,709
Canada	304
Brazil	507
Argentina	1,677
Other American countries	860
Australia and New Zealand	149
Total	5,206
Not specified	18,741
Grand Total	736,358

II. THE ESTABLISHMENT OF AGRICULTURAL SETTLEMENTS

Before the destruction of their National Homeland in Palestine by the Romans the economic structure of the Jews was like that of any other people in the ancient civilized world. The majority of them derived their livelihood from farming. Even in the first centuries following their expulsion from Palestine many Jews in the Diaspora and those who remained in, or subsequently returned to, Palestine owned land and tilled the ground. But gradually restrictive laws were introduced preventing them from owning land and plying certain trades, thus forcing them to become largely a people of city dwellers, merchants, and middle men, alienated from farm and factory.

The Jewish Colonization Program in Palestine which began in the last quarter of the 19th century had as its aim not only the rebuilding of the Jewish National Homeland, but also the normalization of the life of the Jewish people. The return of the Jews to Palestine meant also a return to the soil and to all sorts of productive forms of labor which constitute the basis of a normal economic structure. The task of remaking the Jews into a people of farmers and laborers was no less formidable an undertaking than the transformation of the desert places of Palestine into blossoming and life-sustaining fields, gardens and orchards.

The young immigrants who came to Palestine in the First Aliyah in 1882 from Russia, Poland and Rumania had practically no farming experience. They were encouraged and aided by the Chovevei Zion organization whose central office was in Odessa, Russia. They succeeded in purchasing some land and founded the first three settlements: Rishon Letzion south of Jaffa in Judaea Zikhron Ya'akov, in Samaria, and Rosh Pinna, in Upper Galilee. The following year they established the colony of Yissud Hama'alah, on the shore of Lake Hule, and they resettled Petach Tikvah which had temporarily been abandoned by its original settlers who had been unable to cope with the deadly malaria which infested that whole region.

The inexperience of the Pioneers, their financial difficulties, and the scourge of malaria would have wrecked this beginning of the Jewish colonization program in Palestine in spite of the super-human heroism of the Pioneers. The situation was saved by Baron Edmund de Rothschild of Paris who had become interested in the plight of the colonists and sent them money and instructors and induced them to make vine-growing the basis of their farming economy. He placed the majority of the newly founded settlements under his care and advanced vast sums of money towards their support. Altogether, he is said to have invested the equivalent of 5,600,000 pounds in the Jewish agricultural settlements in Palestine.

In spite of the generous help which the early settlers received from Baron Rothschild this first modern colonization effort in Palestine was not a success. In the first place, their dependence on the Baron's support robbed them of all initiative and creative joy and killed their pioneering spirit. The cultivation of vineyards transformed the colonists into a kind of Jewish plantation owners, acting as overseers, while the actual work was being done by Arab labor. Furthermore, the one-crop system of cultivation made the settlers too dependent on the uncertainties and fluctuations of market prices. The Baron's officials who were supervising and administering the colonies were assimilated French Jews who had no understanding of, and sympathy with, the aims and ideals which the East European Pioneers brought with them.

In the year 1900 Baron Rothschild entrusted the care of the colonies which he supported to the Jewish Colonization Association. This organization was founded in 1891 by Baron Maurice de Hirsch whose aim was to help resettle Russian Jews in non-European countries. In time this society acquired some experience in agricultural colonization. It established a training farm at Sejera, in Lower Galilee, where hundreds of Jewish workers received instruction in farm work, including a knowledge in handling and repairing farm tools. The policy of the Jewish Colonization Association was not to make the settlers the wards of the organization, as was the case with Baron Rothschild. The settlers received the land, farm implements and live stock, but it was on a loan basis. Furthermore, only those who had been trained could become full-fledged settlers. Under the influence of the Jewish Colonization Association the settlers switched from the cultivation of vine to the raising of wheat. It was maintained that wheat would make the settlers less dependent on world markets, and at the same time provide part of their food requirements. But this shift from vine to wheat had all the defects of the single-crop cultivation system. Large tracts of land had to be utilised which necessitated the use of hired Arab labor. There was a growing conviction among the Pioneers that unless they do the work themselves, the normalization of the economic life of the Jewish people will not be accomplished, and thus one of the chief goals of the rebuilding of the Jewish National Homeland will be forfeited. Furthermore, with the exception of Galilee, Palestine, on account of the frequent droughts, does not lend itself to large scale cultivation of wheat.

A new era began in the history of the Jewish Agricultural Program in Palestine when the newly established Zionist Organization decided to make Jewish agricultural activities in Palestine a part of its program. In the year of 1900 a Fund was set up, known as the National Fund, whose task it was to purchase land and prepare it for cultivation. Much of the land purchased by the National Fund, though bought at exorbitant prices from the Arabs, was at the time of purchase uncultivable soil, i.e. swampland, rocky hills, and land covered with sand dunes. The land thus acquired became the perpetual property of the Jewish people. The National Fund not only purchased the ground but financed the clearing of the soil for cultivation. Some areas needed months, or years, of such preparatory work before it was rendered fit for cultivation. In 1920 another Fund was organized, the Foundation Fund, to finance the purchase or erection of the buildings and the acquisition of livestock. The land bought with National Fund money was distributed to the settlers on the following conditions: 1) The land was leased to them on a 49 year basis after which time they could renew the lease, or pass it on to their descendants, who must subscribe to the same conditions. For all practical purposes the settlers own the land as long as they live up to the agreement; 2) the settlers make an annual 2% payment on the money invested in the land; 3) the settlers agree to work the farms themselves, i.e. to use no hired labor except in unusual circumstances; 4) the settlers commit themselves to a diversified, i.e. mixed-type of crop farming.

By the process of trial and error at least three types of agricultural settlements were evolved in Palestine on land acquired by the National Fund.

1. THE KVUTZA OR KIBBUTZ

This is a cooperative or group settlement. In the beginning, most or all of the members of this type of settlements were young single men. In time many of them got married, while some of the later newcomers were married couples. These young men of the

Kvutza were imbued with a zeal for, and a devotion to, the Zionist ideal of the reconstruction of the Jewish National Home. The Kvutza is governed by a committee elected by the members from among themselves. The work is assigned to the various members. They all eat in the central dining room. Married couples have their separate sleeping quarters. All children are cared for by a nursing and teaching staff. This leaves both parents free to work. Evening and holidays the parents and their children spend their time together. All the needs of the individual members are cared for by the Settlement. Not only is all the work in the Settlement done in common, but even the sales and purchases of the Settlement are carried on by a sales and purchasing cooperative. Many cooperative settlements have industrial establishments where much industrial work is being done, especially in the winter months.

Neither the Zionist Organization prior to 1948, nor the Government of the State of Israel since 1948, were directly involved in the development of the Kvutza type of settlement. It is a creation of a certain group of pioneering idealists. The whole scheme rests on a purely voluntary basis. A member may leave the Kvutza any time he chooses. It has certain advantages not found in any other form of agricultural economy. It tends to have a low overhead, it is capable of producing a large output at a low production cost. It provides an excellent training ground for new immigrants who have no agricultural knowledge. Exposed to frequent attacks from unfriendly natives and marauding bands of desert Bedouins, the Kvutza colonies proved better capable of defending themselves against outside attacks.

But this form of settlement has its obvious drawbacks. Many people are by temperament ill-suited to this sort of group life. This is especially true of families. There is a growing conviction that while in a transitional, pioneering era the Kvutza had played a most important role in the rebuilding of Palestine, it has no permanent future after the country has been rebuilt and achieved complete normalcy. The first Kvutza was founded in Dagania in 1910.[13]

2. THE MOSHAV OVDIM

This is the second type of agricultural settlement which sprang up on National Fund soil. It is the smallholders type of settlement, consisting of small farms, one such farm per family. Each family is responsible for the upkeep of its farm. The size of the land allotted to each family depends on whether the land is irrigated or not. From 5 to 7 acres of irrigated land, or from 12 to 15 acres of non-irrigated land, is considered sufficient to support one family. If the non-irrigated land acquires irrigation it is reduced in size and the excess distributed to new settlers.

The principles governing the use of this land by the smallholder are in general the same as those applying to the Kvutza. The land is given to the smallholder family on a heritable lease, i.e. at the end of each 49 years the farmer is entitled to renew the lease for another 49 years. He has the right to pass the land on to his children with the same conditions binding on them. Self-labor applies to the family farms as well as to the cooperative farms. This means that the farmer has to work the farm himself. An annuity of 2% of the cost of the farm is paid by the farmer. In case of accident or sickness the other farmers of the settlement are obligated to assist in the work of the incapacitated farmer. All matters relating to the whole settlement are decided at a Town-meeting. All selling and purchasing is done on a cooperative basis. The first smallholders settlement was organized in Nahalal in 1921.[14]

3. THE MOSHAV SHITUFI

In addition to the first two kinds of farming communities described above, a third variety sprang up, the Moshav Shitufi, which combined features common to the first two. Each family has its own private dwelling place. But the Settlement land is owned and farmed in common by all settlers.[15] Like the Kvutza the Moshav Shitufi tends also to develop industrial enterprises.

These three types of farming settlements were founded on National Fund land. They all had to agree to the same fundamental principles as mentioned above. The farmer could not sell the land when for one reason or another he was tempted to leave the farm; the land by law belongs to the Jewish people. If the farmer chooses to stay on the land, it belongs to him for all practical purposes. The idea back of this was to prevent land speculation, and to develop a Jewish farming class. Both of these objectives have been achieved.

4. THE MOSHAVA

Alongside the settlements which arose on National Fund land there were private settlements where the land was bought by the immigrant with his own money. These farms are managed along the same lines as any other privately-owned farm. They work their farms themselves, or with hired labor if they wish.

From 1882—which marks the beginning of the modern Jewish colonization work in Palestine—to 1947, i.e. in the 65 year interval, 277 agricultural settlements were founded.[16] In the first 6½ years since the State of Israel was established 537 new agricultural settlements were created.[17] Most of the new immigrants, especially those with families, prefer the smallholders type of village.

Notes to Chapter 8

[1] Alex Bein, *The Return To The Soil* (The Youth and Hechalutz Department of the Zionist Organization: Jerusalem, 1952), p. 234.

[2] Ibid., pp. 332-3.

[3] Ibid., pp. 443-4.

[4] Ibid., p. 443.

[5] Ibid., p. 443.

[6] Ibid., p. 442.

[7] Ibid., pp. 446-7.

[8] Ibid., pp. 503-4.

[9] Ibid., p. 510.

[10] *State Of Israel, Facts And Figures, 1955;* published by the Israel Office of Information, New York City.

[11] Ibid.

[12] Alex Bein, Op. Cit., pp. 28-31.

[13] Ibid., p. 65.

[14] Ibid., pp. 293-4.

[15] Ibid., p. 485.

[16] Ibid., p. 530.

[17] *State Of Israel, Facts And Figures, 1955.*

CHAPTER 9

THE REUNION BETWEEN THE JEWISH PEOPLE
AND THEIR ANCIENT HOMELAND
(continued)

III. THE REJUVENATION OF THE SOIL

    1. The Drainage of Swamps

    2. The Reclamation of the Barren Uplands

    3. Afforestation

    4. Irrigation

IV. THE REVIVAL OF AGRICULTURE

    1. Diversified Versus One-Crop Farming

    2. Garden Vegetables

    3. Citrus Fruits

    4. Other Fruits

    5. The Cultivation of Cotton

    6. The Rehabilitation of Palestine's Livestock and Poultry

V. THE DEVELOPMENT OF INDUSTRY: THE DISCOVERY OF
NATURAL RESOURCES IN THE LAND OF ISRAEL

    1. The Dead Sea Chemicals

    2. Phosphates

    3. Ceramic Materials

    4. Copper

    5. Manganese

    6. Iron Ore

    7. Oil

VI. THE DEVELOPMENT OF THE NEGEV

CHAPTER 9

THE REUNION BETWEEN THE JEWISH PEOPLE
AND THEIR ANCIENT HOMELAND

(continued)

III. The Rejuvenation Of The Soil

The early Pioneers, most of whom came from Russia, were city people unversed in agriculture. In making plans for their future work as farmers in Palestine they were influenced by conditions of farm life in Russia. They had an idea that all they had to do when they arrived in Palestine was to plough and plant and in due time gather in the harvest. They were soon to learn through bitter experience that the impoverished soil of Palestine was going to require altogether different treatment than the rich soil of the Ukraine from whose regions most of the early pioneers had come. While they gained valuable information from the Arab peasants in Palestine the Jewish Pioneers were well aware that by using the antiquated methods of the Arabs they will never build up a Jewish Homeland in Palestine. The soil of Palestine, which in ancient days was rich and fertile and capable of supporting from three to five million people, had been ruined while the Jewish people were in dispersion. It was a soil comparable to a sick and moribund human being.

Accordingly, the most urgent problem confronting the Jewish Pioneers was how to revive the wasted soil of Palestine. Here their lack of agricultural knowledge was at once a handicap and a blessing. They were eager to learn all they could and from any source. The Agricultural School at Mikveh Israel established near Jaffa in 1870, the training farm set up at Sejera in 1907, the Rechovoth Agricultural Experiment Station founded in 1921, all these were ready to supply the necessary information on the treatment of the soil and the kinds of crops most suitable for cultivation in Palestine.

The preliminary phase in the modern Jewish agricultural work in Palestine consisted, therefore, of rejuvenating the soil, of restoring it to a healthful condition. This work of reclaiming the impoverished soil often took months, and even years, of careful and loving nursing. Stones had to be gathered up and carried away; grubs dug up and removed; heaps of manure which lay idle on Arab farms were bought

139

and used to cover the soil; leguminous crops were planted and ploughed under to enrich the soil; deep ploughing was introduced in place of the shallow ploughing practiced by the Arab peasant.

The reclamation methods applied by the Jewish Pioneers varied, of course, with the terrain of the country. The swamplands of the valleys, the rocky uplands of the Judaean hills, and the arid and parched ground of the desert, all required a different approach. Accordingly, the reclamation work assumed several forms:

1. THE DRAINAGE OF SWAMPS

Large stretches of the land which the Jews bought from the Arabs were swampland, the breeding ground of the anopheles mosquito harboring the malaria germ. The object of draining these swamps was threefold: 1) To convert useless into fertile ground; 2) to wipe out the breeding nests of the deadly malaria; 3) to make it possible to utilize for irrigation purposes water resources which otherwise went to waste.

From the very beginning of the Jewish colonization program in Palestine the Jewish Pioneers were draining and clearing swamps and marshes. One of the largest swamp areas which the Jews drained while Palestine was ruled by the British Mandatory Power was the Emek territory. The work began there in 1922 and was completed in two years. The work was carried on entirely by Jewish labor. Many of the young Jewish immigrants who were engaged in this drainage project had never done heavy manual work in their native land. Often they had to work standing up to their chest in stagnant water. Many of them died, others were broken physically.[1] By 1924 most of the malaria menace was eliminated and some 25,000 acres of useless, but fertile, land was recovered for agriculture. Today some of the most flourishing communities stand in areas which prior to the present Jewish Return had been deadly swampland. One of these is Petach Tikvah. Established by a group of Jerusalem Jews in 1878, it had to be abandoned after two years' heroic struggle against malaria. But after two or three years the Jewish settlers returned, and began to drain the smaller swamps and plant the Australian eucalyptus trees which absorb much moisture. Following World War One the Zionist Organization completed drainage operations of the district. When the Jews commenced their work in this area there lived in this vicinity some four hundred malaria-infected Arabs. By 1950, two years after the reestablishment of the State of Israel, the population in this flourishing and healthy community numbered 31,500.[2]

Chadera, founded in 1891, was afflicted with malaria no less than Petach Tikvah. Many of the original settlers succumbed to the disease. Baron Rothschild hired laborers from Sudan for the drainage work which relieved the situation somewhat. But it was not until 1930 that modern drainage and control methods were applied which completely eradicated the disease. The long rows of graves on its cemetery, where lie buried the brave people who sacrificed their lives to make the land habitable, are mute evidence of the grim struggle carried on for years.

Chadera was the first large Jewish settlement consisting of 8,500 acres of swampland bought from the Arabs at an exorbitant price. "Today Chadera's many groves of giant eucalyptus trees, its orange, lemon and grapefruit orchards, its fine macadamized roads, street lighting, municipal water supply and comfortable homes, are far different from the former deadly swamps and impassable trails, and from the food shortage, poverty and suffering of the early years."[3]

One of the greatest swamp drainage projects undertaken to date by the Israel Government is the drainage of the Hule region. The Hule basin is a triangular valley of some 45,000 acres of land lying in the northeastern corner of Israel, in which area there are three streams, the Hasbani, Leddan and Banias, merging to form the river Jordan. The southern part of this valley consisted of 7000 acres of marshland, and the Lake Hule which occupied an additional 3500 acres. The Hule valley was in ancient times one of the most fertile regions of Palestine. It had a reputation of growing the richest crops in the country.

The reclamation of the Hule basin had been the dream of Zionist planners since 1906. In 1934 the Palestine Land Development Company acquired the concession for developing the Hule basin. But the work was not really begun until 1950. A special nature reserve of 750 acres surrounded by land-walls was built to preserve the historic appearance of the Lake Hule with its rich natural vegetation and wildlife. The Hule basin and its surrounding vicinity have been freed of malaria-carrying anopheles mosquitoes which had been the scourge of this area for centuries. About a hundred million cubic meters of water, previously lost through evaporation, have been gained for irrigation purposes. 45,000 acres of most fertile farmland, capable of supporting some 100,000 people, have been recovered.[4]

2. THE RECLAMATION OF THE BARREN UPLANDS

The barren uplands and mountain slopes presented a different reclamation problem. The soil submerged under water in the swamps was essentially good soil, as fertile when drainage operations began as centuries ago when there were no swamps in the area. Once the stagnant swamp waters were drained and the choked off springs and streams, whose seepage perpetuated the swamps, channeled into different directions, the soil was ready for agricultural use. It was different with the barren hills. There was no soil on them to begin with, the soil having been washed away and carried off to the valleys and later into the sea during centuries of neglect and misuse.

The apparent hopelessness of this situation did not, however, discourage the Jewish Pioneers from attempting a solution. Stones which accumulated for centuries were blasted and carried away, the roots of ancient trees were dug up and removed. Large quantities of fertilizer were brought in to revive the soil which escaped erosion. Trees were planted on the bare areas unfit for any cultivation. Terrace walls were erected on the hill slopes to stop further erosion. The waters rushing down from mountain springs were directed into newly-built channels. Step by step the landscape changed its appearance beyond recognition. Where there was once a desolate, stony, and barren hill area, there are now fruit orchards, growing delicious plums, peaches, apricots, and vines producing good table grapes; also dairy farms, producing large quantities of milk and butter; poultry farms, supplying large numbers of eggs; market gardening, growing an abundance of vegetables. An example of such a settlement is Kiryath Anavim founded in 1920 on the rocky hills of Judaea west of Jerusalem, where previously "the only growing things were occasional thorn bushes and dwarf trees."[5]

3. AFFORESTATION

When the Jewish Pioneers arrived in Palestine they found the country denuded of trees. Afforestation, therefore, became one of the chief goals of the Jewish agricultural program. Large tracts of land unsuitable for any other form of cultivation were utilized for planting trees. Experiments taught the Pioneers the kind of trees best suitable to the soil and climate of Palestine. Australian eucalyptuses were found especially good because they absorb large quantities of moisture. Consequently they were used in the wet lowlands. "Most adaptable of all were conifers, notably the Aleppo pine, which could strike roots in sandy, rocky or swampy soil unsuitable for any other form of cultivation."[6] Millions of trees have been and are still being planted. This will prove of enormous benefit to the country, since forests are good sources of lumber and timber, and, in addition, they contribute to the conservation of water as they cause great absorption of rain water. Carob trees have also been planted. They are an important source of concentrated fodder. This reforestation program has already changed the face of the land. In the first sixteen years since Israel became an independent state 83 million trees were planted. Since then additional millions of trees have been planted.[7]

4. IRRIGATION

According to the amount of rainfall the Palestine climate can be divided into the dry season, from May to November, and the rainy season, embracing the remainder of the year. Some regions of the country, as for example Galilee, receive an abundance of rain, while the south experiences frequent droughts. But as long as good water conservation measures are practiced the water resources of the country are adequate to support a sizeable population.

During the first several decades of the Jewish agricultural program in Palestine little was done to increase the water resources of the country. Shortage of funds, the abundance of land, and the lack of scientific knowledge were some of the reasons for the inactivity in this direction. With the increase of the number of immigrants a more rational and economic utilization of the available land became imperative. It was found that the average family can support itself comfortably from the intensive cultivation of five to seven acres of well irrigated land while if the land was non-irrigated, at least twenty acres may be necessary. Consequently, a search for water was begun. Many wells were sunk in the same manner as the native Arabs were doing. But these were dug superficially and the yield of water was poor. In time, however, American well-boring machines were imported and deep drilling operations were begun. The search for water received a considerable boost with the arrival of the German Jewish refugees among whom there was a certain number of irrigation engineers. With the use of modern scientific methods the locating of underground water supplies was attended with much greater success. Before 1933—the beginning of German Jewish immigration into Palestine—successful water drillings amounted to 32 per cent, after 1933 the proportion rose to 77 per cent; while the average yield of water per well increased from 8.6 to 55 cubic meters per hour. Hundreds of deep wells were sunk making available large reservoirs of underground water. This has opened up whole new areas for cultivation.[8]

In 1937 the Mekoroth Water Company was established and when the State came into existence in 1948 Mekoroth became the national water company, carrying out most of the irrigation projects of the Government. The Tahal is the Israel Water Planning Authority. Since the establishment of the State many new sources of water have been located. Artificial lakes were constructed to store rain and to prevent floods. In 1956 a Master Water Plan was adopted incorporating the Jordan Valley Authority project by the United States soil conservationist, Walter C. Lowdermilk. The purpose of this Plan is to make use of every available source of water before it is lost to the Dead Sea or the Mediterranean. In 1964, a 154-mile network of pipes, forming part of the Master Water Plan, began to deliver water from the Sea of Gallilee in the north to farms and towns in the arid south. There are five such satellite irrigation projects. Upon completion, this Master Water Plan is expected to bring into use all available natural waters within the geographical borders of Israel. In the southern port of Eilat there is a desalinization plant where sea water is being converted into drinking water by a new process invented by an Israeli scientist. The United States is cooperating with Israel in the construction of an atomic plant designed to provide power for desalinization of sea water. If successful, these activities by Israeli scientists may open up vast stretches of the Negev desert for agriculture, industry and the settlement of many hundreds of thousands of people.

IV. THE REVIVAL OF AGRICULTURE

1. DIVERSIFIED VERSUS ONE-CROP FARMING

Under the influence of Baron Rothschild the colonists who were the recipients of his financial assistance introduced the cultivation of vine. When control of these colonies passed to the Jewish Colonization Association of Paris the colonists were advised to shift to growing of wheat. The purpose of this was to make them less dependent on the vagaries of a world market, and at the same time provide some of the food requirements of the colonists themselves. In time it became apparent that wheat growing partakes of many of the shortcomings of any one-crop type of farming. In the first place, large tracts of land had to be utilized, while to accommodate an ever-increasing immigrant population individual farm holdings had to be small.

Then, also, large wheat growing farms had to depend on hired labor which was an objectionable feature as explained previously. The climate of Palestine with the exception of Galilee is unsuitable for growing of wheat. Last, but not least, the cultivation of wheat did not entirely free the colonists of dependence on world markets.

Consequently, when the Zionist Organization began to settle the Jewish immigrants on Jewish National Fund lands one of the stipulations was that they engage in diversified, i.e. mixed, farming. The advantages of mixed farming are the following: 1) The individual farms can be small, thus conserving the land; 2) hired labor is unnecessary; 3) the farmer grows the food for his family and the fodder for his livestock; 4) the steady growth of urban centers provide a steady market for vegetables and fruits.

The fact that the Jewish immigrants were city people in their countries and consequently were unversed in agriculture was in the long run a blessing in disguise. Having no farming tradition to hold them down as is the case of the peasant of the Middle East, the Jewish immigrants were open-minded and anxious to learn the newest and most scientific methods. Farm machines were imported in ever-increasing numbers and used extensively. Tractors, steel rollers, potato planting machines, sprinklers, grain drills, gang plows, mowing and threshing machines were brought in, and mechanized farming methods were introduced on the Jewish farms. Deep plowing, the liberal use of good fertilizers, and crop rotation, all these new measures made Jewish farming methods equal to the best in the world.

2. GARDEN VEGETABLES

Prior to the arrival of the Jewish immigrants the variety of vegetables grown in Palestine was small. The discovery of underground water supplies, and the introduction of diversified farming made it possible to grow large quantities of vegetables. There is a supply of fresh vegetables all year round as summer vegetables are being grown in the winter months in the tropical parts of the Jordan Valley.[9] Not only have existing varieties of vegetables been improved, but new ones have been introduced, such as asparagus, sweet potato, red cabbage and rhubarb. The application of good ventilating methods helped to prevent premature sprouting of potatoes, thus facilitating their storage during hot summer months. This enabled the Jewish farmers to grow potatoes in large quantities.[10] The Jews have also introduced the cultivation of sugar beets and sugar cane on a commercial scale.

3. CITRUS FRUITS

Lowdermilk states that "the most outstanding achievement of
Palestine agriculture is the scientific production of citrus fruits."[11]
The Jewish colonists improved the native orange of Palestine and
introduced the Washington navel and Valencia oranges, as well as
the grapefruit. "Generally speaking, the citrus groves in Palestine
closely resemble those of Southern California, and in some ways the
Palestinian fruit seemed superior to that of California. . . . Expansion
on a large scale began after Jewish research established improved
methods of planting, picking, packing and marketing. Nowhere in
the world have I found citrus groves cultivated as intensively and
scientifically as in Palestine."[12]

4. OTHER FRUITS

The Jewish immigrants also introduced a variety of delicious
fruits. They are growing the European apples on a commercial scale.
Plums, peaches, pears, bananas, and "a large array of subtropical
fruits—pineapple, mango, avocado, guava, passion fruit, papaya,
persimmon, cherimoa, and others"[13]—are a Jewish innovation.

5. THE CULTIVATION OF COTTON

Cotton growing in Israel was introduced in 1952 by Mr. Sam
Hamburg, a California cotton and sugar beet farmer, and consultant
to the Israel Department of Agriculture. It was found that cotton
can be grown anywhere in Israel, including the Negev. Tests performed in Britain showed that the quality of Israel's cotton is equal
to the world's finest fibers. A cotton gin was imported from Texas
and set up in Beisan, the gin was installed by experts from Texas,
who also trained Israeli workers in the art of ginning and baling
Israel's long-fiber cotton.

6. THE REHABILITATION OF PALESTINE'S LIVESTOCK AND POULTRY

The Jewish achievements in the dairy industry are no less spec-
tacular. The Jewish immigrants found the native Arab cow to be a
rundown and neglected animal whose supply of milk and meat is very
low. This Arab cow averaged about 1,540 pounds of milk a year.
At first the Jewish colonists imported European cows but they could
not thrive in the Palestinian climate. Finally they began to cross
Syrian and Lebanese breeds with Holsteins from Holland and Jerseys
from England, and they evolved a new strain of Palestinian cow
doing well in the Palestinian climate and producing a high output in

milk and meat. This cow yields an average of 8,800 pounds of milk a year which is slightly higher than the average annual milk output of the test cows under observation of the United States Department of Agriculture.[14] Lowdermilk relates in his book *Palestine, Land of Promise,* that during his visit to Palestine negotiations were completed to export this superior "Jewish Cow" to India.[15]

The native Palestinian, fat tail, sheep has also received its due amount of attention from the Jewish colonists. By a process of selection they have improved the native breed to a degree where its annual milk output averages 330 pounds, while the native Arab sheep gives only on the average of 88 pounds a year. Similarly, the native goat was also improved by the same process of selection resulting in a yearly output around 1575 pounds of milk against some 612 pounds of yearly average for the Arab goat.[16]

Arab poultry was in the same run-down state as its livestock. The native Arab hen is a neglected, scrawny fowl, permitted to shift for itself and laying on an average of 70 small eggs per year. The Jewish colonists have introduced the leghorn hen and crossed it with native breeds and produced a superior strain yielding 150 large eggs per year.

V. The Development Of Industry: The Discovery Of Natural Resources In The Land Of Israel

Before the Jewish colonization work had begun there was practically no industry in Palestine. At the end of World War One Palestine industry consisted of a few Arab soap factories, some flour mills, a number of workshops for the manufacture of religious items, and the large wine cellars in the Jewish colonies of Rishon Letzion and Zikhron Ya'akov. The obstacles in the path of the industrial development of the country were many and varied of which the following were the most outstanding:

The Jewish colonists were at first primarily interested in reviving the devastated and ruined soil of the Land and restoring the agricultural economy of the country. They were aware of the fact that no new life is possible in the country unless its soil is first brought back to life. Then, also, the revitalization of the soil was in their mind inseparably associated with the physical and spiritual rehabilitation of the Jewish people. For centuries the Jews were forbidden to own land, they were barred from useful trades, and were thus forced into non-productive occupations. The rebuilders of Zion set out to reverse this process. To normalize Jewish life was one of the chief aims of the Jewish colonization program in the Land of Israel. The Jewish Pioneers were convinced that Jewish life can never be normalized unless the Jew returns to the soil, and Jewish farming becomes the basis of the Jewish economy in the Land of Israel.

However, this emphasis on agriculture was in the course of time modified by experience and sheer necessity. The colonists gradually gained conviction of the essential interdependence of agriculture and industry in modern life. It was also becoming evident that without a well-developed industrial program the resettlement of large numbers of Jews in the Land will be impossible. Consequently, the ideological approach to the soil and agriculture as a stepping stone to the rehabilitation of the Jewish personality was in time extended to all forms of labor and the "conquest of labor" became no less important than the "conquest of soil."

A second factor which seriously impeded the development of industry was the scarcity of local raw materials and the lack of cheap sources of mechanical power.

A third great obstacle in the industrial development of the country was the peculiar tariff policy under which Palestine functioned under the British Mandate. In accordance with Article 18 of the Mandate created by the League of Nations the principle of free trade was applied to Palestine as a mandated territory.[17] This lack of tariff protection made of Palestine a virtual dumping ground for goods manufactured in countries which were members of the League of Nations, which meant from practically all over the world.

The growth of industry has been so rapid that any detailed description would be obsolete upon the publication of this book. Suffice it to say, that in an incredibly short period Israel became the most industrialized country in the Near East. This has been made possible, in large part, by the intensive search for, and consequent discovery of, certain indispensable minerals in the country.

With the Old Testament as a guide a frantic search was begun for the presence of minerals in the country. That minerals did exist was inferred from the Pentateuch describing the Land of Promise not only as a "land flowing with milk and honey" but also "whose stones are iron, and out of whose hills thou mayest dig copper" (Deuteronomy 8:9). It was also known that King Solomon exploited some of the mineral resources. The remains of his copper mines and smelting foundries were actually located in the southern Negev. For centuries during the dispersion of the Jews from the Land these mineral deposits were either unknown or ignored.

Shortly after the reestablishment of the State of Israel the Government ordered a survey of the mineral resources of the country. In May 1949, one year after the Proclamation of Independence, the surveying agency submitted a preliminary report indicating the presence of an impressive number of minerals. The list of the minerals discovered in the Negev included phosphates, copper, manganese, felspar, mica, glass sand, ball clay, iron, bitumen-bearing rock, gypsum and others. The Israel Mining Corporation was then established to direct further geological surveys and formulate plans to exploit the mineral deposits.

1. THE DEAD SEA CHEMICALS

Prior to the establishment of the State the Dead Sea minerals were the only minerals to be exploited commercially. Palestine Potash, Ltd. was established by Moses Novomeysky, a Jewish mining engineer from Siberia, who spent many years investigating Dead Sea chemicals and who obtained the concession to exploit these chemicals.[18] Prior to 1948 this company operated two plants at both the northern and southern shores of the Dead Sea. During the War of Independence the northern works were destroyed, while the southern works remained idle between 1948 and 1952. A new company was then set up to resume operations, and production was begun in June 1953. The Dead Sea is said to have practically an inexhaustible quantity of valuable minerals. Its salts comprise magnesium chloride (142.4 gms. per litre), sodium chloride (82.4 gms. per litre), calcium chloride (33 gms. per litre), potassium chloride (11.8 gms. per litre), magnesium bromide (3.9 gms. per litre) and small quantities of calcium sulphate (1.3 gms. per litre). Before 1948 the yearly output of Dead Sea potash was 60,000 tons. This production is considerably higher now.

2. PHOSPHATES

Phosphate deposits were found in an area of 10,000 acres, in the Negev, to contain 100 million tons. 1,000 acres in this general area contain 15 million tons of phosphate rock. These deposits have not only made Israel completely independent of imports of this highly essential fertilizer, but there is already enough surplus for export to other countries.

3. CERAMIC MATERIALS

The Negev Ceramic and Quartz, Ltd. holds licences to explore and exploit clay, glass sand, felspar and quartz in the Negev area. The activities of this company have made it possible to eliminate completely the imports of glass sand and the sharp curtailment of imports of ball clay and fire clay.

4. COPPER

Proved copper reserves in the Timna region, about 25 kilometers north of Eilat, near the site of King Solomon's mines, total about 23 million tons. Further reserves are estimated at 30-35 million tons.

5. MANGANESE

About 5 kilometers west of the copper deposits in the Negev they found deposits of manganese ore. These are estimated to contain 1 million tons.

6. IRON ORE

Iron Ore was first discovered in the Negev area. Proven reserves are estimated at 5 million tons. While this iron ore has relatively poor iron content quality it is expected to improve with proper preparation. Several years later iron ore deposits were found at Mount Ramim, in Galilee, containing 40 million tons of iron ore of good quality. It is believed that these iron deposits are the most important metal ore find besides the copper deposits in the Negev.

7. OIL

In 1950 the Israel Government asked Max. W. and Douglas Ball, oil and gas consultants of Washington, D.C., to survey the territory of the State of Israel for oil deposits. These experts submitted an optimistic report to the Government, and their findings were published in the Bulletin of the American Association of Petroleum Geologists in January 1953. In the conclusion of their report they made the following statement: "Every geologic province [of the State of Israel] has some oil and gas possibilities; none can be written off. . . . Thus the possibilities of two of Israel's eight geologic provinces are obscure, of two are fair to good, and of four are good. The four whose possibilities are good include the three largest provinces, and cover more than three-fourths of the country."[19]

Drilling for oil began in Israel in 1953. Seven oil companies began to search for oil. Ten drills done by all the seven companies proved unsuccessful. The Lapidot-Israel Oil Prospectors, an Israel company, started the eleventh drill, and this time at Heletz, in the northwestern Negev. This was the exact site where the British Iraq Petroleum Company had been drilling in 1947. This company drilled to a depth of 3,464 feet and struck no oil. When hostilities broke out between the Jews and Arabs in 1947 it suspended drilling operations. The Lapidot-Israel Oil Prospectors went down deeper, and when it reached a depth of 4,905 feet a fountain of oil shot up 60 feet high. It was an hour and 40 minutes before they succeeded to close the jet, and in this time they filled 71 barrels with oil. The chemists at the Weizmann Institute who analyzed the oil reported that it contained 30.5 degrees A.P.I.*, and was as of good quality as the Bahrein and Egyptian oil.

The news of the oil find spread through the country like a wild-fire. People embraced each other, sang and wept. They knew very well the importance of the oil discovery for the economic and defense situation of their country. The oil was struck on September 22, 1955.

Gas was struck in 1958. In 1966, 200,000 tons of oil were pumped, covering 8 per cent of Israel's fuel needs. In the same year eight gas wells produced the equivalent of 59,000 tons of fuel oil.[20]

VI. The Development Of The Negev

The desert forming the southern part of the State of Israel is designated by the Hebrew word Negev. The whole territory of the State of Israel, prior to the June 1967 war, was 8,048 square miles large, about the size of the State of New Jersey. Over half of this territory, about 5000 square miles, is occupied by the Negev desert.

The following description of the adjoining areas of the Sinai Peninsula and southern Palestine by Major C. S. Jarvis, for 14 years British Governor of Sinai, gives us a vivid picture of what these areas used to be before the advent of the Arabs. "What strikes one very forcibly about Central Sinai, particularly the northeastern portion near the Palestine frontier, is the extent to which this area was farmed and exploited in the past. Every single wadi† has been scientifically dammed for its whole length by orderly rows of large stones, the sides of the hills are in many places terraced for olives and vines, the re-

---

* A.P.I.—American Petroleum Institute, a term indicating the specific gravity of crude oil.

† Gully, wash, which fills during the rainy season.

mains of small walled orchards exist everywhere, and, dotted about in the hills, there are dozens, possibly hundreds, of water reservoirs called harabas by the Arabs. These harabas are underground chambers carved out of the virgin rock, and some of them are of vast size with natural pillars left by the masons to support the roof. They are always placed by the side of some wadi so that the flood will flow into them and fill them, and if every one were cleaned out and repaired there would be sufficient water in this area to support twenty times the population that now exists."[21]

Referring to the work done in this part of the Middle East by the archaeologist C. L. Woodley, Jarvis continues: "In his opinion the occupation of Palestine and Syria by the Romans from the first century onwards, and the state of order and public security that ensued as the result caused the population of these countries to increase so enormously that the surplus had to go forth into the wilderness and eke out an existence by utilizing and improving the natural resources of an otherwise harsh and barren land.

Both Palestine and Syria were exceedingly prosperous, and prosperity brought trade from all parts of the world. Some of the merchandize came from the East and much of it landed at either Suez or Akaba, which meant that the now barren lands of Eastern Sinai and Southern Palestine were on the direct route of the merchants who traveled northwards. This trade caused towns to spring up where the natural resources in ordinary times would not entirely justify their existence; the merchants required camels and transport animals, and the animals needed forage, and so every inch of ground that could produce crops was brought into cultivation. Where soil did not exist it was produced by the simple, if laborious, expedient of building walls on barren hillsides and not a drop of water was allowed to run to waste. The wadis after rains filled first the harabas or reservoirs and the water was then conducted to the fields and pastures below. Lawrence* was of the opinion that the rainfall in those days was no greater than it is today—the great results were obtained by making the fullest use of every drop of water that fell...

With the Mohammedan invasion and the occupation of the country by the haphazard Bedouin all this civilization and prosperity disappeared in a very short time. The harabas were allowed to fill with silt so that there was no water supply, the dams broke and were not

---

* T. E. Lawrence, known as "Lawrence of Arabia"

repaired, the orchard walls fell down and goats and camels ate the trees, and in a century, probably much less, the Arab had the country as he really likes it—a howling waterless wilderness, in the midst of which he sits complaining that he is a poor man, has no food, and his wife has to go fifteen miles a day to fetch water from some haraba which a good-natured but weak-minded Governor has cleaned out for him. I am not quite certain if it is either good nature or weak-mindedness that has caused me to do so much for the Arab that he could have done very easily himself. I think it is due to sheer exasperation at seeing a good piece of desert land go to waste for want of a dam to collect the rainfall, and women walking all the hours of daylight to fetch water because their despicable husbands are too lazy to spend ten days digging out the silt from a first-class reservoir a hundred yards away."[22]

In another communication the former British Governor of the Sinai Peninsula has this to say with reference to the Negev district of Palestine: "When Rome went, public security went. There were no police and no central authority, and these towns out in the desert were cut off from civilization. They were subjected to Bedouin raids. There was no initiative, no urge to work, and general stagnation set in, as is always the case when the Bedouin nomad gets the upper hand. They probably hung on for one to three hundred years, and then I suppose gradually the people died out or left these towns and went to some more suitable spots. After this the Arabs' camels broke through the fencing and started to eat the trees and the whole area went very rapidly back to desert."[23]

Nelson Glueck, the American Jewish archaeologist, uncovered the remains of 225 sites of ancient Negev communities. The region was literally dotted with hundreds of towns and villages. With the Bible as his guide Glueck rediscovered King Solomon's copper mines a few miles north of Eilat, the southernmost tip of the Negev.

The above findings merely corroborate information culled from the Bible. The casual remark in Genesis that Abraham took large herds of sheep and oxen through the country south of Beersheba proves the existence in Abraham's day of water and grazing land in the Negev. With this lead from the Bible the Jewish Pioneers undertook a careful search through the hills of this region and actually located the remains of an intricate drainage system designed to conserve every drop of water. They reconstructed the dykes and drains of the Biblical period and within one year there was sufficient grazing land to feed a herd of 300 sheep.

In 1943 three Jewish experimental colonies were established in the Negev desert. Their work definitely revealed the possibility of reclaiming the desert to its former fertile condition by means of irrigation, modern soil conservation methods and any special treatments which the soil of the desert may require. Today, large-scale water projects constructed since the State of Israel had come into existence, are already bringing large water supplies into the Negev. This has already made the cultivation of many thousands of acres of the Negev lands possible. Scores of settlements have been established. Over 200,000 Israeli Jews live now in the Negev. The Negev is already producing harvests of wheat, barley and hay. Sugar beets, corn, peanuts, potatoes, cabbage, tomatoes, carrots, cucumbers, fruit trees, grapes and watermelons are being now grown in the Negev. Spring potatoes, melons and tomatoes are being exported to European lands and the British Isles out of season. When fully developed the Negev will become Israel's main food growing center. It is claimed that with the increasing use of desalinized sea water the Negev may be able to accommodate an additional four or five million people.[24]

In addition to being Israel's potentially largest food source, the Negev is already the chief store-house of the country's mineral resources. The Dead Sea is located here with its vast, practically unlimited, supplies of potassium chloride; the valuable phosphates lie in the Negev; glass sand is found there; while the first oil deposits were discovered in the Negev towards the end of the summer of 1955.

With this we conclude this rather sketchy description of Israel's all-out war against the desolations of the Negev country. The wilderness of this region is gradually being rolled back and this part of the country is being restored to its ancient life-sustaining condition. The words of Israel's Prophets are being fulfilled beyond all expectation, and this before our very eyes. "The wilderness and the dry land shall be glad; and the desert shall rejoice, and blossom as the rose" (Isaiah 35:1).

Notes to Chapter 9

1 Alex Bein, *The Return To The Soil* (The Youth and Hechalutz Department of the Zionist Organization: Jerusalem, 1952), p. 234.

2 Walter Clay Lowdermilk, *Palestine, Land Of Promise* (Harper and Brothers: New York, 1944), Second Edition, p. 135; Alex Bein, Op. Cit., p. 568.

3 Walter Clay Lowdermilk, *"Jewish Colonization In Palestine"*, article in the *Menorah Journal* (Camden, New Jersey), Autumn 1940.

4 *Israel Digest*, June 24, 1955; published by the Israel Office of Information, New York, N. Y. Also, Walter C. Lowdermilk, *"A New Agriculture In An Old Land"*, article in the *The Atlantic Monthly* (Boston), November, 1961. Used by permission.

5 Walter Clay Lowdermilk, *Palestine, Land Of Promise*, p. 138. Used by permission.

6 Alex Bein, Op. Cit., p. 203.

7 *Agriculture, Israel 1954;* published by the Israel Office of Information, New York, N. Y. Also, Robert St. John, *Israel*, (Life World Library, Time Inc.: New York, 1962, 1965), p. 84.

8 Alex Bein, Op. Cit., pp. 453-4. Also, Walter Clay Lowdermilk, Op. Cit., pp. 89-90.

9 Walter Clay Lowdermilk, Op. Cit., p. 93.

10 Ibid.

11 Ibid., p. 94.

12 Ibid., pp. 94-5.

13 Morris Hindus, *In Search Of A Future* (Doubleday and Company, Inc., Garden City, New York, 1949), p. 229. Used by permission.

14 Ibid., pp. 219-220.

15 Walter Clay Lowdermilk, Op. Cit., p. 91.

16 Maurice Hindus, Op. Cit., p. 221.

17 Walter Clay Lowdermilk, Op. Cit., p. 105.

18 Ibid., p. 117.

19 Max W. Ball and Douglas Ball, *"Oil Prospects In Israel"*, article in the *Bulletin Of The American Association Of Petroleum Geologists* (Tulsa, Oklahoma) January, 1953. Used by permission.

20 *Facts About Israel, 1967.* p. 113; published by the Government of Israel.

21 C. S. Jarvis, *Three Deserts* (John Murray: London, 1936), pp. 128-9. Used by permission.

22 Ibid., pp. 129-131.

23 C. S. Jarvis, *"Southern Palestine And Its Possibilities For Settlement"*, article in *Royal Central Asian Society Journal* (London), vol. xxv, April 1938. Used by permission.

24 Robert St. John, Op. Cit., p. 87.

PART THREE

A Message Of Hope For A Time Of Trouble

"And there shall come forth a shoot out of the stump of Jesse*, and a twig shall grow forth out of his roots. And the Spirit of the LORD shall rest upon him, the spirit of wisdom, and understanding, the spirit of counsel and might, the spirit of knowledge and the fear of the LORD. And his delight shall be in the fear of the LORD. He shall not judge by what his eyes see, or decide by what his ears hear. But with righteousness he shall judge the poor, and decide with equity for the meek of the earth; and he shall smite the earth with the rod of his mouth, and with the breath of his lips he shall slay the wicked. Righteousness shall be the girdle of his waist, and faithfulness the girdle of his loins. The wolf shall dwell with the lamb, and the leopard shall lie down with the kid, and the calf and the lion and the fatling together, and a little child shall lead them. The cow and the bear shall feed; their young shall lie down together; and the lion shall eat straw like the ox. The sucking child shall play over the hole of the asp, and the weaned child shall put his hand on the adder's den. They shall not hurt or destroy in all my holy mountain; for the earth shall be full of the knowledge of the LORD as the waters cover the sea.

In that day the root of Jesse shall stand as an ensign to the peoples; him shall the nations seek, and his dwellings shall be glorious.

In that day the LORD will extend his hand yet a second time to recover the remnant which is left of his people, from Assyria, from Egypt, from Pathros, from Ethiopia, from Elam, from Shinar, from Hamath, and from the coastlands of the sea. He will raise an ensign for the nations, and will assemble the outcasts of Israel, and gather the dispersed of Judah from the four corners of the earth" (Isaiah 11: 1-12).

---

* "Jesse" stands here for the Davidic dynasty.

"Behold my servant* whom I uphold, my chosen, in whom my soul delights; I have put my Spirit upon him, he will bring forth justice to the nations. He will not cry nor lift up his voice, or make it heard in the street. A bruised reed he will not break, and a dimly burning wick he will not quench; he will faithfully bring forth justice. He will not fail or be discouraged till he has established justice in the earth; and the coastlands wait for his law.

Thus says God, the LORD, who created the heavens and stretched them out, who spread forth the earth and what comes from it, who gives breath to the people upon it and spirit to those who walk in it. 'I am the LORD, I have called you in righteousness, I have taken you by the hand and kept you; I have given you as a covenant to the people, a light to the nations. To open the eyes that are blind, to bring out the prisoners from the dungeon, from the prison those who sit in darkness' " (Isaiah 42: 1-7).

"It shall come to pass in the latter days that the mountain of the house of the LORD shall be established as the highest of the mountains, and shall be raised up above the hills; and peoples shall flow to it. And many nations shall come, and say: 'Come, let us go up to the mountain of the LORD, to the house of the God of Jacob; that he may teach us his ways, and we may walk in his paths'; for out of Zion shall go forth the law, and the word of the LORD from Jerusalem. He shall judge between many peoples, and shall decide for strong nations afar off; and they shall beat their swords into plowshares, and their spears into pruning hooks; nation shall not lift up sword against nation, neither shall they learn war any more. But they shall sit every man under his vine and under his fig tree, and none shall make them afraid; for the mouth of the LORD of hosts has spoken" (Micah 4: 1-4).

"And all the assembly kept silence; and they listened to Barnabas and Paul as they related what signs and wonders God had done through them among the Gentiles. After they finished speaking, James replied, "Brethren, listen to me. Symeon** has related how

---

* According to the Jewish Targum the servant introduced to us here is Israel's Messiah. Isaiah 11 stresses Messiah's royal dignity and kingly office. Isaiah 42 is the first of several passages in this portion of Isaiah portraying the Messiah as the Suffering Servant of Jehovah who redeems Israel and the nations through His atoning death and resurrection (See Isaiah 49: 1-9; 50: 4-9; 52: 13-15; 53: 1-12).

** Symeon, i.e., Simon Peter.

God first visited the Gentiles, to take out of them a people for his name. And with this the words of the prophets agree, as it is written. After this I will return*, and I will rebuild the dwelling of David, which has fallen; I will rebuild its ruins, and I will set it up. That the rest of men may seek the Lord, and the Gentiles who are called by my name. Says the Lord, who has made these things known from of old' " (Acts 15: 12-18).**

"For if their*** exclusion from the pale of salvation has meant the reconciliation of the rest of mankind to God, what would their inclusion mean? It would be nothing less than life from the dead!" (Romans 11:15. J. B. Phillips' *The New Testament* in Modern English).

"Now I don't want you, my brothers, to start imagining things, and I must therefore share with you my knowledge of God's secret plan. It is this, that the partial insensibility which has come to Israel is only to last until the full number of the Gentiles has been called. Once this has happened, all Israel will be saved, as the Scripture says:

There shall come out of Zion the deliverer;
He shall turn away ungodliness from Jacob:
And this is my covenant unto them.
When I shall take away their sins"
(Romans 11: 25-27. J. B. Phillips' *The New Testament* in Modern English).

---

* This passage from Amos 9 is applied here to the Second Coming of Jesus Christ.

** The sense of this passage is that only a partial conversion of mankind is to take place as a result of Christ's First Coming; that the restoration of Israel and the conversion of the rest of mankind is the purpose of Christ's Second Coming.

*** their, i.e., the Jews'.

CHAPTER 10

A DIVINE FORECAST OF THE DESTINY OF EGYPT

CHAPTER 10

A DIVINE FORECAST OF THE DESTINY OF EGYPT

I. EGYPT UNDER DIVINE JUDGMENT

The State of Israel was established in compliance with a resolution passed by the United Nations. The Arab nations decided to defy the decision of the United Nations and they invaded Israel from the north, east, and south in a determined effort to destroy the reconstituted State. In the first twenty-five years of its existence the State of Israel was engaged in four wars with the neighboring Arab states. Egypt, the most populous of these Arab states, was the principal contender on the Arab side in these four wars.

Egypt is one of the oldest countries in existence. It has a recorded history of more than five thousand years. Israel's encounter with Egypt goes back to the beginning of Israel's existence. Egypt was the first nation which pursued a policy of genocide designed to exterminate the Hebrew people (Exodus 1:15-22). It was especially with reference to Egypt that God is said to have declared to Abraham that He will judge that nation which will oppress his descendants (Genesis 15:13-14). The disasters heaped upon Egypt in the period of Israel's Exodus were only the beginning of the judgments which were in store for Egypt as seen from the following Divine statement conveyed through Moses to the Egyptian king of the Exodus period.

"For by now I could have put forth my hand and struck you and your people with pestilence, and you would have been cut off from the earth; but for this purpose have I let you live, to show you my power, so that my name may be declared throughout all the earth" (Exodus 9:15-16).

It was by the name of Jehovah that God began His work of redemption in the Exodus period. It was by this name that He delivered Israel from Egyptian bondage, led them through the wilderness, and brought them into the Promised Land, in order that through Israel His salvation may reach all mankind. The above statement declares that in dealing with Egypt God had intended to become known as the God of judgment ("to show you my power") and the God of redemption ("and that my name"—i.e., the name of Jehovah, the God of redemption—"may be declared throughout all the earth"). Many nations of antiquity ceased to exist. Egypt, one of the oldest nations, was permitted to survive ("for this purpose have I let you live") in order that her long history may continue to be a witness

160

of the fact that God is a God of judgment and also a God of redemption.

The element of Divine judgment was spelled out in a Divine message delivered through the prophet Ezekiel centuries after the Exodus period.

"In the tenth year, in the tenth month, in the twelfth day of the month, the word of Jehovah came unto me saying, Son of man, set thy face against Pharaoh king of Egypt, and prophesy against him, and against all Egypt; speak, and say, Thus saith the Lord Jehovah: Behold, I am against thee, Pharaoh king of Egypt, the great monster that lieth in the midst of his rivers, that hath said, My river is mine own, and I have made it for myself. . . . Therefore thus saith the Lord Jehovah: Behold, I will bring a sword upon thee, and will cut off from thee man and beast. And the land of Egypt shall be a desolation and a waste; and they shall know that I am Jehovah. Because he hath said, The river is mine, and I have made it; therefore, behold, I am against thee, and against thy rivers, and I will make the land of Egypt an utter waste and desolation, from the tower of Seveneh[1] even unto the border of Ethiopia. . . . It shall be the barest of the kingdoms; neither shall it any more lift itself up above the nations: and I will diminish them, that they shall no more rule over the nations" (Ezekiel 29:1-3, 8-10, 15). The statement, "the river is mine own and I have made it" has reference to the belief fostered among the Egyptian people that their king is a god, and therefore it was he who made the Nile River upon which Egypt's life depended. Many rulers in antiquity were invested with divine honors, but they were regarded as essentially human. The Egyptian king, however, was considered as divine by nature. The Egyptians were taught to believe that all was well with them as long as the Egyptian throne was occupied by a king who was a god. He controlled the life-giving waters of the Nile. He held sway over all the forces of nature on which the welfare of Egypt depended. He ruled Egypt in his lifetime, and he exercised strong influence over the country from his abode in the afterlife. Loyalty to their king or to their respective masters of lower rank assured the Egyptians continued life after death.

Idolatry is severely dealt with in the Bible, but not because God cares much if man decides to play God. The condemnation of idolatry stems from its disastrous moral and social consequences. For idolatry is the deification of man's works and human ideology. A deified political or ideological system is a dictatorial system, and the modern world has had firsthand knowledge of the infinite evils of which dictatorships are capable since the Communists seized power in Russia in 1917.

In ancient Egypt man's sin of political and ideological deification with all its evils attained the highest degree in the ancient world. The land belonged to the state, and to the state-controlled temples, and to the officials that were allied with the state. The peasants who formed the bulk of the population were no more than serfs. They produced the food and fiber for the country; they were compelled to dig irrigation canals and clean them; and they were forced to build the pyramids—those gigantic royal burial places which perpetuated the myth of the immortality of the Egyptian dictatorial system as embodied in the king. The lot of the Egyptian peasant was a wretched one indeed! Egypt was permitted to survive in order that she may be a living demonstration to the remainder of the world of God's wrath against the deification of ideological or political systems.

The wheels of Divine justice often grind very slowly, but they grind, nonetheless, surely. The judgments pronounced in the Ezekiel statement took centuries to work themselves out fully. In 525 B.C. Egypt was conquered by Persia. With the defeat of Persia by Alexander the Great, Egypt became the dominion of this Greek-Macedonian world ruler. After his death Alexander's world empire was divided among four of his generals, and Egypt fell to the share of Ptolemy, one of them. The Ptolemies held Egypt for three hundred years, after which it was incorporated into the Roman Empire. It remained a province of the Roman Empire for 670 years. In A.D. 641 Egypt was overrun by the Muslim Arabs, and for thirteen centuries she was ruled by various Muslim powers as one of the provinces of their dominions. From the thirteenth to the sixteenth century Egypt was ruled by the Mamluks, who were Circassian and Kurdish slaves and who originated in Central Asia. In 1517 the Ottoman Turks expelled the Mamluks and made Egypt a province of the Turkish Empire. In 1917, four hundred years later, the Allies in the First World War liberated Egypt from Turkish rule and set her on a path which led her to political independence after having been under foreign rule for some 2,500 years.

II. EGYPT'S RESTORATION PREDICTED

Egypt was preserved not only to be a witness of God's judgment upon the idolatry of ideological and political dictatorships; she was kept alive to show also that the same God who brought judgments upon her is able and willing to bring about her national regeneration. The subject of Egypt's revival is set forth in the second half of chapter 19 in the book of Isaiah. We will quote several excerpts.

"In that day the Egyptians will be like women, and tremble with fear before the hand which the LORD of hosts shakes over them. And the land of Judah will become a terror to the Egyptians; every one to whom it is mentioned will fear because of the purpose which the LORD of hosts has purposed against them.

. . . In that day there will be an altar to the LORD in the midst of the land of Egypt, and a pillar to the LORD at its border. It will be a sign and a witness to the LORD of hosts in the land of Egypt; when they cry to the LORD because of oppressors he will send them a savior, and will defend and deliver them. And the LORD will make himself known to the Egyptians; and the Egyptians will know the LORD in that day and worship with sacrifice and burnt offering, and they will make vows to the LORD and perform them. And the LORD will smite Egypt, smiting and healing, and they will return to the LORD, and he will heed their supplications and heal them.

In that day there will be a highway from Egypt to Assyria, and the Assyrian will come into Egypt, and the Egyptian into Assyria, and the Egyptians will worship with the Assyrians.

In that day Israel will be the third with Egypt and Assyria, a blessing in the midst of the earth, whom the LORD of hosts has blessed, saying, "Blessed be Egypt my people, and Assyria the work of my hands, and Israel my heritage" (Isaiah 19:16-17, 19-25).

III. THE PERIODS OF "SMITING" AND "HEALING" IN EGYPT'S HISTORY

The key to the proper understanding of the above prophetic declaration is the two phrases in the Isaiah statement: "smiting and healing" and "in that day." The phrase "smiting and healing" suggests that when the period of regeneration begins in the history of Egypt it will not be a continuous, uninterrupted process, but rather that times of recovery may be temporarily arrested and followed by intervals of adversity. This prophetic forecast has had literal fulfillment in Egyptian history. During the three hundred years under the Greek Ptolemies and during the 670 years under the Roman Empire, Egypt was in close contact with European civilization of that day, and during the early Christian centuries Egypt was one of the great intellectual and Christian centers of the ancient world. It was a period of "healing" which lasted over nine centuries.

This period of "healing" came to an end with the Arab invasion of Egypt in the seventh century of our era. Another period of "smiting" had begun which brought about intellectual and economic stagnation. This period of "smiting" lasted about twelve centuries until Napoleon opened up Egypt once again to the influence of European civilization.

The full extent of what happened to Egypt in the twelve centuries of Muslim rule was described by European travelers who visited Egypt in the second half of the eighteenth century. Bruce, an Englishman who went to Egypt to locate the source of the Nile River, said in his report that "more brutal, unjust, tyrannical, oppressive, avaricious miscreants there is not on earth than the members of the government in Cairo."[2] C. F. Volney, who visited Egypt in 1783–1785 gave the following description of conditions: "All that one sees, one hears, announces that one is in the country of slavery and tyranny. One speaks only of civic troubles, of public misery, of extortion, of bastinados, and of murder. No safety for life and property. The blood of human beings is shed like that of an ox. The officer on his rounds at night, and the officer on his circuits during the day, judge, condemn, and execute in the twinkling of an eye—without appeal. The public officials accompany them, and at the first order the head of some unfortunate one falls into the leather sac where it is received lest it soil the place."[3]

Jabarti, an Egyptian historian in the early nineteenth century, describes Egyptian society as presenting a picture of intellectual barrenness and cultural stagnation.[4] Sharaqawi, a prominent religious leader in the Napoleonic period, represents his countrymen as being deceitful, cunning, weak in character, and fearful of those in authority over them.[5] Historians of the last century of Egyptian isolation from European civilization inform us that the native population pined away under the heavy burden of taxation and forced labor. The irrigation canals and cultural works were neglected, leading to a deterioration of the whole economy. In Pharaonic times Egypt was capable of supporting around seven million people. During the prosperity years of the Greek and Roman periods the population of Egypt increased to over ten million. In the eighteenth century—after twelve centuries of Muslim rule—Egypt's population dwindled to 2½ million. It was the Muslim period of twelve centuries that witnessed the awful fulfillment of the Ezekiel prophecy: "It [Egypt] shall be the basest of the kingdoms; neither shall it anymore lift itself up above the nations; and I will diminish them, that they shall no more rule over the nations."

A second period of "healing" began with the British occupation of Egypt in 1882. Among the many evils which existed in Egypt prior to the British occupation were the following: (1) the *courbash*. For thousands of years Egyptian governments took the position that the only way to manage Egyptians is to flog them. When the British entered Egypt the flogging instrument was the *courbash*, a strip of hippopotamus hide which tapered off at the end. It was used on every occasion when punishment or coercion was required. The British outlawed the use of the *courbash* and put an end to a system of government by flogging.

(2) The *corvée*, or compulsory labor system. The annual rise of the waters of the Nile River fills with mud the irrigation canals which transport the waters from the Nile to the outlying areas of the country. This mud has to be cleaned out regularly. Egypt, geographically part of the North African desert, has no rain to speak of, and its survival depends on the annual rise of the Nile River and the irrigation canals. For the canals to function properly they have to be cleared of the mud which the overflowing Nile deposits in them. The annual clearing of the canals required the work of about ⅛ of the population laboring for ninety days. The work was compulsory. The British did away with this compulsory labor system and substituted in its place paid labor, subsidizing this paid labor from the British treasury whenever it became necessary. The British insisted that a man should not be flogged if he refused to work; and if he did work, he should get paid for it.

(3) The *bakshish*, or bribery. In no country, we are told, was corruption more widespread than in Egypt in the days preceding the British occupation. Everybody, as it were, took bribes. The contractor bribed the government official to obtain a contract on terms most advantageous to himself, and he would then bribe the Clerk of the Works in order that he should not inquire too carefully whether the terms of the contract had been strictly adhered to. The subordinate official would bribe his superior in order to obtain a promotion. The landowner bribed the government engineer in order that he should receive more irrigation water for his fields than was his due. The judge was bribed by both defendant and plaintiff, and his verdict was usually given in favor of the highest bidder. The village officials were bribed to accord exemption from *corvée* and from military service. The police were bribed by everybody who had the misfortune to fall into their hands.[6]

Lord Cromer, who was deeply involved in the rehabilitation of

Egypt initiated by the British, gives credit for the revival of Egypt to a group of dedicated Englishmen. The success of their labors depended upon "whether the Egyptian cultivator was, or was not, to be allowed to reap the fruits of his labor; whether after supplying the wants of the State, he was to be left with barely enough to keep body and soul together, or whether he was to enjoy some degree of rustic ease; whether he was to be eternally condemned to live in a wretched hut, or whether he might have an opportuniy given to him of improving his dwelling-house; whether he should or should not have water supplied to his fields in due season; whether his disputes with his neighbors should be settled by a judge who decided them on principles of law, or whether he should be left to the callous caprice of some individual ignorant of law and cognizant only of *bakshish;* whether, if he were ill, he should be able to go to a well-kept hospital, or whether he should be unable to obtain any better medical assistance than that which could be given to his watchdog or his donkey; whether a school in which something useful could be learned should be provided his children, or whether they should be left in the hands of teachers whose highest knowledge consisted in being able to intone a few texts [from the Koran], which they themselves only half understood; whether, if he suffered from mental aberration, he should be properly treated in a well-kept [mental] institution, or whether he should be chained to a post and undergo the treatment of a wild beast; in short, whether he, and the ten million Egyptians who were like him, were or were not to have a chance afforded to them of taking a few steps upward on the ladder of moral and material improvement. . . . All these things have been accomplished by the small body of Englishmen who, in various capacities, and with but little direct support or assistance from their government or its representatives, have of late years devoted their energies to the work of Egyptian regeneration."[7]

It was stated before that the two phrases in the second half of Isaiah 19 which have a special bearing on the subject of Egypt's revival are "smiting and healing," and "in that day." The phrase "in that day" occurs six times. In Isaiah the phrase "in that day" has a Messianic connotation and it points to a time associated with the coming of the Messiah. This same phrase is used by Isaiah in chapter 11, acknowledged by Jews and Christians as one of the great Messianic chapters in the Old Testament.

"In that day the root of Jesse[8] shall stand as an ensign to the peoples; him shall the nations seek, and his dwellings shall be glorious.

In that day the Lord will extend his hand yet a second time to recover the remnant which is left of his people, from Assyria, from Egypt, from Pathros, from Ethiopia, from Elam, from Shinar, from Hamath, and from the coastlands of the sea" (Isaiah 11:10-11).

The phrase "in that day" stands at the head of the second half of Isaiah 19. At the very outset of this great prophetic statement concerning the future revival of Egypt we are told that in the period associated with the coming of the Messiah "the land of Judah will become a terror to the Egyptians; every one to whom it is mentioned will fear because of the purpose which the LORD of hosts has purposed against them" (Isaiah 19:17). In the same year of 1882 in which the British landed their occupation force in Egypt a group of East European Jews arrived in the ancient land of their forefathers. It was the first of several waves of immigrants whose work of reconstruction paved the way for the reconstitution of the ancient Jewish State. When the present State of Israel came into existence in 1948 Egypt placed herself at the head of the Arab nations which were determined to uproot the newly constituted State of Israel. The Egyptians were defeated in 1948 and in 1956. In 1967 the Egyptian dictator Nasser assembled a huge army in the Sinai Peninsula, including hundreds of tanks and airplanes, while his ships blockaded the entrance of the Gulf of Akaba. To all appearances Israel was doomed. But what had taken place stunned the whole world. In about three or four days Nasser's military might in the Sinai Desert was routed and the Israeli forces occupied the Sinai Peninsula.

Rearmed by Russia and equipped with the most modern, sophisticated weapons, Egypt tried again in October 1973. Israel was unprepared for this assault and paid a big price because of it. But even in this war she landed a force on the west side of the Suez Canal in Egypt proper; took thousands of Egyptians prisoners of war; and, had the war been permitted to go on another two or three days, she would have destroyed or forced the surrender of the flower of the Egyptian army. "And the land of Judah will become a terror to the Egyptians; every one to whom it is mentioned will fear because of the purpose which the LORD of hosts has purposed against them."

The phrase "in that day" indicates that the full regeneration of Egypt will not take place until the Messiah comes, and the coming of the Messiah in the teachings of the Old Testament is equivalent to the return of Jesus in accordance with the New Testament. "And the LORD will make himself known to the Egyptians; and the

Egyptians will know the LORD in that day and worship with sacrifice and burnt offering,[9] and they will make vows to the LORD and perform them" (Isaiah 19:21).

This spiritual rebirth will not be limited to Egypt. It will affect also Assyria. Assyria and its successor Babylon were the great world powers of the Mesopotamian valley—present-day Iraq. For centuries rivalry and wars existed between the world power centered in the Mesopotamian valley and Egypt—the great power centered in the Nile valley. Israel, sandwiched in-between these two superpowers, was frequently a battle ground of the two opposing armies. The prophet declares that in the new world which will emerge when the Messianic Kingdom of God will be established on earth the intense and deadly rivalry between the two great powers of the Middle East— Egypt and Assyria (modern Iraq)—will have ceased.

"In that day there will be a highway from Egypt to Assyria, and the Assyrian will come into Egypt, and the Egyptian into Assyria, and the Egyptians will worship with the Assyrians" (Isaiah 19:23).

Together with a nationally restored and spiritually regenerated Israel these two powers will form a triple alliance which will result not only in a transformation of the Middle East, but in a blessing to the whole world.

"In that day Israel will be the third with Egypt and Assyria, a blessing in the midst of the earth, whom the LORD of hosts has blessed, saying 'Blessed be Egypt my people, and Assyria the work of my hands, and Israel my heritage'" (Isaiah 19:24-25).

Notes to Chapter 10

1 Seveneh—the modern Aswan.

2 See his *Travels to Discover the Source of the Nile*, 1768, vol. 1, p. 26; quoted by the Earl of Cromer in *Modern Egypt* (Macmillan Co.: New York, 1916), vol. 2, p. 166.

3 C. F. Volney, *Travels Through Syria and Egypt on the Years 1783, 1784 and 1785* (London: 1788), vol. 1, p. 162.

4 See, P. J. Vatikiotis, *The Modern History of Egypt* (Frederick A. Praeger: New York, 1969), p. 90.

5 Ibid, p. 93.

6 The Earl of Cromer, Op. Cit., vol. 2, p. 421.

7 Ibid, pp. 454-5, 556-7.

8 An allusion to the Davidic descent of the Messiah; Jesse was David's father.

9 To Isaiah "worship with sacrifice and burnt offering, etc.," meant to worship the God of Biblical revelation.

CHAPTER 11

WHY THE JEWS RETURNED TO THE LAND OF ISRAEL: A BIBLICAL VIEW OF THE HOLOCAUST

CHAPTER 11

WHY THE JEWS RETURNED TO THE LAND OF ISRAEL: A BIBLICAL VIEW OF THE HOLOCAUST

I. THE PROPHECY OF JEREMIAH 16:14-17

Prior to the proclamation of the Balfour Declaration in 1917 the vast majority of Jews lived in Europe. Even at the beginning of the Second World War the bulk of the Jewish people were still found in Europe. The destruction of six million European Jews by the Nazis in the Second World War, the reconstitution of the State of Israel in 1948, and the exodus of Jews from European and Arab lands marked the end of the longest era in Jewish history known as the Great Dispersion. The largest number of Jews live now on the American continent and in Israel. History knows of no other instance of a people which, while separated from the country of its national origin for some nineteen centuries, not only retained its national identity but also, at the end of these many centuries of dispersion, returned to the land of its ancestors and reestablished there its national homeland. The only satisfactory explanation for this extraordinary phenomenon is found in the Bible, as seen, for example, from the prophetic statements cited below:

"Therefore, behold, the days are coming, says the LORD, when it shall no longer be said, 'As the LORD lives who brought up the people of Israel out of the land of Egypt,' but 'As the LORD lives who brought up the people of Israel out of the north country and out of all the countries where he had driven them.' For I will bring them back to their own land which I gave to their fathers" (Jeremiah 16:14-15). Notice carefully that it was *God* who *drove* them out of their land, and it is *God* who will *bring* them back out of all the countries where He had driven them. But how will God bring them back? Here is the answer.

"Behold, I am sending for many fishers, says the LORD, and they shall catch them; and afterwards I will send for many hunters, and they shall hunt them from every mountain and every hill, and out of the clefts of the rocks. For my eyes are upon all their ways; they are not hid from me, nor is their iniquity concealed from my eyes" (Jeremiah 16:16-17). The above passage clearly indicates that the Jews will not return voluntarily to the land of Israel. They will have to be fished out and hunted down from their places of residence in the various Gentile countries.

Some Bible expositors interpret the last passage in Jeremiah as referring to the thoroughness with which the Babylonian deportation of the Jews will be accomplished; others maintain that the passage speaks of a future ingathering of the Jews other than that which had taken place after the Babylonian exile. Jewish history has proven that the substance of the above passage has never been so literally fulfilled as during the Nazi period. Through His prophets God announced that as He drove Israel out of her land so will He drive them back to their land. This compulsory character of Israel's return to the land of Israel is described more clearly in the Ezekiel prophecy cited below.

II. THE PROPHECY OF EZEKIEL 20:32-38

This subject of the compulsory return of the Jews to the land of their ancestors is presented in greater detail in the following passage from Ezekiel, a contemporary of Jeremiah.

"What is in your mind shall never happen—the thought, 'Let us be like the nations, like the tribes of the countries, and worship wood and stone.' " How God will prevent the Jews from becoming like the other nations is described in the next passage.

"As I live, says the Lord GOD, surely with a mighty hand and an outstretched arm, and with wrath poured out, I will be king over you. I will bring you out from the peoples and gather you out of the countries where you are scattered, with a mighty hand and an outstretched arm, and with wrath poured out; and I will bring you into the wilderness of the peoples and there I will enter into judgment with you face to face. As I entered into judgment with your fathers in the wilderness of the land of Egypt, so I will enter into judgment with you, says the Lord GOD. I will make you pass under the rod, and I will let you go in by number. I will purge out the rebels from among you, and those who transgress against me; I will bring them out of the land where they sojourn, but they shall not enter the land of Israel. Then you will know that I am the LORD" (Ezekiel 20:32-38).

Israel was chosen by God to be a channel through which God's redemptive purpose would reach all nations. If Israel was to accomplish the purpose for which she was called into existence, she had to remain separated from the ungodly ways of the world. She was to be " . . . a people dwelling alone, and not reckoning itself among the nations!" (Numbers 23:9b).

But consciously or not, through her whole history Israel struggled against the necessity of national apartness imposed on her. Samuel was upset not so much because the representatives of the people demanded that he set up a monarchical form of government, but because they desired to be governed like the other nations (1 Samuel 8:4-9).

As with many other prophetic utterances in the Old Testament, the Ezekiel statement was occasioned by certain contemporary events. In the days of Jeremiah and Ezekiel the big event was the downfall of the Judean kingdom and the deportation of its people to Babylon. A sizable portion of the Jews deported to Babylon were doing everything to adopt the ways of the Gentiles and merge completely with the people of the host country. Had this trend been permitted to go on unchecked, the Jews in the Babylonian exile would have lost their national identity, there would have been no rebuilding of the Judean State, and the Jews would have ceased to exist. It was this situation which, in the first place, called forth the strong statement by Ezekiel. However, as is the case with many of the other prophecies of the Old Testament, there is also a long range element in the fulfillment of the prophetic declaration of Ezekiel. As a matter of fact, the full thrust of this prophetic message encompassed all subsequent Jewish history, and its complete fulfilllment has only taken place in our own generation.

III. THE "WILDERNESS OF THE NATIONS" PERIOD IN JEWISH HISTORY

The clue to a proper understanding of the Ezekiel message is the statement in Ezekiel about the "wilderness of Egypt" and the "wilderness of the nations": "And I will bring you into the wilderness of the peoples [nations], and there I will enter into judgment with you face to face. As I entered into judgment with your fathers in the wilderness of the land of Egypt, so I will enter into judgment with you, says the Lord GOD." Following their departure from Egypt the Israelites could have arrived in the Promised Land in several weeks if they had followed the short route. But they were prevented from taking the short route and were kept wandering in the wilderness for forty years. One reason for this was to permit the older generation to die out in the wilderness of Egypt. They were the people whose roots were deep in the soil of Egypt, who preferred the relative security of their life of bondage in Egypt to the uncertainties of beginning a new life as a free people in the Promised Land. Another reason for the long sojourn of the Israelites in the wilderness of

Egypt was to isolate them from the surrounding nations, in order that they may develop a national awareness of their own, that they may become molded into one people, the people of God.

However, through the whole period of the first Israelitish Commonwealth, from the days of the judges to the last Judean king, the people of Israel continued to imitate the heathen ways of the surrounding nations, until it became necessary for God to drive them out from the Land of Israel. The Babylonian exile was the beginning of a new period of Jewish history called by Ezekiel "the wilderness of the nations" since the Babylonian empire was composed of many nations. Within seventy years this chapter, or phase, of the "wilderness of the nations" history was terminated, and many of the Jewish exiles returned to Judea to rebuild the land. But some five hundred years later the Jews were driven out again from the Land of Israel, this time by the Romans, and the second phase of the "wilderness of the nations" period in their history had begun, known as the Great Dispersion which lasted some nineteen centuries. In the wilderness of Egypt the very geography of the region isolated the Hebrews from the surrounding nations. In the "wilderness of the nations" of the Great Dispersion the Jews were kept isolated from the other nations by ghetto walls erected around Jewish settlements in European countries, reinforced by a wall of hatred and discrimination which was no less impenetrable than the physical walls surrounding the Jewish ghettos.

During the long centuries of this "wilderness of the nations" period the Jews, though scattered in many countries, formed one monolithic people, held together by Gentile anti-Semitism from without, and by the religion of Talmudic Judaism from within. When in the aftermath of the French Revolution the ghetto walls were removed and the Jews were permitted to enter the general stream of the life of the countries of their residence, the religion of traditional Judaism began to decompose at its first contact with the fresh air of Jewish emancipation.

In the post-emancipation era the Jewish people became divided ideologically into three large groups: Orthodox Judaism; Liberal Judaism; and Jewish Socialism. Orthodox Judaism was basically a continuation of the traditional Judaism of the ghetto centuries. Liberal Judaism was born in Germany; it evolved the Reform Synagogue and revised the Prayer Book from which it deleted all references to a personal Messiah and Jewish national restoration in the Land of Israel. Liberal Judaism spread from Germany to other coun-

tries of central and western Europe, and from western Europe to
America. In eastern Europe, where the Jews were never fully eman-
cipated until after the First World War, the ideas of Liberal Judaism
were transplanted by the Haskalah movement, an offspring of German Liberal Judaism. In the neo-Hebrew language the word "haskalah" meant "enlightenment" or "liberalism." In eastern Europe the
Haskalah was a movement advocating the abandonment of Jewish
"exclusiveness and acquiring the knowledge, manners and aspirations of the nations among whom they dwell."[1] In time, Liberal
Judaism in the West and the Haskalah in eastern Europe became
increasingly secular in their outlook.

The third large ideological group was Jewish Socialism. Jewish
Socialists were the leaders of the large Jewish working class in eastern
Europe, and they propagated among the Jewish laboring masses the
atheistic and materialistic philosophy of European Socialism.

To all appearances the emancipation of the European Jews brought
to an end the "wilderness of the nations" era of Jewish history, and
Jewish life assumed a direction which ran counter to that marked
out for the Jewish people by the will of God as recorded in the Bible.

IV.   THE CONNECTION BETWEEN THE HOLOCAUST AND
      THE REESTABLISHMENT OF THE STATE OF ISRAEL

But God was not taken by surprise by all these developments, and
His ultimate purpose for Israel and the nations of the earth cannot
be thwarted. Within fifty years from the time the Jews were granted
equal civil rights in western Europe, a backlash reaction sprang up
in Germany from where it spread to other places, seeking to deprive
the Jews of their newly won liberties. This new racial or economic
anti-Semitism became more intense in the turmoil which followed
the First World War, and it reached its fearful consummation in the
Nazi holocaust.

The word "holocaust" means total destruction. In the Nazi period
of some ten or twelve years six million Jews and millions of non-Jews
perished at the hands of the Nazis. In the movie *The Hiding Place,*
which recounts the story of a Dutch Christian family who was sent
to the concentration camps for using their home as a hiding place
for Jews, there is a scene in which one of the women inmates asks
the Ten Boom sisters what is so great about their God. If He is
righteous, then why does He permit them to suffer; if He is a God of
love and compassion, then He is not almighty, seeing that He does
nothing to set them free. If we fail to detect a Divine purpose in

history, we cannot see that periods of suffering, while brought on by evil men, may yet serve to advance a Divine purpose in history, and when this has been accomplished, a particular period of suffering comes to an end to give mankind another chance to repent and change its course. If, moreover, we as individuals do not have the Biblical hope, and this brief individual life is all we possess, then when adversity strikes and our puny world collapses about us we are unable to see that at the end of the long and dark tunnel there is an exit into a world of sunshine, fresh air, and freedom.

The Nazi period was a Divine judgment upon the West, the consequences of which are still round about us. In his massive history of the Second World War Winston Churchill, one of the principal leaders of World War Two, cites abundant evidence to the effect that on several occasions prior to the outbreak of the Second World War Hitler could have been stopped by England and France. For the failure of England and France to go to the help of Czechoslovakia— with whom France had had a mutual defense treaty—when Hitler invaded it, both England and France, the leaders of the Western world at that time, paid a fearful price. The Nazi period was God's judgment upon the many sins of omission and commission of the Western world.

But the Nazi period was also a Divine judgment upon the Jewish people of Europe. However hard may have been the lot of the Jews in the Middle Ages, they endured their hardships with fortitude because they were conscious of suffering for their religious convictions. The millions of Jews whom the Nazis removed from the countries of their sojourn in occupied Europe and assembled in concentration camps to be exterminated did not know why all this happened to them. If we read the holocaust literature, one of the significant things we learn is that those concentration camp inmates who knew why they were placed there found it easier to bear their lot than those who did not, and often survived hardships easier even when they may have been physically less fit.

The Jewish concentration camp inmates did not know why they were there. They were not there because they were religious or irreligious, because they were rich or poor, because they were capitalists or socialists; they were there because they were Jews. And in the years between the end of the French Revolution and World War Two the word "Jew" was emptied of its religious meaning for most Jews. They became like all other nations, worshiping material things and pursuing secular goals. The tragedy of the Jews in the Nazi period was that they suffered without a cause.

The Jews who were taken to Babylon in the first deportation were called by Jeremiah the "good figs." They were the patriots, they were the cream of the crop, they were the backbone of the nation. And yet, Jeremiah, Ezekiel, and all other Biblical writers who dealt with the Babylonian disaster considered it a Divine judgment upon the Judean State.[2]

The vast majority of the six million Jews—men, women, and children—tortured to death by the Nazis were good, upright, and honest people. They were the "good figs." Nevertheless, the Nazi holocaust was a Divine judgment upon the Jewish people as much as the Babylonian episode was. It was a judgment on Talmudic Judaism which displaced the Bible to the periphery of Jewish life and put in its center the religion of the Talmud, a religion of dos and don'ts, a religion composed of the words of men rather than the Word of God, a religion which has grown increasingly irrelevant to the needs of the individual Jew, a religion which has turned many Jews into skeptics and atheists.

The Nazi holocaust was also a Divine judgment on Liberal Judaism which sprang up in Germany and which propagated a secular religion which has abandoned the Biblical Messianic hope and the hope of a restoration in the Land of Israel.

Finally, the Nazi holocaust was a Divine judgment on the Jewish Socialists who were telling the thousands of their Jewish followers that atheistic Socialism would bring in the millennium. They lived to see Russia, the center of Marxist Socialism, enter into an alliance with Hitler Germany and after World War Two become the world center of anti-Semitism.

But the six million Jews destroyed in the Nazi holocaust did not die in vain. When at the end of the Second World War the civilized part of the world came to know what had taken place in the concentration camps, the shock, compassion, and sense of guilt experienced by that part of the world led the United Nations to pass a resolution authorizing the Jews to reconstitute their ancient State in the Land of Israel. The abominable behavior of the Arab–Communist bloc, which on November 14, 1975 called Zionism a racist ideology, proves that the creation of the State of Israel in 1948 was the result of God's perfect timing. Had it not been done then, humanly speaking, there might have been no State of Israel now.[3]

The Jews from European and Arab lands, who like a mighty flood have poured into the State of Israel since its reconstitution, were not immigrants who went there of their free will. They were uprooted from the countries of their birth or residence, broken in body and spirit, refugees from a hostile non-Jewish world. Their return to the Land of Israel was a fulfillment of the Jeremiah and Ezekiel prophecies. The Nazis were the fishers and hunters of the Jeremiah passage. They sought out every person with some Jewish blood in his veins and removed him from the countries of his birth or residence. It was God who drove the Jewish people out of the Land of Israel, it was the same God who drove them back to the Land of Israel. "What is in your mind shall never happen—the thought, 'Let us be like the nations, like the tribes of the countries, and worship wood and stone.' As I live, says the Lord GOD, surely with a mighty hand and an outstretched arm, and with wrath poured out, I will be king over you. I will bring you out from the peoples and gather you out of the countries where you are scattered, with a mighty hand and an outstretched arm, and with wrath poured out" (Ezekiel 20:32-34).

Notes to Chapter 11

1 *The Jewish Encyclopedia* (Funk and Wagnalls Co.: New York, 1912), vol. 6, p. 256a.

2 Biblical references dealing with this subject are too numerous to cite; see, e.g., Isaiah 42:24-25.

3 See, Jacob Katz, "Was the Holocaust Predictable?", article in *Commentary* (New York), May 1975, p. 48.

CHAPTER 12

THE MEANING OF THE PRESENT JEWISH RESTORATION

I. THE HUMAN ASPECT

II. THE DIVINE ASPECT

    1. Jacob and Israel

       a. Both Jacob and the Jewish People Became Exiled From Their Native Land.

       b. Both Jacob and the Jewish People Intended to Remain in Their Adopted Countries.

       c. Both Jacob and the Jewish People Relied Principally on Human Resources.

    2. "Israel—Prophetic Vision And Historical Fulfillment".

CHAPTER 12

THE MEANING OF THE PRESENT JEWISH RESTORATION

I. THE HUMAN ASPECT

At this juncture of history Russia is Israel's most deadly enemy. There is a good reason for it. Israel's remarkable achievements in an incredibly short period pose a great challenge to the claims of communism. They are a living demonstration of what every one of the developing nations can do for itself without selling its soul to communism. Israel has proven that it is possible even for the poorest among the nations to have social justice and equality of economic opportunity without depriving its citizens of their human dignity and personal liberties. Many Israeli scientists go to Asia and Africa to share with their people Israel's know-how. Many young people from the less developed countries come to Israel for a period of study, and upon their return home they spread the news of Israel's accomplishments.

The following are a number of statements by various observers about the meaning of the Israel experiment for the Middle East and the world at large.

"So far from having proved a failure, Zionism has proved the one great success that has emanated from the Great War*. It has been like a miracle, for it has transformed deserts into fertility, marshes into the joyous abodes of free men, and the barren sands along the shores into vineyards and orange groves. . . One would, indeed, search the world in vain for anything to compare to the creative value of the Jewish colonizing work in Palestine. It isn't merely that the land is blossoming and bearing fruit once more; not merely that where starvation and poverty reigned, comfort and affluence now abound. That is but the least part of it. The great thing is that a race long denied access to the soil are now revivified by contact with the soil, building up their manhood and their self-respect by hard work. In eyes where fear ever lurked there are now keen glances of men who look out on life and their fellows with level eyes. It is humanity, and not the soil, that is being really enriched".[1]—The Very Reverend Norman Maclean

---

* The First World War

179

King Abdullah of Transjordan: 'I was astonished at what I saw at the Jewish colonies when I traveled from Jenin to Lydda. . . They have colonized the sand dunes, extracted their water, quickened them to life and transformed into a paradise'.[2]

"He* told me that the Arab world, even at the top, was far from unwilling to cooperate with the Jews. The entire Middle East needed the intelligence, ingenuity and productive capacity they represented". He said: 'Whether the present Arab leadership likes it or not we must realize that what the Jews are doing in Palestine must be done for all of the Middle East, if we are to take our rightful place in the community of nations.' In his opinion real democracy could come to the Middle East only through economic development of the whole area in cooperation with the Jewish community in Palestine."[3]— Bartley C. Crum

T. E. Lawrence, better known as Lawrence of Arabia and a great friend of the Arabs, is quoted as having declared: 'I am decidedly in favor of Zionism. Indeed, I look on the Jews as the natural importers of that Western leaven which is so necessary for the countries of the Middle East'.[4] To a representative of the Jewish Agency he said: 'The problem of Zionism is the problem of the third generation. It is the grandsons of your immigrants who will make it succeed or fail, but the odds are so much in its favor that the experiment is worth backing; and I back it not because of the Jews, but because a regenerated Palestine is going to raise the whole moral and material status of its Middle East neighbors'.[5]

Edgar A. Mowrer, newspaper columnist and foreign correspondent, had this to say: "In roughly twenty-five years [the Jews] now have transformed a semi-desert into one of the garden spots in the world. They have established the only industrial center in a thousand mile radius. . . Welcome or unwelcome, it is the Jews who, more even than the French or British, have goaded Egyptians and Arabs into making the effort that alone may one day enable them to sit among the great peoples—as their ancestors did".[6]

The following statements are by Dr. Lowdermilk, a world authority on soil conservation, formerly assistant chief of the United States Soil Conservation Service. He was sent by the United Nations on two extended missions to Israel to help solve the land and water problems. "Twentieth-century Israelites, coming back to the land of their patriarchs did not find the bountiful land Moses had described

---

* An influential Middle East Arab

three thousand years ago as 'a land wherein thou shalt eat bread without scarceness, thou shalt not lack anything in it.' Instead, they came to malarial swamps, which killed off many pioneer settlers before drainage was completed. They found rocky hills from which three feet or more of soil had been washed off to bedrock, exposing white limestone skeletons of the hills. Ancient stone terraces built to level land on slopes were generally in ruins. Thousands of former hill villages were heaps of weather-beaten stones. . .

This long decline, shared by North Africa and the Near East, began in A.D. 640 with the first invasion of nomads out of Arabia. Then followed more invasions, ravages of wars, and heavy tax burdens laid on by conquerors as feudal landlords cruelly exploited peasant farmers. The remarkable refinements in agriculture and animal husbandry attained by the Roman-Byzantine civilization were blotted out. Wastage of soils and waters set in and destroyed the productivity of the land and reduced survivors to poverty and misery. . . Palestine by the 1880's*, was a man-made ruin of a once flourishing land.

In 1938 and 1939, on a general survey across North Africa and the Middle East for our Department of Agriculture, I discovered that Jewish agricultural colonists had bought 'unprofitable' lands from the Arabs, albeit at very high prices. They had achieved the finest reclamation of old lands that I had seen on three continents. Although formerly city dwellers, they had trained themselves to be excellent farmers, eager to do better.

This amazing success of Jewish land reclamation was due in large part to one important ingredient-the dynamic and idealistic spirit of the people. They believed redemption could not be achieved with hired labor but only with intelligent self-labor by those inspired with a passionate love for these rocky, eroded slopes and malarial swamps. They had the courage and indomitable spirit to do what was necessary on a terrain that would have frustrated people with less vision and courage. Now, after almost two thousand years of homelessness, about two million Jews are at last free citizens in their own country, small and half desert as it is. Here they work on their own land and in their own industries."[7]

In a book published in 1944, Lowdermilk makes the following concluding observation: "On 14 percent of the cultivated area

---

* When the first phase of the Present Jewish Return to Palestine began.

and 6 percent of the total area of Mandated Palestine, a people with faith and devotion born of long tradition has changed desolation into fertile fields, fruitful orchards and reforested slopes. Ancient cities have been rebuilt and the commerce on their streets quickened, long-unknown resources have been brought into the light of day and sent to the distant marts of the world. After the centuries of darkness which crushed the hopes of Palestine's miserable inhabitants, a new force has come into the land and made it live again. The possibility of a new day for the entire Near East is hidden in the fertile lands, the flourishing villages and cities, the cooperatives and the factories of Jewish Palestine.

If the forces of reclamation and progress Jewish settlers have introduced are permitted to continue, Palestine may well be the leaven that will transform the other lands of the Near East . . .[It] can serve as the example, the demonstration, the lever, that will lift the entire Near East from its present desolate condition to a dignified place in a free world."[8]

At a conference on Middle East problems Lowdermilk said: "I am convinced, after studying the relation of peoples to their lands in twenty-six different countries, that these Jewish colonists have done something new under the sun; they are working out a lasting adjustment of a people to their land in which all peoples of the world should be interested. By a balanced combination of scientific agriculture and industry, and a voluntary cooperative social system, they have managed to achieve a European standard of living in the midst of the backward, depressed subsistence economy of the Middle East. Their approach to the problem of industrializing subsistence agrarian economies promises a new day not only for Palestine and for the Middle East, but for the world at large."[9]

Finally, the following additional statement by Mr. Crum: "For Palestine Jewry represents the power of a collective and unbreakable moral decision, which short of a massacre of the entire population, is bound to prevail. I did not fully comprehend the great positive influence of this moral decision until I had seen the Middle East and compared the poverty, the disease, and the humiliation of Egypt with the cleanliness, the well-being, and the dignity of the people in Palestine. Then I understood how much the unfettered development of the Jewish people in Palestine could mean to the whole of the Middle East, for it could bring to the Middle East the good in Western civilization—not by domination, but by example." [10]

In another passage Mr. Crum speaks of the need of a firm and an enlightened American policy in the Middle East. "To determine this foreign policy," he says, "we have one of two paths before us. We can throw our lot with the forces of reaction who prop up feudalistic regimes in the Arab States . . .; who believe they can successfully continue the same processes of exploitation in the future which have proved successful in the past. Or we can throw our lot in with the progressive forces in the Middle East. We can recognize that there is a slow rising of its peoples, and that we must place ourselves on the side of this inevitable development toward literacy, health, and a decent way of life. I say to my fellow Americans that not only for the sake of the masses of the Middle East, but for the sake of world peace, we must encourage this development, a development of which Jewish Palestine is thus far the outstanding example holding great promise for the future of all its neighbors. Therefore, it follows that support for the Jewish National Home is the first and logical step to take on this path toward the advancement of a democratic way of life in that area of the world."[11]

The following are several excerpts from a book by the late President John F. Kennedy:

"Israel is the bright light now shining in the Middle East. We, and ultimately Israel's neighbors, have much to learn from this center of democratic illumination, of unprecedented economic development, of human pioneering and intelligence and perseverance.

In 1939 I first saw Palestine, then an unhappy land under alien rule, and to a large extent then a barren land. In the words of Israel Zangwill: 'The land without a people waited for the people without a land.' In 1951, I traveled again to the land by the River Jordan, to see firsthand the new State of Israel. The transformation that had taken place was hard to believe.

For in those twelve years, a nation had been born, a desert had been reclaimed, and the most tragic victims of World War II—the survivors of the concentration camps and ghettos—had found a home . . .

There have always been skeptics scoffing at the possibility of making deserts bloom and rocky soils productive. In this regard, our own history as a nation and Israel's have many parallels—in the diversity of their origins, in their capacity to reach the unattainable, in the receptivity to new ideas and social experimentation.

In this country, throughout much of the nineteenth century, warnings were repeatedly proclaimed that mid-America and its plains beyond the 100th Parallel could never be settled and made productive . . . But on the Great American Plains—as decades later in the great Palestinian plains and valleys—determined settlers learned the truth of the epigram that 'Rain follows the plow.' By 1881 a great Western town builder and scientist, Charles Dana Wilber, was saying: 'In this miracle of progress, the plow was the advance messenger— the unerring prophet—the procuring cause.'

These words sound deep resonances in the minds and memories of those who have observed the gradual Zionist fulfillment in Israel. History records several such break-throughs—great efforts to which spiritual conviction and human endurance have combined to make realities out of prophecies. The Puritans in Massachusetts, the Mormons in Salt Lake City, the Scotch-Irish in the Western territories were all imbued with the truth of the old Jewish thought that a people can have only as much sky over its head as it has land under its feet . . .

I cannot hope—nor pretend—to solve all of the complex riddles of the Middle East. But I would like to suggest some perspectives which might help to clarify our thinking about that area and to indicate what lines our longer-range efforts might take. To do this requires first of all, that we dispel a prevalent myth about the Middle East.

This myth—with which you are all too familiar—is the assertion that it is Zionism which has been the unsettling and fevered infection in the Middle East, the belief that without Israel there would somehow be a natural harmony throughout the Middle East and Arab world. Quite apart from the values and hopes which the State of Israel enshrines—and the past injuries which it redeems—it twists reality to suggest that it is the democratic tendency of Israel which has injected discord and dissension into the Near East. Even by the coldest calculations, the removal of Israel would not alter the basic crisis in the area. For, if there is any lesson which the melancholy events of the last two years and more taught us, it is that, though Arab states are generally united in opposition to Israel, their political unities do not rise above this negative position. The basic rivalries within the Arab world, the quarrels over boundaries, the tensions involved in lifting their economies from stagnation, the cross pressures of nationalism—all of these factors would still be there, even if there were no Israel.

The Middle East illustrates the twin heritage of modern nationalism. In one of its aspects it reflects a positive search for political freedom and self-development; in another, it is the residue of disintegration and the destruction of old moorings. The Arab states, though some have had significantly varying lines of development, have all too often used Israel as a scapegoat and anti-Zionism as a policy to divert attention away from the hard tasks of national and regional development, and from special area problems . . . Israel today stands as an example for all the Middle East, in spotlighting how economic modernization may be spurred and accelerated against high odds, great physical barriers, and constantly growing populations, as well as against all Communist blandishments . . .

The choice today is not between either the Arab states or Israel. Ways must be found of supporting the legitimate aspirations of each. The United States, whose President was first to recognize the new State of Israel, need have no apologies—indeed should pride itself—for the action it took. But neither should we foreclose any effort which promises a regeneration of a much wider segment of the Middle East.

The Jewish state found its fulfillment during a time when it bore witness, to use the words of Markham, to humanity betrayed, 'plundered, profaned, and disinherited.'

But it is yet possible that history will record this event as only the prelude to the betterment and therapy, not merely of a strip of land, but of a broad expanse of almost continental dimensions. Whether such a challenge will be seized cannot be determined by the United States alone. But as we observe the inspiring experience of Israel, we know that we must make the effort—and that we can once again demonstrate that 'Rain follows the plow.' "[12]

The statement below is by two eminent Catholic priests.

"Israel came into being with the active support of the world community. We can think of no better title to her sovereignty than the sponsorship of a majority of nations at the time of her birth. Yet, her claim does not rest with international law alone; it is also based on the work of her hands. A former generation drained malaria-infested marshes, the former and the present ones have turned barren land into gardens. Not only has Israel made the desert bloom, she has created the economic, social, and cultural conditions for a just, a truly human, society. Israel's leaders have accepted the challenge of the Balfour Declaration (November 2, 1917) and turned her into a homeland for all Jews who wish or need to live there. In fact, so solid has her advance been that this tiny country is able to send teams of highly gifted and skilled men to developing countries, thereby doing her share in making the community of man a happy reality.

Even if all this were not so, Israelis now have lived in the land of their forefathers—from which, incidentally, Jews were never fully absent—for almost twenty years. They have taken root there, children were born, men and women died, couples married, and solidiers fought. It seems to us that as a living person has a right to go on living—a right that no neighbor or society can deny him—so a commonwealth as alive as Israel has a right to peaceful existence. We thus affirm Israel's right to stay securely on the soil which her farmers, workers, thinkers, and teachers have reclaimed by the sweat of their brows. As Christians, we must go even further: The people of Israel not only have a right to live—they have a vocation to live for the Lord. We hope that it will be granted them to bear witness to the God of Abraham, Isaac, and Jacob on His favored land, as never before."[13]

II. THE DIVINE ASPECT

1. JACOB AND ISRAEL

The Jewish people stand in a closer relationship to Jacob than to any other Biblical character. Though Abraham was the first person to be called a Hebrew, it is seldom that the Jews are spoken of in the Old Testament as the children of Abraham. Though Moses laid the foundation of Jewish nationality and the faith of Israel, Jews are never referred to as the sons of Moses. Jacob and Israel, the two names of Isaac's younger son, are the two names by which the Jewish people are most frequently designated in the Old Testament. Bible students have for a long time been impressed with certain striking similarities in the life story of Jacob and the history of the Jewish people. The reestablishment of the Jewish State in Palestine in 1948 is certainly one of the greatest events in Jewish history. In the following study we wish to examine certain common features in the story of Jacob and the history of the Jews as pertaining especially to the reestablishment of the present State of Israel.

a. Both Jacob and the Jewish People Became Exiled From Their Native Land.

Jacob was compelled to leave his homeland because of his feud with his brother Esau. The New Testament calls Esau an immoral and irreligious character (Hebrews 12:16). Nevertheless, according to the Genesis record Jacob dealt with Esau in an unbrotherly way. When one day Esau came home downhearted, not caring whether he lived or died, Jacob took advantage of Esau's despondent mood and prevailed on him to sell his birthright. Esau was the firstborn, and in ancient times the first born held a privileged position.

When Isaac became old and began to lose his sight, thinking that he was approaching the end of his earthly pilgrimage, he decided to confirm to Esau priority and leadership in the Abrahamic covenant. Accordingly, he summoned Esau one day and gave him instructions to prepare a feast, probably with the intention of solemnizing the occasion. Rebecca was determined to prevent this from happening. She knew her two sons far better than their father. She was convinced that by character and inborn tendencies Jacob was more fit for leadership in the Abrahamic covenant than Esau. Subsequent events proved Rebecca right. Esau was a reckless individual, with little or no appreciation of spiritual values, who lived chiefly for the transient and material things of life. Jacob, though scheming and ready to grasp at every advantage, manifested none of the shallowness of character which Esau exhibited. Jacob had ambition and perseverance, and his inner make-up contained sound and genuine elements which, when cleansed from the purely selfish and personal aims, were capable of being consecrated to God's service.[14]

And so while Esau was out in the field, hunting for some game in compliance with his father's request, Jacob, acting under the promptings of his mother, impersonated his brother Esau. He took to his father's room the meal which Rebecca had prepared in accordance with Isaac's directions issued to Esau, and he received from Isaac the blessing intended for Esau, which conferred upon him leadership in the Abrahamic covenant. This deception was made possible because of Isaac's loss of sight. In doing this Jacob lied to his father about his true identity, and he even implied that God aided in the execution of his plot.

When upon his return from the field Esau discovered what had transpired during his absence, he vowed that he would kill his brother after Isaac's death. By this time Isaac realized that in wishing to confer upon Esau leadership in the Abrahamic covenant he had not acted in the best interests of the Divine purpose. But the damage was already done. Accordingly, Isaac and Rebecca advised their younger son Jacob to leave Canaan and seek temporary refuge in Haran, in the home of Laban, who was Rebecca's brother.

Thus Jacob became an exile from his native land because of his dishonest and his unbrotherly behavior towards Esau. Having deceived his father, Jacob in turn was deceived on several occasions by his uncle Laban; while in subsequent years he was deceived by his sons in connection with the Joseph incident. Having destroyed the domestic tranquility in his parental home, Jacob experienced little peace and happiness in his own married life; and when in his old age he settled in Egypt he admitted to Pharaoh that his years had been attended with much evil.

Israel, too, was banished from her native land, once in the days of the First Temple, and again in the period of the Second Temple. Had northern Israel heeded the warnings of men like Amos and Hosea, there would have been no destruction of her national life; had the southern Judaean kingdom followed the advice and pleadings of Jeremiah there would have been no Babylonian exile. There is strong historical evidence that the destruction of Palestine by Rome could also have been avoided had reason and restraint prevailed on the Jewish side. Everywhere in the Old Testament Israel's dispersion from her land is attributed to her disobedience. The Prayer Book of the post-Biblical period has maintained the same position as seen from the statement: "Because of our sins we were exiled from our land, and because of our iniquities we were dispersed from our soil."

b. Both Jacob and the Jewish People Intended to Remain in Their Adopted Countries.

Jacob spent twenty years in Haran. There he married, raised a family, and in due time became fairly prosperous. There was no good reason why he should have desired to go back to Canaan and there is no clear indication that he intended to go back. But just as soon as he gained a sense of belonging in his new environment he was made to feel that he was not wanted there (Genesis 31:1-2). It was this unpleasant realization which caused him to think of returning to his native land.

This experience of Jacob became a recurring phenomenon in Jewish history. Jews have been Zionists, in the sense of longing to regain their country, since they became a people without a country as a result of the destruction of their homeland by Rome. But as long as they were treated even half-decently in the lands of their dispersion, their interest in a national reconstitution in Palestine lacked a real or practical foundation. But again and again it seemed to happen that whenever the Jews would begin to feel at home in the countries of their adoption some new flare-up of anti-Jewish feeling would take place and remind them that they are undesirable aliens. About the middle of the 19th century the Jews in Germany and in other parts of Western Europe became convinced that a new day had dawned for the Jews. At a Rabbinical conference in Germany in 1845 it was voted to delete from the Prayer Book all references to a Jewish restoration in Palestine. The German Jews, who were the pioneers in the movement of liberal Judaism, had no more need to think of Zion and Jerusalem: Germany was their Zion and Berlin their Jerusalem.

Within twenty-five years from that optimistic conference a recrudescence of intense antisemitism took place in Germany; and before a century was over the bulk of European Jews, including the German Jews, were destroyed. Some of the German Jews who managed to escape found their way to Palestine and there they helped to rebuild the very same Zion which was repudiated by their grandfathers and even by their fathers.

c. Both Jacob and the Jewish People Relied Principally on Human Resources.

Laban, Jacob's uncle who later became his father-in-law, was a master in trickery and subterfuge. When Jacob gained the consent of his wives to move to Canaan, he decided to conceal this decision from Laban. He feared that Laban might seek to prevent his return, or failing in this, to detain his family. Laban did not discover Jacob's depature until three days later. He then assembled an armed band and overtook Jacob's company near the border of Canaan. There is no telling what Laban and his armed companions might have done to Jacob. What saved Jacob from Laban's power was not his own cleverness or human resourcefulness, but a Divine warning given to Laban in a dream the night before his encounter with Jacob. It was God's intervention that saved Jacob.

When Jacob crossed the border into Canaan he had another opponent to cope with. The manly thing to have done would have been to send a message to Esau, to confess that he had wronged him in the past, and to ask for pardon and a reconciliation. This evidently Jacob did not do. Consequently, when he heard that Esau was marching towards him at the head of 400 armed men, Jacob became terrified; he prostrated himself before God in prayer, confessed his utter unworthiness and pleaded for Divine help.

God answered Jacob's prayer, as He often does with many of us, not exactly as Jacob desired, but in accordance with his need. The answer to his prayer came in the course of a spiritual struggle with a mysterious Divine person beside the brook of Jabbok, lasting all night. Out of this contest Jacob emerged with his pride humbled, and emptied of his excessive self-confidence. The spraining of his hip, making it difficult for him to stand on his feet unsupported, only symbolized Jacob's failure to work out his destiny by his human resources alone.

Until the end of the 18th century the Jews knew of no solution to their problem other than a religious solution: They looked for the coming of the Messiah who would bring about their national restoration in Palestine. A decided change in this attitude had taken place in the 19th century. While the orthodox segment of Jewry continued to adhere to the traditional position, increasing numbers adopted a secular approach to the Jewish problem. By and large, the Jews who had chosen this non-religious approach consisted of two main divisions; the liberal Jews and Jewish socialists formed one group, the Zionists made up the second division. The liberal Jews and the Jewish socialists believed that with changing circumstances Jews will be able to live happily in the countries of their residence; while the Zionists maintained that the Jewish position in the world will never become normal unless and until a Jewish state is re-established in Palestine.

The position of liberal Judaism on this subject was spelled out at the above-mentioned Rabbinical assembly in Germany in 1845. "In our days," declared one of the participants in that Rabbinical conference, ". . .the ideals of justice and the brotherhood of men have been so strengthened through the laws and institutions of modern States, that they can never again be shattered; we are witnessing an ever nearer approach of the establishment of the Kingdom of God on earth through the strivings of mankind."[15] Within a century from the date of that conference liberal Judaism, which had such an unbounded faith in the goodness and perfectibility of human nature, witnessed the most cruel manifestation of human barbarism ever recorded in the annals of human savagery. Those whose parents asserted with so much confidence that their newly-won freedoms can never be shattered, were deprived by the State of the right to stay alive. Millions of European Jews, men, women and children, were torn away from their homes and loved ones, and deported in cattle trains to extermination centers. Those few who somehow managed to survive went into hiding and lived the life of fugitives in constant dread of being detected. The Kingdom of God concerning which the German Jews were so certain as being realized through strivings of mankind turned out to be the kingdom of Satan, a veritable hell on earth.

As to the Jewish socialists, they kept repeating the sterotyped socialist assertion that antisemitism is the child of capitalism, and that with the demise of capitalism antisemitism will die a natural death. The Jewish masses of eastern Europe had the bitter experience of seeing Soviet Russia enter into an alliance with Nazi Germany which made it possible for Hitler to start the Second World War. In the post-World War Two period the same socialist Soviet Russia has been pursuing a strong anti-Jewish policy.

Modern Zionism arose in the second half of the 19th century. It differed from traditional Zionism in that it held that Jews need not wait for a Messiah in order to regain Palestine; in fact, many of the adherents of modern Zionism have given up belief in a personal Messiah. Zionism advocated a Jewish emigration to Palestine with the purpose of rebuilding the land and reestablishing the Jewish State. Zionists voiced the conviction that the Zionist program can be realized by means of Jewish manpower, Jewish money, and with the help of political diplomacy, in other words, by human resources alone.

Up to the First World War Zionism derived its main strength, moral, spiritual and material, from the large Jewish centers in Russia and Poland. What happened since the days of World War One put a strange twist into the Zionists program. As a result of the communist revolution in Russia in World War One, Russian Jewry was cut off from the rest of the Jews; while the Jews of Poland, some 3½ million strong, perished at the hands of the Nazis in World War Two. The loss of Russian and Polish Jewry was a veritable calamity for Zionism, since Russian and Polish Jews supplied Zionism with the manpower and much of the money it needed to carry out the Zionist program.

There was in store for Zionism yet another unpleasant surprise. When it drew up its program Zionism never took into account the presence of Arabs in Palestine. When the British government issued in 1917 the Balfour Declaration promising to assist the Jews to re-establish their national homeland in Palestine, Arab leadership of that day viewed the Zionist movement with deep sympathy and promised its help in the accomplishment of its goals. It looked upon the revival of Jewish nationhood in Palestine as likely to be of great benefit to the revival of Arabism in the Middle East. But for a variety of factors this enlightened Arab attitude quickly underwent a complete about-face change, and the Arabs in Palestine began to display increasing opposition to the Zionist idea. Zionist leadership simply did not know how to deal with this Arab opposition, even as Jacob knew not how to handle his feud with Esau upon his return to Canaan.

When in 1947 the United Nations passed a resolution calling for a division of Palestine into a Jewish and Arab state, the neighboring Arab countries marched their armies into Palestine with the intention of preventing the formation of a Jewish State. The Palestinian Jews numbered only about 600,000 people, including men, women, and children. Confronted by the approaching Arab onslaught the small Jewish community could count on no outside help. Like their forefather Jacob beside the brook of Jabbok, they were left alone, alone in their utter helplessness. What transpired there within the following few weeks and months was viewed by many of the Palestinian Jews as a miraculous event. With their bare hands, as it were, they rose up and expelled the invaders from the territory which became the State of Israel.

As a direct outgrowth of the Arab invasion of Palestine several hundred thousand Palestinian Arabs became war refugees; while hundreds of thousands of Jews were expelled from Arab countries penniless. The Jews in the newly-formed State of Israel took these Jewish refugees into their hearts and homes, even as post-war Western Germany, though overpopulated, took in millions of German refugees from the neighboring regions of what is now Poland and Czechoslovakia. But the Arab countries which through their invasion of Palestine created the Arab refugee problem refused to take in their Arab kinsmen even though some Arab lands are underpopulated.

But there is no denying the fact that the sudden withdrawal of several hundred thousand Palestinian Arabs as the direct consequence of the Arab war on Palestine made the task of the establishment of the State of Israel much easier.

The United Nations resolution of 1947 calling for the formation of a Jewish State in Palestine was the immediate response of the civilized, especially the Western, world to the shock produced at the end of World War Two when the full story of the sufferings of the Jews under the Nazis became known. It appears that when the question of the reconstitution of Palestine began to be considered by members of the British Government in World War One, it was Weizmann who, on behalf of the Zionists, proposed to Lord Cecil, then assistant to the Secretary of Foreign Affairs, that Palestine be made into a British Protectorate. The Jews of the whole world, Weizman said to Lord Cecil, had faith in England and they trusted her.[16] The Zionists had utmost confidence that under a British Protectorate the Jews would be able to accomplish the reconstruction of Palestine. Under the Conservative Chamberlain just before the outbreak of World War Two, and under the Laborite Bevin soon after the end of World War Two, England, in whom the Jews put their trust, did all in its power to nullify the aim of the Balfour Declaration and the Palestine Mandate which she had assumed under the League of Nations. When the United Nations resolution, mentioned above, came up for a vote, England opposed the formation of a Jewish State in Palestine. In fact, events culminating in the establishment of the State of Israel were so swift and so unexpected that the Zionists themselves were caught by surprise. The State of Israel came into existence not exactly the way the Zionists planned. The rebirth of the State of Israel was a catastrophic event, the immediate outgrowth of the Jewish disaster in the Second World War which in its magnitude stands next to the destruction of Jewish Palestine by the Roman Empire.

But this is not all. It was one thing to establish the State of Israel, and quite another thing to keep it alive. And yet at this writing, twenty years later, Israel is probably the most advanced country in the Middle East, economically, industrially and scientifically. How are we to account for it? There is no denying that the generous flow of financial help from American Jews had been a great contributing factor. But Israel would have been in a precarious condition if she had to depend entirely on financial help from

American Jews. It is Western Germany that played a most important part in the phenomenal economic development of Israel. Under the Reparations Agreement of 1952 between West Germany and Israel, Germany allocated some 850 million dollars for Israel in compensation for Jewish properties expropriated by the Nazis. This sum was paid not in cash but in equipment and goods. Reparation money financed the acquisition of 49 ships for Israel's merchant fleet, and equipment for the expansion of some 1500 industrial plants. Many of the ships which ply the oceans were built in German ports; many of the Israeli factories were equipped by the Germans; many of the machines, tools and instruments which keep Israeli factories running were made in Germany. Thus, the development of the industrial and commercial economy of the State of Israel was in a large measure aided through the labor and ingenuity of a country which in the Nazi period set out to put an end to all Jewish existence; and it was accomplished with the material assets of Jews destroyed by the Nazis, many of which Jews may have been, while alive, indifferent, if not actually opposed, to the idea of a reconstitution of a Jewish State in Palestine. How strange and mysterious are the ways of God and the means He uses to accomplish His purpose! And what a lesson we are taught by Israel's history concerning the futility of depending on human resources alone!

2. "ISRAEL—PROPHETIC VISION AND HISTORICAL FULFILLMENT."

The material which follows below is from a contribution to another work by William F. Albright, world-famous Biblical archaeologist and for many years professor of Semitic languages at Johns Hopkins University. It is included in this study at Dr. Albright's suggestion in response to this writer's request.

"No other phenomenon in history is quite so extraordinary as the unique event represented by the Restoration of Israel in the sixth and fifth centuries B. C. E. At no other time in world history, so far as is known, has a people been destroyed, and then come back after a lapse of time and reestablished itself. It is utterly out of the question to seek a parallel for the recurrence of Israel's restoration after twenty-five hundred years of further history.

This doubly unique phenomenon demands explanation. If we look at some of the elements involved, we first turn, naturally, to the land, the land to which Israel returned because it had been the home of Israel from its beginning as a people; then, to the people Israel;

and finally, to the Restoration itself. How is such a thing possible? How did it happen?

First, the Land. Palestine was little and poor. Greece also was little and poor, but Palestine was still poorer and smaller. Yet this land became the home of Israel, the focus of Israelite aspirations in the Diaspora, the point to which Israel always hoped to return, and, finally, the reestablished home of the Israelite people . . .

Palestine has always challenged its settlers—the climate is unpredictable and rainfall can never be foreseen. It challenged Israel's power of resistance to nature as well as her ability to resist the foes which surrounded her: Israel had to sustain cycles of famine, as well as every possible attack of nature from invasions of locusts to epidemics among animals and plants. The land itself was a challenge because of its rugged terrain.

And from this land which challenged the energy of its people, there emerged a people of singular vitality; in spite of the fact that this people had been—to quote the Torah—an 'ereb rab and asafsuf,' or as translated inadequately in the Authorized Version, 'a mixed multitude'. We may paraphrase 'ereb rab and asafsuf' as a hopeless mixture of elements having no merit whatever in the eyes of any people proud of its own alleged purity of race, a mob with a mixed plebeian background of nomads, slaves, and bandits. We are given, in the Bible, a vivid picture of Moses' constant struggle with this people, trying to hammer it into some sort of unified nation . . .

Israel's history begins with a great man. It has been popular in recent decades to dismiss Moses as a reflection of the spirit of the people (ruah ha-am), or as a figure which grew out of traditions dealing with different persons and situations in the dawn of Israel's history. But we can have no such phenomenon as Israel without a great founder. It is impossible to imagine such a creation without a Moses. Furthermore, it is impossible to imagine the monotheistic faith of this people without a man to bring the Torah* to it. Through this early monotheism, which Moses was able to impress upon his people, Israel became not only a nation but also a unified religious congregation . . .

There had been monotheisms before. One of them we know quite well—the monotheism of Egypt in the century immediately preceding Moses. Though poor as compared with that of the Bible, it was

---

* The Sinai revelation.

nevertheless a monotheism. Israel, however, had more than mere ethical monotheism. It had the conviction that a formal pact existed between the sole God of the universe and His people Israel. This berit, symbolized by the Ark of the Covenant, was a treaty in which God promised to favor Israel and to maintain an eternal pact with her if she obeyed His commands, which included both cultic and ethical content ..

Nowhere in history have we anything comparable to the Prophets of Israel ... Year after year, generation after generation and century after century, the Prophets felt themselves called upon to rebuke their kings, their nobles, their priests, and their people... The Prophets are our eternal heritage from Israel. Between 750 and 700 B.C.E., and again between 620 and 580 B.C.E., they taught the inevitable destruction of Israel because of its rebellion against God. They also taught the restoration of Israel ... The Prophets believed not only that God would destroy Israel and restore it at a later time, but also that the restoration would come as a result of divine grace or hesed ...

Recent scholars have devoted a great deal of time, especially in this country and England, trying to disprove the Biblical tradition of the Exile and Restoration. They say that there was no thorough destruction or complete devastation, that there was no real Exile, no Babylonian Captivity, and, of course, no Restoration. There are scholars who say that we cannot rely on the prophecies of Jeremiah and Ezekiel, alleging that they are apocryphal. They reject the historical content of Chronicles and Ezra, claiming that they are also apocryphal.

And what is the reason for such a violent onslaught against the historicity of precisely those parts of the Bible which were regarded by the classical literary critics of the nineteenth century as being the most reliable of all? The reason is very simple: it rests in the extreme melioristic evolutionism of the Victorian Age and its aftermath, which is even now dying very slowly among British and Americans. This is particularly true in our own country because we have not yet really suffered from the crises of our age... Of course there was an Exile, a Captivity, and a Restoration. Year by year archaeologists make finds which have disproved the contentions of these scholars even in detail ..."

In the Hellenistic and Roman periods a new group of men arose in Israel, the dreamers and apocalypticists. "These dreamers kept the spiritual aspirations of Israel alive. They expected a Messiah

and a Messianic Age. Dr. Gershom Scholem's authoritative survey of
the history of the Messianic movement in Jewry* vividly shows that
there has never been a period in which there were not Messianic
movements in Israel. But more important than these Messianic
movements within Israel was Christian and Moslem influence.
Thanks to Christianity and Islam Judaism has never been allowed to
forget the Messianic Age promised by the Prophets. This they did
in two ways. First, and most important, the Christian and Moslem
persecution forced the Jews to keep Judaism alive if they were to
maintain their national existence at all . . .

We must remember that all through this period there were also
Christian and Moslem rulers who invited the Jews to take refuge
in their countries, popes who supported the Jews and befriended
them, and ordinary Gentiles who helped them in every possible way.
There never was a time when there were not Christian friends of
Jews.

Second, we have a positive Christian effort that developed in the
nineteenth century, and since then has become very important. It is
the increased recognition by Christian writers and preachers, both
conservative and liberal, of the world role of Judaism, of the fact
that the existence and the continued prosperity of the Jewish people
are an index of the good will and the spiritual vitality of Christianity.
A large section of Christendom, mainly Protestant, has emphasized
the truth of Old Testament prophecy. . . Unquestionably, Christian
expectations of the second coming of Christ have helped to keep
alive Messianic expectations in modern Jewry, both by direct and
indirect influence. The Zionist movement is, after all, historically a
special form of Messianic expectation . . .

Both Jews and Christians have thus played a role in keeping alive
the hope of Restoration. And so Restoration came. It came with the
great founders of Zionism, with men like Eliezer Ben Yehuda, who
reestablished the Hebrew language as a living tongue in Israel, with
men like Chaim Weizmann and David Ben Gurion. It came with men
who are dreamers and scholars and doers, like Yitzhak Ben Zvi, the
head of the new Jewish State, and like the young archaeologist
Yigael Yadin, son of my old friend Eleazer Sukenik, who has not
only begun a brilliant career as a scholar but also became one of the
greatest single military geniuses of the past decade. These men have

---

* (Major Trends in Jewish Mysticism.)

continued to dream. They have—often without knowing it, because some were not religious and did not believe in prophecy—carried on the prophetic tradition of Israel, incorporating it into a reality which has made nonsense of the predictions of every non-prophetic soul, including myself. I never dreamed that there would be an actual Jewish State in Israel, and I must often have asserted its 'impossibility'. Yet Israel exists, and the vision has been fulfilled.

What is going to happen next? Are the words of the Prophets merely archaic survivals of a naive age? Not at all. God will keep His covenant with His people, if His people obey the Divine commands. God is fulfilling the predictions made through His servants, the Prophets, although some of those who have brought the dream of Restoration to fulfillment would certainly not have been imagined by the Tannaitic or Amoraic rabbis, or by the great orthodox teachers of the Middle Ages. I am thinking particularly of a certain Viennese journalist,* or a certain Russian who began the study of medicine only to leave it for Zionism**, or a certain Manchester chemist***, also born in Eastern Europe. I suspect that the Prophets themselves would have been greatly surprised at some of their successors."[17]

---

* (Theodor Herzl, 1860-1904.)

** (Eliezer Ben Yehuda, 1858-1922.)

*** (Chaim Weizmann, 1874-1952.)

Notes to Chapter 12

[1] The Very Reverend Norman Maclean, *His Terrible Swift Sword*, pp. 27, 43.

[2] Quoted in *The Jewish Plan For Palestine* (The Jewish Agency For Palestine: Jerusalem, 1947), p. 121.

[3] Bartley C. Crum, *Behind The Silken Curtain* (Simon and Schuster: New York, 1947), pp. 187, 189.

[4] Quoted by Bartley C. Crum, Op. Cit., pp. 291-2.

[5] Quoted by L. B. Namier, *In The Margin Of History* (Macmillan and Co.: London, 1939), pp. 281-2. Used by permission.

[6] Edgar A. Mowrer in *Problems Of The Middle East* by New York University School of Education (The American Christian Palestine Committee: New York, 1947), p. 102.

[7] Walter C. Lowdermilk, *"A New Agriculture In An Old Land"*, article in *The Atlantic Monthly* (Boston), November 1961. Used by permission.

8 Walter C. Lowdermilk, *Palestine, Land Of Promise* (Harper & Brothers: New York, 1944), pp. 228-9.

9 Walter C. Lowdermilk in *Problems Of The Middle East* by New York University School of Education (The American Christian Palestine Committee: New York, 1947), p. 9.

10 Bartley C. Crum, Op. Cit., p. 290.

11 Ibid., p. 291.

12 John F. Kennedy, *The Strategy Of Peace* (Harper & Brothers: New York, 1960), pp. 118-123. Used by permission.

13 Monsignor John M. Oesterreicher and Reverend Edward G. Flannery, *"A Statement Of Conscience"*, article in *The American Zionist* (New York), February, 1968. Used by permission.

14 S. R. Driver, *The Book Of Genesis* (Methuen & Co.: London, 1904), p. 249.

15 David Philipson, *The Reform Movement In Judaism* (The Macmillan Company: New York, 1931), p. 178.

16 Chaim Weizmann, *Trial and Error* (The Jewish Publication Society of America: Philadelphia, 1949), vol. 1, p. 191.

17 William F. Albright, *"Israel—Prophetic Vision and Historical Fulfillment"*, in *Israel: Its Role In Civilization*, edited by Moshe Davis (Harper & Brothers: New York, 1956), pp. 31-38. Used by permission of The Jewish Theological Seminary of America.

CHAPTER 13

"AND JERUSALEM WILL BE TRODDEN DOWN BY THE GENTILES, UNTIL THE TIMES OF THE GENTILES ARE FULFILLED" (Luke 21:24).

I. THE TIMES OF THE GENTILES

II. THE TIMES OF THE GENTILES IN DANIEL 2

1. The Human Image Of Nebuchadnezzar's Dream

2. The Golden Age Of Ancient Mythology

3. Daniel's Interpretation Of Nebuchadnezzar's Image

4. The Message For Israel In Daniel 2

5. The Universal And Jewish Phase Of The Times Of The Gentiles

6. Divine Judgment On The Times Of The Gentiles

"AND JERUSALEM WILL BE TRODDEN DOWN BY THE GENTILES, UNTIL THE TIMES OF THE GENTILES ARE FULFILLED" (Luke 21:24).

The above words are part of a statement in which Jesus Christ had predicted the destruction of the Jewish State, about thirty-seven years prior to its accomplishment by pagan Rome. "But when you see Jerusalem surrounded by armies, then know that its desolation has come near. Then let those who are in Judea flee to the mountains, and let those who are inside the city depart, and let not those who are out in the country enter it. For these are days of vengeance, to fulfill all that is written. Alas for those who are with child and for those who give suck in those days! For great distress shall be upon the earth and wrath upon this people. They will fall by the edge of the sword, and be led captive among all nations; *and Jerusalem will be trodden down by the Gentiles, until the times of the Gentiles are fulfilled*" (Luke 21: 20—24).

In the opening days of June 1967 Israel was for the third time, since the reconstitution of the new State, fighting for her survival. Only several days before, Egypt's dictator Nasser called for the annihilation of Israel. On May 22, 1967, Nasser announced a blockade of the Gulf of Akaba, which is the entrance to Israel's southern port of Eilat. Through this port Israel brings in about 90 percent of her oil supplies and handles her trade with Asian and African countries. War broke out on Monday, June 5, 1967. On the southern front Egypt had 80,000 troops; on the eastern border Jordan had 40,000 men, with 20,000 additional men ordered into Jordan by Saudi Arabia; on the northern front there were 40,000 Syrians with a contingent of 5,000 soldiers from Iraq. Israel's regular army numbered only 70,000 men, with 230,000 reserves. The Arab nations opposing Israel numbered about 110 million people, while Israel had a population of only 2½ million.

The Arabs had 1,090 planes, Israel—350 planes. The Arabs were in possession of 2,700 tanks, Israel—800 tanks. The Arabs possessed a navy consisting of 205 ships, Israel—19 ships.

Arrayed against Israel on the southern front alone were 900 tanks, hundreds of high performance jet planes, Russian-built missiles and giant rockets.

Israel struck Monday morning, June 5, 1967. In four hours Nasser's air force was smashed, and 25 of the most vital Arab air bases were wrecked. In sixty hours Israel destroyed the Jordanian, Syrian, and Iraqi air forces. In six days hostilities were brought to a halt. The war cost Israel 679 dead; the Egyptians suffered about 20,000 death casualties; 2,000 Syrians and 8,000 Jordanians were killed. Israel captured over a hundred Patton and Centurion tanks, and over 700 Russian tanks, many in good condition, hundreds of intact artillery pieces, thousands of tons of ammunition.

When hostilities ceased Israel had reached the Suez Canal, occupied the Straits of Tiran, the Gaza Strip, the Syrian Golan Heights from which artillery had kept the Israeli border villages under frequent fire, old Jerusalem, and the west bank of the river Jordan. Thus within six days Israel regained much of the area of the Biblical Promised Land with the old city of Jerusalem, and the Western Wall which is the only remaining part of the Jerusalem Temple.

In concluding his Report on this stunning Israeli victory, General Marshall, a soldier since World War One and a military analyst, has this to say: "When the [Israeli] reserves stacked arms a few days later, and with their friends in the standing force looked back, not exultantly but with a frightful pride in the achievement of their arms, they told one another that superior shooting accounted for the smash victory. But as did their civilian neighbors, they also spoke of the 'miracle'. Many things about the way they did it transcended technical explanation and mortal understanding."[1]

I. THE TIMES OF THE GENTILES

To return to the statement by Jesus Christ concerning the destruction of the Jewish State by the Romans. This destruction, He implied, would last until the end of the Times of the Gentiles. What does the phrase the "Times of the Gentiles" mean? In my book *The Rebirth of the State of Israel* I suggested that in the Old Testament Hebrew the English word "Gentile" or "Gentiles" means nation or nations. In this sense even Israel is at times designated by the same word "Goy" which the English versions translate "Gentile" or "Gentiles". But by and large Israel is called "am" translated by the English word "people", whereas the noun "Gentile" or "Gentiles" designates in the Bible any non-Jewish nation. With the emergence of Israel, the word "Gentile" assumed a religious, in addition to its racial connotation, i.e., a Gentile was a person or a nation which stood outside of Biblical revelation.

The next question which needs to be cleared up is the meaning of the expression the "Times of the Gentiles". For the answer we must go to the eleventh chapter of Genesis where the Tower of Babel event is recorded. The story begins with an account of a migration of a segment of the human race, some time after the great Flood, into the Mesopotamian Valley called Shinar in the Hebrew. "And they said to one another, 'Come let us make bricks, and burn them thoroughly'. And they had [been using] brick for stone, and bitumen for mortar. Then they said, 'Come let us build ourselves a city,* and a tower with its top in the heavens, and let us make a name for ourselves. . . And the LORD said, 'Behold, they are one people, and they have all one language; and this is only the beginning of what they will do; and nothing that they propose to do will now be impossible or them. . . . So the LORD scattered them over the face of all the earth, and they left off building the city" (Genesis 11:3-4, 6, 8).

A careful analysis of this passage will convince us that it was written by one who had a true knowledge of the topography of the Mesopotamian Valley where this episode is said to have taken place. In the absence of stone Mesopotamians used mud which they molded into bricks, and applied heat to harden the bricks. Since the area abounded in bitumen, this material served as mortar to hold the bricks together. The "tower with its top in the heavens" describes the towering temples of the Sumerians, the original inhabitants of the lower region of Mesopotamia.

We have in the above description the first recorded attempt on the part of a segment of mankind—some time after the great Flood— to erect a world civilization. "Come, let us build ourselves a city . . . lest we be scattered abroad". Perhaps the expansionist activities of Nimrod reported in the preceding chapter are related to the Tower of Babel event: "Cush became the father of Nimrod: he** was the first on earth to be a mighty man, "a mighty conqueror".[2] He was a mighty hunter before the LORD; the beginning[3] of his kingdom was

---

* State
** Nimrod.

Babel, Erech, and Accad, all of them in the land of Shinar"[4] (Genesis 10: 8-10).

Political power and conquest combined with the power of man-made organized religion, were to be the instruments with which this first world-state was to be erected. The inspiration and driving power of the whole enterprise was a desire for the glorification of man—"let us make a name for ourselves." The whole undertaking ended in a dismal failure. Mankind was not unified. The sinfulness of human nature makes a world system dominated by one big power potentially dangerous for the welfare of mankind. This is the inner meaning of the statement: "Behold, they are one people, and they have all one language; and this is only the beginning of what they will do; and [if permitted to go on] nothing that they propose to do will now be impossible for them" (Genesis 11:6). This being so, a world fragmented into a multitude of nations is the lesser of two evils, and from the Biblical point of view this state of affairs is more desirable and is to continue until mankind's redemption has been accomplished.

The Times of the Gentiles or the Times of the Nations is the period of world history which has its beginning in the Tower of Babel event. It is characterized by man's persistent efforts to unify the world by human means alone. It is a secularist, humanist, world system which seeks to shape man's destiny in ignorance of, or in opposition to, the redemptive purpose of Biblical revelation.

The same eleventh chapter of Genesis records the beginning of another historical movement, a movement initiated by God with the call of Abraham. In bidding Abraham to leave his native land and proceed to Canaan which was to become the eternal possession of the Jewish people, God said to Abraham, "and I will make thy name great". The builders of the Tower of Babel enterprise were out to make a name for themselves and they achieved nothing but disorder and confusion. What they failed to achieve Abraham obtained from God's hand. Today, some 4,000 years later, some 1,400 million people, Jews, Christians and Muslims, trace their religious ideas and their spiritual heritage back to Abraham.

In the call of Abraham it was hinted that there will be hostility between the ungodly system—the Times of the Nations—and the divine world order begun with Abraham. "I will bless those who bless thee, and him who curses thee I will curse" (Genesis 12:3).

II. The Times Of The Gentiles In Daniel 2

1. the human image of nebuchadnezzar's dream.

The collapse of the Babel scheme did not spell the end of un-redeemed man's dream for world unification under the supremacy of one centralizing power. A condensed and comprehensive Biblical view of this subject is presented in Nebuchadnezzar's image as related in the second chapter of Daniel. Nebuchadnezzar was the founder of the Babylonian empire. Among the nations which he subdued and incorporated into his empire was the Judaean kingdom with the depor-tation to Babylon of a portion of the Judaean population. Among these captives was a young man Daniel. In the beginning of his reign Nebuchadnezzar saw in his sleep a certain strange human image. The following is a description of Nebuchadnezzar's vision and its meaning as interpreted by Daniel:

"Daniel answered the king, 'No wise men, enchanters, magicians, or astrologers can show to the king the mystery which the king has asked. But there is a God in heaven who reveals mysteries, and he has made known to King Nebuchadnezzar what shall be in the latter days. Your dream and the visions of your head as you lay in bed are these. . .

You saw, O king, and behold, a great image. This image, mighty and of exceeding brightness, stood before you, and its appearance was frightening. The head of this image was of fine gold, its breast and arms of silver, its belly and thighs of brass. Its legs of iron, its feet partly of iron and partly of clay. As you looked, a stone was cut out by no human hand, and it smote the image on its feet of iron and clay, and broke them in pieces. Then the iron, the clay, the brass, the silver, and the gold, all together were broken in pieces, and became like the chaff of the summer threshing floors; and the wind carried them away, so that not a trace of them could be found; but the stone that struck the image became a great mountain and filled the whole earth.

This was the dream; now we will tell the king the interpretation. You, O king, the king of kings, to whom the God of heaven has given the kingdom, the power, and the might, and the glory. And into whose hand he has given, wherever they dwell, the sons of men, the beasts of the field, and the birds of the air, making you rule over them all: you are the head of gold. After you shall arise another kingdom inferior to you, and yet a third kingdom of brass, which shall rule over the earth. And there shall be a fourth kingdom, strong as iron, because iron breaks to pieces and shatters all things; and like iron which crushes, it shall break and crush all these. And as you saw the feet and toes partly of potter's clay and partly of iron, it shall be a divided kingdom; but some of the firmness of iron shall be in it, just as you saw iron mixed with miry clay. And as the toes of the feet were partly iron and partly clay, so the kingdom shall be partly strong and partly brittle. As you saw the iron mixed with miry clay, so they will mix with one another in marriage, but they will not hold together, just as iron does not mix with clay. And in the days of those kings the God of heaven will set up a kingdom which shall never be destroyed, nor shall its sovereignty be left to another people; but it shall break in pieces all these kingdoms and bring them to an end, and it shall stand for ever. Just as you saw that a stone was cut out of the mountain by no human hand and that it broke in pieces the iron, the brass, the clay, the silver and the gold, a great God has made known to the king what shall be hereafter; the dream is certain, and its interpretation sure" (Daniel 2:27-28, 31-45).

2. THE GOLDEN AGE OF ANCIENT MYTHOLOGY.

There was a widespread belief in the ancient pagan world that human history is a repetitive series of epochs, similar to the cycles of the seasons and years. This idea finds expression in the following Greek poem which dates back to the middle of the 9th century B.C., about three centuries preceding Nebuchadnezzar's dream.

"First of all the deathless gods who dwell on Olympus made a golden race of mortal men who lived in the time of Cronos[5] when he was reigning in heaven. And they lived like gods without sorrow of heart, remote and free from toil and grief: miserable age rested not on them; but with legs and arms never failing they made merry with feasting beyond the reach of all evils. When they died, it was as though they were overcome with sleep, and they had all good things; for the fruitful earth unforced bare them fruit abundantly and without stint. They dwelt in ease and peace upon their lands with many good things, rich in flocks and loved by the blessed gods.

But after the earth had covered this generation . . . then they who dwell on Olympus made a second generation which was of silver and less noble by far. It was like the golden race neither in body nor in spirit. A child was brought up at his good mother's side an hundred years, an utter simpleton, playing childishly in his own home. But when they were full grown and were come to the full measure of their prime, they lived only a little time and that in sorrow because of their foolishness, for they could not keep from sinning and from wronging one another, nor would they serve immortals, nor sacrifice on the holy altars of the blessed ones as it is right for men to do wherever they dwell. Then Zeus the son of Cronos was angry and put them away, because they would not give honor to the blessed gods who live on Olympus.

But when earth had covered this generation also . . . Zeus the Father made a third generation of mortal men, a brazen race, sprung from ash-trees; and it was in no way equal to the silver age, but was terrible and strong. . . Great was their strength and unconquerable the arms which grew from their shoulders on their strong limbs. Their armor was bronze, and their houses of bronze, and of bronze were their implements: there was no black iron. These were destroyed by their own hands and passed to the dark house of chill Hades, and left no name: terrible though they were, black Death seized them, and they left the bright light of the sun.

But when earth had covered this generation also, Zeus the son of Cronos made yet another, the fourth, upon the fruitful earth, which was nobler and more righteous, a god-like race of hero-men who are called demi-gods, the race before our own, throughout the boundless earth. Grim war and dead battle destroyed a part of them. . . But to the others father Zeus the son of Cronos gave a living and an abode apart from men, and made them dwell at the ends of the earth. . .

And again far-seeing Zeus made yet another generation, the fifth, of men who are upon the bounteous earth. Thereafter, would that I were not among the men of the fifth generation, but either had died before or been born afterwards. For now truly is a race of iron, and men never rest from labor and sorrow by day, and from perishing by night; and the gods shall lay sore trouble upon them. . . And Zeus will destroy this race of mortal men also when they come to have grey hair on the temples at their birth.* The father will not agree with his children, nor the children with their father, nor guest with his host, nor comrade with comrade. Men will dishonor their parents as they grow quickly old, and will carp at them, chiding them with bitter words, hard-hearted they, not knowing the fear of the gods.

---

* "That race will so degenerate that at the last even a newborn child will show the marks of old age." Translator's note.

They will not repay their aged parents the cost of their nurture, for might shall be their right: and one man will sack another's city. There will be no favor for the man who keeps his oath or for the just or for the good; but rather men will praise the evil-doer and his violent dealing. Strength will be right and reverence will cease to be; and the wicked will hurt the worthy man, speaking false words against him, and will swear an oath upon them. Envy, foul-mouthed, delighting in evil, with scowling face, will go along with wretched men one and all. And then Aidos and Nemesis,[6] with their sweet forms wrapped in white robes, will go from the wide-pathed earth and forsake mankind to join the company of the deathless gods: and bitter sorrows will be left for mortal men, and there will be no help against evil."[7]

From the above we can see that mankind's golden era was conceived by the peoples of antiquity as having taken place in the distant past; the present state of the world constitutes a condition of unrelieved gloom. The view concerning the degeneration of human civilization held by the ancients may represent a remnant of the primeval Divine revelation, the original source of which may be seen in the following Biblical passage: "Now the earth was corrupt in God's sight, and the earth was filled with violence. And God saw the earth, and behold, it was corrupt; for all flesh had corrupted their way upon the earth. And God said to Noah, 'I have determined to make an end of all flesh; for the earth is filled with violence through them; behold, I will destroy them with the earth'" (Genesis 6: 11-13). The Bible knows nothing of a golden age in the past. For all practical purposes, the Biblical account begins with man's fall, and the Biblical message from the beginning to the end is concerned with man's redemption and the regeneration of human nature. In the Bible mankind's golden era lies in the future.

From their observation of the recurrent periodicity of the movements of the sun and other heavenly bodies, and of the regularity which characterizes the coming and going of the seasons of the year, the ancients came to think of human events in similar cyclical terms. "They were impressed by the visible order and beauty of the cosmos, and the cosmic law of growth and decay was also the pattern for their understanding of history".[8]

Having unified the known ancient world of his day, Nebuchadnezzar may have been burdened with thoughts of how enduring a structure he had erected, and whether his accomplishments spelled the return of the mythical golden era. His troubled state of mind is reflected in the following words addressed to him by Daniel: "To you, O king, as you lay in bed came thoughts of what would be hereafter, and he who reveals mysteries made known to you what is to be." (Daniel 2:29).

3. DANIEL'S INTERPRETATION OF NEBUCHADNEZZAR'S IMAGE.

For a detailed discussion on Daniel's interpretation of the human image the reader is referred to expository works on Daniel. My own analysis was given in *The Rebirth of the State of Israel*. Here I wish to take up only those elements of Daniel's interpretation which have a bearing on Christ's statement concerning the Times of the Gentiles. From the point of view of Biblical revelation the symbolism of Nebuchadnezzar's human image had a two-fold purpose. In the first place, it was intended to help Nebuchadnezzar find his way to a saving knowledge of the God of Israel as the God of history and of all mankind. To accomplish this Daniel, under Divine inspiration, makes use of Babylonian beliefs as vehicles by which to convey Biblical truth. To begin with, he interprets the meaning of the metals of which the human image of Nebuchadnezzar's vision was composed. The head of gold he identified with Nebuchadnezzar's Babylon. The silver, brass, iron and iron mixed with clay represented the succession of empires which will follow the fall of Nebuchadnezzar's kingdom. So far Daniel's exposition of the mystery of the metallic image was a message of doom for Nebuchadnezzar's Babylon.

The gloomy note, however, was changed with Daniel's reference to the stone cut out from a mountain without human hands, i.e., by Divine instrumentality. This stone smote the whole image and the stone increased and became itself a great mountain which filled the whole earth. In Babylonian mythology the gods were identified with mountains, hence the Babylonian temples were so designed as to imitate mountains. The Babylonian chief deity, Merodach, or Marduk, is styled on one of the tablets as the Great Mountain.[9]

When therefore Daniel spoke of the stone which had demolished the image, and it then became a great mountain, to his Babylonian listeners in the king's palace his words conveyed the idea that after the Babylonian kingdom had been displaced by a succession of other empires it would be handed back to the "Great Mountain" or to the "Great God" whom Daniel's hearers identified with Marduk, Babylon's chief god and patron deity. This is as far as any one could go in seeking to convey to a Babylonian audience the truth concerning the Messianic Kingdom.[10] No wonder that Nebuchadnezzar was so pleased with Daniel's interpretation of the vision of the human image that he showered upon him many gifts and appointed him to an exalted office in the empire (Daniel 2:46-48).

4. THE MESSAGE FOR ISRAEL IN DANIEL 2.

The human image of Nebuchadnezzar's dream had also a message for Israel. In fact, the message for Israel may be the primary object of the vision. The clue to this message is contained in the expression "latter days" used by Daniel in the opening statement of his exposition. "Daniel answered the king, 'No wise men, enchanters, magicians, or astrologers can show to the king the mystery which the king has asked. But there is a God in heaven who reveals mysteries, and he has made known to King Nebuchadnezzar what will be in the latter days" (Daniel 2:27-28). The "latter days" phrase in the Old Testament refers to the end-time of human history in which a group of events take place which culminate in the coming of the Messiah, Israel's full restoration, and the conversion of the nations. In the New Testament these events are linked with the return of Jesus Christ.[11] The first Old Testament figure to use the "latter days" idea was Jacob who before his death delivered to his sons the following prophetic message: "Gather yourselves together that I may tell you that which shall befall you in the latter days . . . The scepter shall not depart from Judah, nor the ruler's staff from between his feet, until Shiloh come, and unto him shall the obedience of the peoples be" (Genesis 49:1, 10). The Targum, and Rashi, the great medieval Jewish Biblical commentator, interpret the word Shiloh as referring to the Messiah. Additional passages in the Old Testament in which the phrase "latter days" occurs are as follows: Numbers 24:14; Isaiah 2:2; Jeremiah 23:20; 30:24; 48:47; 49:39; Ezekiel 38:16; Hosea 3:5; Micah 4:1-4; Daniel 10:14.

There was a danger that the Babylonian exiles might identify the termination of the Babylonian exile with the beginning of the national restoration of Israel as foretold in the prophetic writings. In the revelation granted to Daniel as recorded in the 9th chapter of Daniel he was expressly informed that the end of the Babylonian exile will not inaugurate Israel's full restoration (Daniel 9:1-24). In the message of Nebuchadnezzar's vision we have the first intimation in the book of Daniel of this fact. The "latter days" period, or the end of the Times of the Gentiles, was not to be ushered in with the fall of the Babylonian empire, but after the succession of world empires—identified in the image of Nebuchadnezzar's vision by the gold, silver, brass, iron, and iron mixed with clay—had run its full course.

5. THE UNIVERSAL AND JEWISH PHASE OF THE TIMES OF THE GENTILES.

If we are to know what exactly the Bible teaches concerning the Times of the Gentiles, it is imperative that we should realize that the phrase "Times of the Gentiles" or "Times of the Nations" in the Bible does not allude to world history in general or Gentile history as such, but to a succession of empires or political systems, exerting a world-dominating influence. The metallic image of Nebuchadnezzar's vision is a symbolic representation of the entire period of history which in the Bible goes under the name of the Times of the Gentiles. The first attempt to set up such a world empire is described and interpreted in the Bible in the account of the Tower of Babel event in Genesis 11. The last of these world orders is represented by the feet and toes of the image of Nebuchadnezzar's vision.

Lacking natural barriers, Mesopotamia was exposed to frequent invasions. To assure the safety of this area it was inevitable that in Mesopotamia—the cradle of recorded human history—a movement for world unification through conquest should be initiated. This policy was pursued successively by the Sumerians, Accadians, Amorites, Assyrians and Chaldeans. In the reign of Nebuchadnezzar the Chaldean this ancient Mesopotamian dream of world unification achieved its fullest realization. Nebuchadnezzar was therefore justly identified by Daniel with the head of the image. With the fall of Nebuchadnezzar's dynasty the Mesopotamian—or first—period of the Times of the Gentiles came to an end and was followed by the second period initiated by Medo-Persia, identified by the silver in the image of Nebuchadnezzar's dream.

When in his interpretation of Nebuchadnezzar's vision of the human image Daniel describes the second world empire as inferior to Nebuchadnezzar's empire, he uses the word inferior in the sense that silver, representing the second empire, is inferior in quality as compared with gold, or in the sense of being inferior in location, since the breast and arms representing the second empire would be inferior with relation to the head in a human image in the standing position.

The destruction of the First Jewish Commonwealth by Babylon did not mark the beginning of Gentile supremacy. The Gentile world was supreme long before the destruction of ancient Israel by Babylon. Within seventy years the Babylonian exiles returned and rebuilt the Jewish State. From then on Palestine was in Jewish hands for some five hundred years, even though during most of this period the Jews of Palestine paid allegiance to some outside Gentile power. The "trodding" down of Jerusalem to which Christ referred did not begin until the destruction of Palestine by Rome.

And yet the Jewish phase did begin with the destruction of Jerusalem by Babylon. The reason for this was that this destruction of Jerusalem marked the end of the human line of the Davidic dynasty. From the Biblical standpoint there can be no full and real national restoration of Israel without a simultaneous restoration of the Davidic dynasty. For in accordance with God's promise to David his dynasty was to rule over Israel forever (2 Samuel 7:16). On the eve of the Babylonian exile Ezekiel made the following announcement to Zedekiah, the last Judaean king of the Davidic dynasty:

"And you, O unhallowed wicked one, prince of Israel, whose day has come, the time of your final punishment. Thus says the Lord God: Remove the mitre, and take off the crown; things shall not remain as they are; exalt that which is low, and abase that which is high. A ruin, ruin, ruin I will make it. There shall not be even a trace of it until he comes whose right it is; and to whom I will give it" (Ezekiel 21: 25-27; 21: 30-32 Heb.). Commenting on this passage in the Soncino edition of Ezekiel, Rabbi Fisch states that this passage links the ultimate restoration with the advent of the Messiah.

Thus the Jewish phase of the Times of the Gentiles had its beginning in the fall of the Davidic dynasty; while both the Jewish and the universal phase of the Times of the Gentiles will end with the coming of the Messiah—who on His human side must be of the lineage of David—to restore the Davidic dynasty (Acts 15: 12-18).

6. DIVINE JUDGMENT ON THE TIMES OF THE GENTILES.

The stone which struck the feet of Nebuchadnezzar's image was aimed at the destruction of not merely the feet but of the entire image. "As you looked, a stone was cut out by no human hand, and it smote the image on its feet of iron and clay, and broke them in pieces. Then the iron, the clay, the brass, the silver, the gold, all together were broken in pieces, and became like the chaff of the summer threshing floors; and the wind carried them away, so that not a trace of them could be found" (Daniel 2:34-35). The reason for the destruction of the entire image is that the Bible views the Times of the Gentiles as a continuous period of history, inspired by the same ideal of bringing about world unification based on the principle of humanism and secularism. Hence the Divine judgment at the final stage of the Times of the Gentiles will be a judgment on the whole historical era of the Times of the Gentiles.

That the establishment of God's Kingdom on earth will be preceded by a universal judgment is the clear teaching of the Bible.[12] But the Biblical writers see God's Hand in all of human history. According to them history is under the constant judgment of God. But even as human sinfulness is cumulative in character and will reach the lowest depth of degradation at the time of the End, so are God's judgments also cumulative and will culminate in the great judgment at the end of history. On that day all nations, including Israel, will come under God's judgment.

The following passages describe the judgments upon Israel.

"The word that came to Jeremiah from the LORD. 'Thus says the LORD, the God of Israel: Write in a book all the words that I have spoken to you. For behold, days are coming, says the LORD, when I will restore the fortunes of my people, Israel and Judah, says the LORD, and I will bring them back to the land which I gave to their fathers, and they shall take possession of it.'

But after they will have returned to the Land, and before their final restoration, they will experience great sufferings.

'Thus says the LORD: We have heard a cry of panic, of terror, and no peace. Ask now, and see, can a man bear a child? Why then do I see every man with his hands on his loins like a woman in labor? Why has every face turned pale? Alas! that day is so great there is none like it; it is a time of distress for Jacob; yet he shall be saved out of it.'

And it shall come to pass in that day, says the LORD of hosts, that I will break the yoke from off their neck, and I will burst their bonds, and strangers shall no more make servants of them. But they shall serve the LORD their God and David their king, whom I will raise up for them" (Jeremiah 30: 1-3, 5-9).

That the mention of David has reference to the Messiah, David's descendant, may be seen from the following statement by the same prophet Jeremiah.

"Behold, the days are coming, says the LORD, when I will raise up for David a righteous Branch, and he shall reign as king and deal wisely, and shall execute justice and righteousness in the land. In his days Judah will be saved, and Israel will dwell securely; and this is his name by which he will be called: Jehovah our righteousness" (Jeremiah 23: 5-6).

"Behold, a day of the LORD is coming when the spoil taken from you will be divided in the midst of you. For I will gather all the nations against Jerusalem to battle, and the city shall be taken and the houses plundered and the women ravished; half of the city shall go into exile, but the rest of the people shall not be cut off from the city. Then the LORD will go forth and fight against those nations as when he fought in the day of battle. On that day his feet shall stand on the Mount of Olives which lies before Jerusalem on the east. . . And the LORD will become King over all the earth. . . (Zechariah 14: 1-4, 9). The Jewish Targum interprets the words "as when he fought on the day of battle" as referring to the calamity which overtook the Egyptians at the Red Sea as recorded in the book of Exodus.

The above text is a mere expansion of the description of the same event in the twelfth chapter of Zechariah. A multitude of nations invade the Land of Israel. But Israel is saved by the sudden appearance of her Messiah whom she had pierced in the long ago. In the fourteenth chapter additional features of this same event are furnished, and we are informed that Messiah will appear from the direction of Mount of Olives.

There is a multitude of Bible passages concerning the judgments on the nations in the closing stage of world history. The following by the prophet Joel is a vivid description of this event.

"And I will give portents in the heavens and on the earth, blood and fire and columns of smoke. The sun shall be turned to darkness, and the moon to blood, before the great and terrible day of the LORD comes. . .

For behold, in those days and at that time, when I restore the fortunes of Judah and Jerusalem, I will gather all the nations and bring them down to the valley of Jehoshafat, and I will enter into judgment with them there, on account of my people and my heritage Israel, because they have scattered them among the nations, and have divided up my land. . . Proclaim this among the nations: Prepare war, stir up the mighty men; let all the men of war draw near, let them come up. Beat your plowshares into swords, and your pruning hooks into spears; let [even] the weak say, 'I am a warrior' . . . Put in the sickle, for the harvest is ripe. Go in, tread, for the wine press is full. The vats overflow, for their wickedness is great.

Multitudes, multitudes, in the valley of decision! For the day of the LORD is near in the valley of decision. The sun and the moon are darkened, and the stars withdraw their shining. And the LORD roars from Zion, and utters his voice from Jerusalem, and the heavens and the earth shake. But the LORD is a refuge to his people, a stronghold to the people of Israel" (Joel 2: 30-31; 3: 1-2, 9-10, 13-16; 3: 3-4; 4: 1-2, 9-10, 13-16 Heb.).

That the final restoration of Israel will be preceded by a time of unprecedented trouble in the world is also implied by Jesus Christ. His declaration that Jerusalem will remain under Gentile domination until the Times of the Gentiles will be completed is followed immediately by a description of a worldwide distress.

"And there will be signs in the sun and moon and stars, and upon the earth distress of nations in perplexity at the roaring of the sea and the waves. Men fainting with fear and with foreboding of what is coming on the world; for the powers of the heavens will be shaken. And then they will see the Son of Man[13] coming in a cloud with power and great glory" (Luke 21: 25-27).

Notes to Chapter 13

[1] General S. L. A. Marshall, *The Swift Sword*, The Historical Record of Israel's Victory, June 1967, p. 131. Copyright 1967 by the American Heritage Publishing Co., Inc. and United Press International. Used by permission.

[2] E. A. Speiser, *Genesis, The Anchor Bible* (Doubleday & Company, Inc.: Garden City, New York, 1964), p. 67.

[3] Ibid., p. 64.

[4] The area where the Tower of Babel event is reported to have taken place.

[5] Cronos, the father of Zeus of Greek mythology. The Romans identified Zeus with Jupiter.

[6] Aidos—personification of shame generated in the individual's conscience. Nemesis—personification of retributive justice.

[7] Hesiod, *Works and Days;* English translation by Hugh G. Evelyn-White (S. P. Putnam's Sons: New York, 1926), pp. 11-17. Used by permission.

8 Karl Lowith, *Meaning In History* (The University of Chicago Press: Chicago, 1955), p. 4. Used by permission.

9 Eberhard Schrader's Keilinschriftliche Bibliothek, vol. 4, p. 188; see, Charles Boutflower, *In And Around The Book Of Daniel* (Zondervan Publishing House: Grand Rapids, Michigan, 1963), pp. 41-43.

10 Charles Boutflower, Op. Cit., pp. 46-49.

11 Acts 15: 12-18; Romans 11: 15, 25-27.

12 See, Arthur W. Kac, *The Rebirth Of The State Of Israel: Is It Of God Or Of Men?*, part one, chapter 2.

13 *"Son of Man"*—a Messianic title which Jesus Christ frequently used, and which identifies Him with the Messianic Person in Daniel 7:13.

CHAPTER 14

ARE WE LIVING IN THE LAST PHASE OF THE TIMES OF THE GENTILES?

A. The Daniel Prophecies

I. THE DRIVE FOR WORLD UNION

II. WEAKNESS IN THE MIDST OF STRENGTH

III. A CIVILIZATION WITHOUT A COHESIVE PRINCIPLE

1. The Intellectual Sphere
2. The Social Sphere
3. Concluding Observations

CHAPTER 14

ARE WE LIVING IN THE LAST PHASE OF THE TIMES OF THE GENTILES?

A. The Daniel Prophecies

When the old part of the city of Jerusalem along with the other regions of the Biblical Promised Land passed under Jewish rule as a result of the June 1967 war, many Christians began to wonder whether the world is standing on the threshold of the end-time of history, in accordance with Christ's statement that "Jerusalem shall be trodden down by the Gentiles, until the Times of the Gentiles are fulfilled." We will seek to answer this question chiefly on the basis of the writings of Daniel and the Olivet Prophecy.

I. THE DRIVE FOR WORLD UNION

We saw in the preceding chapter that the metallic image of Nebuchadnezzar's vision was interpreted by Daniel as a representation of a succession of several world empires. The first of these empires was Babylon. "You", Daniel said to Nebuchadnezzar, "are the head of gold" (Daniel 2:38). Not Nebuchadnezzar himself, but Babylon is meant. In Nebuchadnezzar's Babylon the Mesopotamian drive for unification of the ancient world begun in the dim and distant past was crowned with its greatest success. In less than twenty-five years after Nebuchadnezzar's death Mesopotamian world supremacy came to an end.

The silver in the metallic image referred to Medo-Persia. In a vision granted to Daniel on another occasion he saw a ram, representing Persia, gain world power (Daniel 8:1, 3-4, 20). This predictive element of the vision was fulfilled in Daniel's lifetime (Daniel 5:30).

The third world power, symbolized in the metallic image by the brass, is also identified for us in the book of Daniel. In the same vision mentioned above, Daniel saw a he-goat strike down the ram. The he-goat, we are told in the same chapter, represents Greece, i.e., the Macedonian-Greek empire of Alexander the Great (Daniel 8:5-8, 21-22).

218

The identity of the fourth kingdom, indicated by the iron, is not disclosed in Daniel's writings. But from history we know that after a certain lapse of time following the dismemberment of Alexander's empire Rome moved up to the forefront of world history. Much of what Daniel has said concerning the fourth kingdom is a fit description of the Roman State. It was to be "strong as iron"; in Daniel's day iron was the last word in physical power at man's disposal. "Like iron which crushes, it shall break and crush all these"— is a true description of the severity with which Rome put down all resistance to her rule. The Roman empire was larger than any of the preceding three world empires. She occupied a vast area of some 2,000 miles in width, and over 3,000 miles in length, embracing parts of Asia, Africa and Europe. In the Roman empire the ancient world's dream of world union and world peace found its greatest fulfillment.

During the period of history which goes under the name of the Times of the Gentiles all three divisions of mankind which branched off from Noah's descendants have had an opportunity to try their hand at world government. The Hamitic Sumerians of Mesopotamia were the first group; they were followed by the Semites; then came the Japhethites—the third and last division. Japhethic world rule began with Persia, designated by the silver in Nebuchadnezzar's metallic image, and has continued to this day. Persia is the Asiatic branch of the Indo-European, or Aryan, portion of mankind. The third empire of Alexander the Great, and the fourth, or Roman, were also Japhethic states. In the beginning of the twentieth century three continents were peopled with Europeans while the remaining two—Asia and Africa—were in a large measure under European control. America and Russia, the two most powerful nations in the world of today, are Japhethic nations.

The metallic image of Nebuchadnezzar is a graphic representation of the Times of the Gentiles. The gold, silver, brass, iron, and iron plus clay symbolize the five divisions of the Times of the Gentiles: The Mesopotamian, the Persian, the Greek, the Roman, and the fifth—or last—period designated by the iron plus clay of the feet and toes of the metallic image. The burden of the message of the metallic image in the second chapter of Daniel is centered on the feet and toes, i.e., on the last stage of the Times of the Gentiles. "There is a God in heaven who reveals mysteries, and he has made known to King Nebuchadnezzar what will be in the latter days"

(Daniel 2:28). This is why more is said about the feet—and—toes period than about any of the preceding periods.

It is this fifth period of the history of the Times of the Gentiles which shall be shattered by Divine instrumentality. The fourth, or Roman, empire was not struck down by direct Divine intervention. Its western part was defeated in the fifth century by the invading Germanic tribes from the north; while the eastern portion was overcome a thousand years later by the Turks. The last stage of the history of the Times of the Gentiles, identified by the feet and toes of Nebuchadnezzar's metallic image, comes to a catastrophic end by God's intervening power. "And as you [Nebuchadnezzar] looked, a stone was cut out by no human hand, and it smote the image on its feet of iron and clay, and broke them in pieces" (Daniel 2:34). This is an event which is yet to take place.

During each of the first four divisions of the Times of the Gentiles the civilized and known world of that day had been unified under the leadership of the dominating world power of that day. It is therefore reasonable to assume that in the last period of the Times of the Gentiles the world will also become united under the direction of a certain world power. As a matter of fact, Western civilization has been long at work preparing the modern world for world union. "Since about A.D. 1500", the historian Toynbee declares, "mankind has been gathered into a single world-wide society. . . . The Western handiwork that has made this union possible has not been carried out with open eyes, like David's unselfish labors for the benefit of Solomon; it has been performed in heedless ignorance of its purpose, like the labors of the animalculae that build a coral reef up from the bottom of the sea till at length an atoll rises above the waves. But our Western-built scaffolding is made of less durable materials than that. The most obvious ingredient in it is technology, and man cannot live by technology alone. In the fullness of time, when the ecumenical house of many mansions stands firmly on its own foundations and the temporary Western technological scaffolding falls away—as I have no doubt that it will—I believe it will become manifest that the foundations are firm at last because they have been carried down to the bedrock of religion." [1]

In another place Toynbee declares that Western civilization "is the only expansion of a civilization to date that has been literally world-wide in the sense of extending over the whole habitable portion of the earth's surface; and owing to the 'conquest of space and time' by modern mechanical means, the spread of the network of Western material civilization has brought the different parts of the world into far closer physical contact than ever before."[2] Western civilization which has brought about this cultural unification of the world is the outgrowth of Graeco-Roman civilization of the fourth empire of Nebuchadnezzar's metallic image, even as the feet and toes are extensions of its legs.

But a mere cultural unification of the world will not suffice. There is a growing conviction in the world today that nothing short of a political union of the world under one world government is needed if the world is to escape nuclear destruction and to be saved from the chaotic and political impasse in which we find ourselves today.[3]

According to Biblical teachings mankind will at the end of the Times of the Gentiles make a last mighty effort to bring about world unification, and at this time it will succeed, though for a short time only. The head of this world government is referred to as the beast (Daniel 7, Revelation 13). It will be a government led and inspired by the Evil one as never before in the history of the world. "And they worshipped the dragon [i.e., Satan] because he gave his authority unto the beast; and they worshipped the beast, saying, Who is like unto the beast? And who is able to make war with him? And there was given unto him a mouth, speaking great things and blasphemies; and there was given to him authority to continue forty and two months. And he opened his mouth for blasphemies against God, to blaspheme his name, and his tabernacle, even them that dwell in heaven. And it was given unto him [authority] to make war with the saints, and to overcome them: and there was given to him authority over every tribe, and people and tongue and nation" (Revelation 13: 4-7).

The above is a description of the government of a unified world, holding in its mighty grip the nations of the earth, presided over by a blasphemous beastly tyrant, under the inspiration of Satan himself. But his reign will last only three and a half years. After this short period of time this human world government will be destroyed by God's intervention, and the world will become unified indeed, but under God's rule. Under the leadership of the Messiah the kingdoms of this earth will become transformed into the Kingdom of God (Revelation 11:15).

II. WEAKNESS IN THE MIDST OF STRENGTH

There are two other phenomena which according to Daniel are to distinguish the final period of the Times of the Gentiles. These two are: Weakness in the midst of strength, and a civilization without a cohesive principle. At no time in human history have these two features been characteristic of the life of the whole world as much as they are today.

The first of these two conditions is set forth in the following passage: "And as the toes of the feet were partly iron and partly clay, so the kingdom shall be partly strong and partly brittle" (Daniel 2:42). Nuclear science has placed at man's disposal incredibly-vast sources of power. He can now crumble whole mountains and sink entire islands. At the same time man has displayed a remarkable inability to solve human problems on a national or international level. The bloody clashes between Russia and China, these two communist giants, the invasion of communist Czechoslovakia by Russia, the growing alienation between Russia and her European satellites and communist parties of other lands, the rising demand among the intellectuals in many communist countries for democratization of the communist system—these developments prove that not all is well in the world of communism.

Similar conditions exist in neutralist and western countries. America has enough nuclear power to obliterate a whole continent in a matter of minutes. And yet the American Government has not been able to prevent minority groups from burning down whole neighborhoods, and criminals from making American cities unsafe for peaceful citizens. "The sense of impotence—of being unable to affect events —is even more acute in facing problems of foreign policy", declares Governor Rockefeller.[4] There was a time, when America was not nearly as powerful as she is now, but an American passport provided an American citizen traveling abroad with all the protection he needed. Now such a passport is hardly any protection at all. Any country, however insignificant, can assume a most insulting attitude towards America and not even create a serious diplomatic incident.

The Western-built scaffolding of world unification, Toynbee declares, is not made of very durable materials. It certainly is not. It is a mixture of extreme strength and extreme weakness. "And as the toes of the feet were partly iron and partly clay, so the kingdom [i.e. the last stage of the Times of the Gentiles] shall be partly strong and partly brittle".

III. A CIVILIZATION WITHOUT A COHESIVE PRINCIPLE

1. THE INTELLECTUAL SPHERE

The second distinguishing feature of the end of the Times of the Gentiles, as symbolized by the feet and toes of the prophecy of Daniel 2, is the lack of a cohesive principle. This must result in the fragmentation of human society and human life. "As you saw the iron mixed with miry clay, so they will mix with one another in marriage, but they will not hold together, just as iron does not mix with clay" (Daniel 2:43).

In one of the great works on the history of Western thought, in the beginning of the chapter on Christianity, the writer states that his analysis of the subject of Christianity will be from the point of view of an outsider. The following is a passage from that chapter. "No one in the Western world can wholly escape the influence of Christianity. Even those who set themselves against what they consider the Christian religion are unavoidably affected by what they oppose. For Christianity has colored the thinking and feeling of nearly seventy generations of Western men and women. Through the work of missionaries it has in the last few centuries followed expanding Western society throughout the world. As a way of life, Christianity in the two thousand years of its existence seemed capable of extraordinary range and variety. In one form or another it has manifested itself throughout the activity of Western man. . .

Christianity is a revealed religion. Its God is perfect, above such human categories as time and space, above the historical process. But Christianity is also a religion much concerned with human conduct on this earth, with its mission in historical time. . . To an observer from outside, Christianity has displayed great ingenuity and adaptability in adjusting itself to the natural world without losing grip on the concept of the supernatural world."[5]

Biblical Christianity has a remarkably well-integrated world-and-life view. It teaches that man is born with a disposition towards evil; that through faith in the atoning death and resurrection of Jesus Christ, through prayer and the study of the Scriptures, human nature can be renewed, man is enabled to live a holy and righteous life, and he gains the assurance of eternal life. Biblical Christianity rejected the pagan concept of history as a recurrence of cycles. In its stead it offered to Western man the Biblical view of history having as its purpose the redemption of man, and as its goal the establishment of the Kingdom of God on earth at the consummation of history as we know it.

Christianity made its appearance in the pagan world when Graeco-Roman civilization had already for several centuries been in a process of decadence. If not for Christianity the fall of the Roman empire in the West would have been a catastrophe. Christianity blunted the violence and tamed the savagery of the Germanic peoples from the north. It saved for posterity what was best in the Graeco-Roman heritage. For centuries it exerted a civilizing effect on the semi-barbarian peoples of Europe. It gave to these peoples a faith to live by. It founded hospitals for the care of the sick, and schools for the training of the young. It promoted the advancement of the social, legal, and political position of the woman. It surrounded married life with a halo of sacredness. It afforded protection to the stranger and help to the unfortunate. "Almost every code in Europe, Charlemagne's capitularies, the laws of the Northern tribes, the Sachsenspiegel, the Anglo-Saxon laws and others, contain touching reference to the Scriptural commands in regard to the stranger and 'far-comer' and enforce the duties of hospitality and mercy."[6]

The influence of the Gospel made itself felt also in man's attitude to the slave. It is true that other factors worked in the direction of the abolition of slavery, such as political and economic considerations. But the Gospel of Christ exercised a powerful influence in this area. As the message of the Bible was circulated among the people, they became imbued with a sense of their human dignity. The Bible produced an atmosphere favoring the gradual change from slavery to serfdom and from serfdom to total freedom.

"It scarcely need be said that all the countless institutions of human compassion and love, which attempted throughout Europe to relieve the horrible misery following the overthrow of the Roman empire, came from Christ. The blessed associations of mercy, the hospitals, asylums, refuges, schools, and centers of charity, which everywhere radiated human mercy and goodwill; the lives of beneficence to which so many noble souls devoted themselves; the innumerable actions of benevolence, philanthrophy, and heroic self-sacrifice which light up these dark ages—these are all from the 'Son of Man'."[7]

Repudiation of Biblical Christianity by Western man has been a gradual process. Some historians claim to find in the Middle Ages the roots of modern secularism. Humanism, also called the Renaissance, which sprang up in the Middle Ages, certainly reveals the beginnings of the modern secular attitude. It exhibited a state of mind which culminated in the rejection of Christianity by many of the foremost representatives of the so-called Enlightenment of the eighteenth century. Since then Western man has become increasingly alienated from the Biblical world-and-life view. Western civilization, which today is the civilization of the world, has returned to the paganism of Graeco-Roman civilization. "I would ask you to agree with me," says Toynbee, "that the tide of Christianity has been ebbing and that our post-Christian Western secular civilization that has emerged is a civilization of the same order as the pre-Christian Graeco-Roman civilization."[8]

Today the inheritance of Biblical Christianity in the West is all but squandered. "Call it a return to paganism or what one will, the fact remains that in the West for three centuries Christian influences upon society, the state and culture have decreased, while secular influences have increased to dominating proportions. In the eighteenth century the upper classes of society broke with the Christian beliefs, and the unity of Western Christendom vanished. . . For two generations influential philosophers in the once-Christian West have ceased to ask, 'Who is God?', 'What is the purpose of history and of the universe?', 'How shall we define man's dignity?', 'What are the permanent aspects of truth and morality?', but instead have been asking, 'Is there a God?', 'Does purpose exist in history and the universe?', 'Is man essentially unique?', and 'Have reason and goodness any objective significance?' "[9]

This return of Western civilization to the secularism of its Graeco-Roman origins gave birth to what is called the Age of Anxiety by the author of another outstanding work on the intellectual history of the West. By "anxiety" this author means "a state of mind combining loneliness of spirit with a sense of loss of control. . . . In this circumstance the individual simply drifts, anxiously awaiting the shock of events which will determine his tomorrow." In the next sentence the author of that work gives the source of Western man's anxiety: "Having kicked over, first Christianity, and then the bourgeois code, [Western man] lives without benefit of a standard of values to which these events might be referred."[10]

The following are some of the manifestations of our present "Age of Anxiety."

"No one knows towards what center human beings are going to gravitate in the near future, and hence the life of the world has become scandalously provisional."—Ortega y Gasset.[11]

". . . Our modern theory of man lost its intellectual center. We acquired instead a complete anarchy of thought. Even in the former times to be sure there was great discrepancy of opinions and theories relating to this problem [of the nature of man]. But there remained at least a general orientation, a frame of reference, to which all individual differences might be referred. . . The real crisis of this problem manifested itself when such a central power capable of directing all individual efforts ceased to exist. . . Theologians, scientists, politicians, sociologists, biologists, phychologists, ethnologists, economists—all approached the problem from their own viewpoints. To combine or unify all these particular aspects and perspectives was impossible. And even within the special fields there was no generally accepted scientific principle. . . That this antagonism of ideas is not merely a grave theoretical problem but an imminent threat to the whole extent of our ethical and cultural way of life admits of no doubt."—Ernst Cassirer.[12]

"Lord of all things, [man] is not lord of himself. He feels lost amid his own abundance. With more means at his disposal, more knowledge, more technique than ever, it turns out that the world today goes the same way as the worst of worlds that have been; it simply drifts. Hence the strange combination of a sense of power and a sense of insecurity which has taken up its abode in the soul of modern man."—Ortega y Gasset.[13]

"Perhaps there has never been a generation so completely rootless, so completely cut off from the intellectual traditions of the race, than the one that has grown up in the 1930's and 1940's." Franklin Le Van Baumer.[14]

One of the distinctive social features of our time is the wide gap separating the generations. This phenomenon is no less true of communist countries than of the West. Though the people of communist Russia have spent the greater part of their lives under communism, there is ample proof that, except for a tiny segment, most of them pay no more than lip service to Marxist philosophy. In spite of all the efforts of the State to indoctrinate them with the tenets of communism, the young intellectuals in communist Russia are yearning for the day when they will be in a position to articulate their thoughts freely, to exchange their ideas with people from non-communist countries, and be permitted to live their lives without the coercive supervision of the State.

In the matter of educating the young people the liberal, open society of the West occupies in certain respects a position which is the very opposite from that of the closed society of communism. In communist lands the young people are taught that everything which is non-communist is bad, and anything which serves to promote Marxist ideology is good. In the West young people are provided with no helpful guidelines. They are left to decide for themselves what is good and what is bad and they are free to choose the one, the other, or neither.

The rationale back of this Western attitude is the desire to be as thoroughly objective as possible and to avoid giving the impression of seeking to exert an undue influence on others. In his discussion of the crisis facing the modern university Moberly declares that this "so-called academic objectivity is a fraud; and the fraud is none the less disastrous and reprehensible because its perpetrators are commonly also its victims and deceive themselves as successfully as they deceive others . . ."[15] "Broadly speaking, the university today is not asking the really fundamental questions. In particular there has been something like a taboo on the treatment of contentious issues of politics and religion. . . [The modern university] abjures any contribution to answering the master-question—How shall a man live? . . . A university can train a student to be a chemist or a linguist. But what he should do with his chemistry or languages when he has acquired them, whether and why injustice and cruelty and fraud are bad and their opposites are good, whether faith in God is a snare and a delusion or is the only basis on which human life can be lived without disaster—all these things the student must find out for himself as best as he may, for a university education can do nothing to help him. If you want a bomb, the chemistry department will teach you how to make it; if you want a cathedral, the department of architecture will teach you how to build it; if you want a healthy body, the department of physiology and medicine will teach you how to tend it. But when you ask whether and why you should want bombs or cathedrals or healthy bodies, the university, on this view, must be content to be dumb and impotent. . . Our predicament then is this: Most students go through our universities without ever having been forced to exercise their minds on the issues which are really momentous."[16] Receiving no helpful guidance from the university the students take their questions to other places. It is thus that they fall an easy prey to totalitarian propaganda.

Nathan M. Pusey, president of Harvard University, once said that "what every young person seeks in college, from liberal education—whether or not he has articulated this—is self-discovery. What he wants most to know is what it means to be a human being, what is expected of him as such, what the world is, and what are the options in it that lie before him, and how he is to get on with others. In short, the really burning question that faces someone trying to live through his mind is what to do with his life? What such a person wants—what we all want is a meaning that becomes a motivating force in our lives. And when we ask this question, whether we are conscious of it or not, we have begun to think religiously and have begun to ask of God."[17]

But that students at the modern university do not achieve this self-discovery and do not find the motivating force for their lives is seen from the following words by one of the graduating class at Yale University. "Most of us", he said, "graduate unsure of life's calling. Yet Yale, which has determined the kind of life we seek, has imposed substantial barriers in the way of that life's accomplishment. The university has demonstrated how the daily existence of most Americans can be criticized, even ridiculed, without prescribing the formula for a useful, rewarding life—and without showing how one can reconcile himself to a ridiculous world."[18]

Commenting on the behavior of the students of the radical left who have recently staged riots at American universities, professor George F. Kennan refers to them as "rebels without a program". "I know", he says, "that behind all the extremisms—all the philosophical errors, all the egocentricities and all the oddities of dress and deportment—we have to do here with troubled and often pathetically appealing people, acting, however wisely or unwisely, out of sincerity and idealism, out of the unwillingness to accept a meaningless life and a purposeless society."[19]

In a speech before the members of the American Law Institute, Erwin N. Griswold, Solicitor General of the United States, and a former dean of the Harvard Law School, manifested a concern at the mass lawlessness at every level of American society. Alluding to student riots he said: "These young people may be in the process of destroying our centers of higher education, and that would be a worse national calamity in the long run than anything that has happened to us."[20] In the early 1930's when this writer had attended college he listened to casual remarks made by university professors in the lecture halls which had a destructive effect on the little religion which many of the students had brought with them from home. Many of our greatest universities have been founded, and some of them endowed, by Christians who were moved by a desire to strengthen the religious life and to promote true learning in America. For about a generation these same universities, through their dedication to the secularist concept of life, have been engaged, directly or indirectly, in undermining the religious foundation of America. One must wonder whether it is not the universities, rather than the students, which are destroying our centers of higher education. "The contemporary uneasiness—especially of our young generation—reflects rebellion against the emptiness of a life which knows only 'practical' problems and material goods and seems to lack in deeper purpose. . . The deepest problem before America, then, is moral or psychological. . . Decades of 'debunking' and materialism have left the young generation without adequate moral support in the face of the challenges of a revolutionary age. . . The contemporary discontent proves among other things that man cannot live by economics alone: he needs quality and purpose in addition to material well-being; he needs significance and meaning beyond physical comfort."—Governor Nelson A. Rockefeller.[21]

2. THE SOCIAL SPHERE

Never before in history has there been such a widespread trend as there is in these days to create a homogeneous human society. In the United Nations there is a coming together of groups of nations which economically and socially stand centuries behind others; of states which rule their peoples with blood and iron alongside other states whose citizens enjoy the utmost in civil and political freedom; of countries which live in peace with their neighbors, and others which pursue a policy of subverting the governments of other countries, both near and far. Is there any wonder that the United Nations organization has consistently displayed a distressing impotence in solving world problems? "Disunited Nations" would have been a more suitable name for this international agency.

The two dominating States in the world today are the United States of America and Soviet Russia. One of the chief aims of the communist revolution in Russia was the formation of a classless society. It destroyed the upper class of Tzarist Russia and eliminated the Kulak-type of peasants. Originally a "Kulak" denoted a peasant of some means. Under Stalin the term Kulak was interpreted to include every peasant who owned more than two cows, and any peasant who was seeking to retain his own parcel of land.[22]

In his determination to collectivize Russian agriculture Stalin ordered in December 1929 the liquidation of the Kulaks as a class. No less than a million families numbering about five million people were deprived of their property, herded into cattle cars and unloaded in the deserts of Central Asia or the lumber regions of the frozen North. Thousands of these people never reached their destination, having succumbed on the way from starvation, disease, and exposure. Many others died in the wilderness of their dispersion.[23]

While forced into submission, yet the Russian peasant never became reconciled to the collective type of farming. The Red Army had to be called out frequently to put down peasant uprisings. Hundreds of officials charged with enforcing collectivization were murdered. Some peasants set fire to their homes and barns, others uprooted fruit trees. Slaughtering of animals became a serious form of sabotage. In 1932, which marked the end of the First Five Year Plan, Soviet Russia had lost half of its cattle and horses, two-fifths of its hogs, and two-thirds of its sheep and goats. In 1953 Khrushchev is said to have complained that there were about nine million fewer cows in Russia than in 1928 when collectivization of Russian farming had begun.[24]

In 1932 about 80 per cent of Russia's farmland had been changed into collective farming. In that year the peasants embarked on another kind of sabotage: they planted only enough to take care of their needs. When Stalin became aware of this he decided to teach the recalcitrant peasants a lesson. In the fall of that year army trucks were sent into the countryside, and they removed all the grain, the fruit, the eggs and vegetables, leaving the peasants to starve. The effect of these measures was a famine which caused the death of countless thousands of people in Russia. Cannibalism was resorted to in many of the stricken areas.[25]

After about 40 years of farm collectivization farm production in the Soviet Union is lower than in many of the major food producing countries. In fact, in some years Russia had to import food. In 1965, we are told, that while Russia cultivated 75 per cent more cropland and used four times more farm workers than the United States she nevertheless produced less than half as much grain as the United States.[26] The same agricultural shortcomings have plagued the other communist countries except Yugoslavia and Poland where permission issued to the peasants to return to private farming was attended by instantaneous rise in food production.[27]

What has become of the Soviet attempt to create a classless Russian society? The slogan of equality adopted by the French Revolution was aimed against the inequalities which stemmed from a system based on privilege and a highly stratified society. In the mass industrial society of today the old stratified social system became obsolete. "But a new kind of stratification has entered into every branch of administration and production. The need for technological and administrative elites declares itself at every level—in government, in industrial organization, on the factory floor, and on the farm—and is likely to increase with the increasing complexity of administrative and productive processes."[28]

In June 1931 when Lenin was dead and Trotsky had been banished into exile Stalin shocked the world by denouncing the doctrine of "levelling" of the classes. He declared that every industry, enterprise, or workshop has its leading groups.[29]

In Soviet Russia today there is neither political, social or economic equality. The extremes of rich and poor, of privileged and underprivileged, are to be found there as in non-communist countries, if not more so.

One of the most important documents on the social system under communism is a book entitled *The New Class*. For writing this book and having it published in the West, Milovan Djilas landed in prison. Before writing this book he was Vice-President of communist Yugoslavia. The following excerpts from this book concern the new ruling class in communist countries.

"The new class may be said to be made up of those who have special privileges and economic preference because of the administrative monopoly they hold. . . The new class is interested in the proletariat and the poor only to the extent necessary for developing production and for maintaining in subjugation the most aggressive and rebellious social forces. The monopoly which the new class establishes in the name of the working class over the whole society is,

primarily, a monopoly over the working class itself. . . Former sons of
the working class are the most steadfast members of the new class. It
has always been the fate of slaves to provide for their masters the
most clever and gifted representatives. In this case a new exploiting
and governing class is born from the exploited class. . ."[30]

"Discrepancies between the pay of workers and party function-
aries are extreme." In communism, "he who grabs power grabs
privileges and indirectly grabs property. Consequently, in communism, power or politics as a profession is the ideal of those who have
the desire or the prospect of living as parasites at the expense of
others. . ."[31]

"More than anything else, the essential aspect of contemporary
communism is the new class of owners and exploiters. . . No other
class in history has been as cohesive and singleminded in defending
itself and in controlling that which it holds—collective and monopolistic ownership and totalitarian authority. . . The new class is as
exclusive as the aristocracy but without aristocracy's refinement and
proud chivalry. . ."[32]

"Property is legally considered social and national property. But,
in actuality, a single group manages it in its own interest. . . In
communism, power and ownership are almost always in the same
hands, but this fact is concealed under a legal guise. . . The formal
owner is the nation. In reality, because of monopolistic administration, only the narrowest stratum of administrators enjoys the rights
of ownership. . . While promising to abolish social differences, [the
new class] must always increase them by acquiring the products of
the nation's workshops and granting privileges to its adherents. . ."[33]

"This is a class whose power over men is the most complete known
to history. . . Having achieved industrialization, the new class can
now do nothing more than strengthen its brute force and pillage the
people."[34]

"Modern apartment houses for the new middle class stand on the
edges of foul slums in Soviet cities. Fine dachas or country vacation
houses are within view of wretched peasant hovels. . . While ordinary
mortals queue up for hours to obtain some of the everyday necessities, the new aristocrats shop at leisure in special stores stocked with
the best the country produces and imported goods. While top officials and managers draw hundreds of rubles a month—plus an array
of perquisites like chauffeured motorcars, choice apartments—millions

on the nether levels struggle to survive on the legal minimum of 45 rubles a month. In factories and institutions the dining rooms are socially graded: first-rate for the important people, third-rate for the workers... The best hospitals are reserved for 'the best people'."[35]

"The old Adam, in short, has prevailed over the new [communist] man. A new class, snobbish as well as arrogant, rules the roost, and below it are other classes, hoping and intriguing for the same comforts and advantages that have moved mortal man since the beginning of time. Only in the lowest depths, in penal camps and exile regions, among the lowest-grade [collective] workers and unskilled laborers, is there a certain equality, the kind Dostoyevsky talked of through one of the characters in his novel *The Possessed:* 'All are slaves and equal in their slavery... Slaves are bound to be equal.' "[36]

In the United States, the center of world democracy, we are witnessing another aspect of the contemporary movement for social equalization. For several years American cities have been in a turmoil over the drive for speedy integration of the Negro population in the life of the country. As one ponders over this situation one recalls to mind the Biblical statement about "visiting the iniquity of the fathers upon the children and the children's children, to the third and fourth generation" (Exodus 34:7). The American colonies could have prevented the use of slave labor; while the task of integrating the Negro people into the mainstream of American life might, for a number of reasons, have been much simpler had it been done soon after the abolition of slavery.

What the country failed to do in the course of a century, is expected to be accomplished in the space of months or several years at most. Then, also, instead of concentrating on improving Negro education to the point where Negroes could take their place in today's complex and computerized economy, much energy is being spent on the social side of integration.

There is much truth in Rockefeller's statement that "the key issue of race is not merely to legislate equality of opportunity: this is in many respects the easiest aspect. Nor is the solution limited to such necessities as jobs, housing, and education. Beyond all these, it must be possible for minority groups to gain a sense of belonging."[37]

However much the racial issue may be responsible for the present tension, for the increasing dislocation of neighborhoods, and for the widening racial rift, what is really wrong with America today is the individual's spiritual alienation. Man's estrangement from God deepens his estrangement from his fellow men.

3. CONCLUDING OBSERVATIONS

In their first attempt to create a world civilization men discovered that while they had an abundance of bitumen to hold the material ingredients of their civilization together, their secular humanism was not sufficient to keep the human element together, and their civilization fell apart. Living at the end of the Times of the Gentiles, we in these days are making the same discovery. We have brought together the various societies and cultures into one world society, living under one physical roof. But all our secular means to wed and weld together the various disparate elements of the present-day Tower of Babel world civilization are proving ineffective: *mankind is as splintered now as it ever has been.* This is an amazing fulfillment of the second feature of the closing phase of the Times of the Gentiles. "As you saw the iron mixed with miry clay, so they will mix with one another in marriage, but they will not hold together, just as iron does not mix with clay" (Daniel 2: 43).

As we approach the end-time of history, symbolized in Daniel, chapter 2, by the feet and toes of Nebuchadnezzar's human image, our world civilization will be marked by the extremes of strength and weakness, of world union and fragmentation of mankind, and in every respect—spiritually, morally, socially, politically and financially—it will stand on feet of crumbling clay. "And as the toes of the feet were partly iron and partly clay, so the kingdom shall be partly strong and partly brittle. As you saw the iron mixed with miry clay, so they will mix with one another in marriage, but they will not hold together, just as iron does not mix with clay" (Daniel 2: 42-43).

And yet there are many aspects in contemporary history—positive as well as negative—which are preparing the way for the establishment of God's universal kingdom on 'earth. As Jesus the Messiah came into the small Mediterranean world in the fullness of time (Galatians 4:4), so will He also come into the larger world of modern history in the fullness of time. Toynbee's words are germane to this subject and will therefore bear repeating: "The most obvious ingredient in it* is its technology, and man cannot live by technology alone.

---

* Present-day Western world civilization

In the fullness of time, when the ecumenical house of many mansions stands firmly on its own foundations and the temporary Western technological scaffolding falls away—as I have no doubt that it will—I believe it will become manifest that the foundations are firm at last because they have been carried down to the bedrock of religion."

Notes to Chapter 14

[1] Arnold Toynbee, *Civilization On Trial And The World And The West* (Oxford University Press: New York); Paperback Edition by Meridian Books, Inc., 1960, pp. 65, 86-7. Used by permission.

[2] Ibid., p. 141.

[3] Arthur W. Kac, *The Rebirth Of The State Of Israel: Is It Of God Or Of Men?* Part Three, Chapter 2.

[4] Nelson A. Rockefeller, *"Policy And The People"*, article in *Foreign Affairs* (New York), January 1968. Used by permission.

[5] Crane Brinton, *Ideas and Men:* The Story Of Western Thought, Second Edition (Prentice-Hall, Inc.: Englewood Cliffs, New Jersey, 1964), p. 105. Copyright by Prentice-Hall 1963; used by permission.

[6] Charles Loring Brace, *Gesta Christi* (A. C. Armstrong & Son: New York, 1885), p. 275.

[7] Ibid., p. 279.

[8] Arnold Toynbee, Op. Cit., p. 202.

[9] Carl F. H. Henry, *"The Christian-Pagan West,"* editorial in *Christianity Today* (Washington, D. C.), December 24, 1956. Used by permission of *Christianity Today*.

[10] Franklin Le Van Baumer, *Main Currents Of Western Thought* (Alfred A. Knopf: New York, 1967), pp. 587-8. Used by permission.

[11] Ortega y Gasset, *The Revolt Of The Masses* (W. W. Norton & Co., Inc.; New York, 1932), p. 195. Copyright 1932 by W. W. Norton & Co., Inc.; copyright renewed 1960; used by permission.

[12] Ernst Cassirer, *An Essay On Man* (Yale University Press: New Haven, Conn., 1944), pp. 21-2. Used by permission.

[13] Ortega y Gassett, Op. Cit., pp. 47-8.

[14] Franklin Le Van Baumer, Op. Cit., p. 594.

[15] Walter Moberly, *The Crisis In The University* (SCM Press, Ltd.: London, 1949), p. 59. Used by permission.

[16] Ibid., pp. 50-52, 70.

[17] Nathan M. Pusey, *"Religion's Role In Liberal Education"*, article in *Religion And Freedom Of Thought*, by Perry Miller, Robert L. Calhoun, Nathan M. Pusey, Reinhold Niebuhr (Doubleday & Company, Inc.: Garden City, N. Y., 1954), p. 51. Used by permission.

[18] *Yale News* (Yale University, New Haven Conn.), May 29, 1962. Used by permission.

[19] George F. Kennan, *"Rebels Without A Program"*, article in the *New York Times* Magazine (New York), January 21, 1968. Copyright 1968 by the New York Times Company. Used by permission.

[20] Quoted in *The Sun* (Baltimore, Md.), May 25, 1968.

[21] Nelson A. Rockefeller, Idem.

[22] Eugene Lyons, *Workers' Paradise Lost* (Funk & Wagnalls: New York, 1967); Paperback Edition by Paperback Library, Inc., New York, 1967, p. 219. Used by permission.

[23] Ibid., p. 220.

[24] Ibid., p. 221.

[25] Ibid., p. 222.

[26] Ibid., p. 212.

[27] Ibid., p. 209.

[28] E. H. Carr, *"A Historical Turning Point: Marx, Lenin, Stalin,"* article in *Revolutionary Russia,* edited by Richard Pipes (Harvard University Press: Cambridge, Mass., 1968), p. 291. Used by permission.

[29] Ibid.

[30] Milovan Djilas, *The New Class* (Frederick A. Praeger: New York, 1957), pp. 30, 42. Used by permission.

[31] Ibid., p. 46.

[32] Ibid., pp. 58-60.

[33] Ibid., pp. 65-6.

[34] Ibid., p. 69.

[35] Eugene Lyons, Op. Cit., pp. 74-5.

[36] Ibid., p. 82.

[37] Nelson A. Rockefeller, Idem.

CHAPTER 15

ARE WE LIVING IN THE LAST PHASE OF THE TIMES OF THE GENTILES?

B. *The Olivet Prophecy*

I. The Proclamation Of The Gospel

II. World-Wide Distress

1. Wars
2. Famine
    a. Overpopulation
    b. Man's Abuse Of The Earth
    c. "Cursed Is The Ground Because Of You."

III. The Liberation Of Palestine From Gentile Rule

IV. A Message Of Hope For A Time Of Trouble

1. The Hope Of Christ's Return Should Generate Faithfulness And Vigilance.
2. "When These Things Begin To Take Place, Look Up And Raise Your Heads, Because Your Redemption Is Drawing Near."

CHAPTER 15

ARE WE LIVING IN THE LAST PHASE OF THE TIMES OF THE GENTILES?

B. The Olivet Prophecy

Jesus Christ brought to a close His teaching ministry in the Jerusalem Temple with a statement implying the imminent destruction of the Temple (Matthew 23:29-39). Following these ominous words He and His small apostolic band left the Temple and proceeded in the direction of the Mount of Olives. On the way one of the apostles made some comment about the splendor and structural massiveness of the Temple. Christ's response was that notwithstanding all its glory and strength the Temple will become a heap of stones. When they all arrived at the foot of the Mount of Olives four of the apostles put to Him the following two questions: (1) When will the predicted destruction of Jerusalem take place; (2) What will be the sign of the end of the age and of His return to earth. The substance of Christ's reply to these two questions constitutes the Olivet prophecy (Matthew 24:1-51, 25:1-46; Mark 13:1-37; Luke 21:5-36).

The fact that the apostles placed the question about the destruction of Jerusalem alongside the question about Christ's return indicates that they viewed both these events as destined to take place simultaneously. There was then a real possibility that the followers of Jesus Christ living in the days of the destruction of Jerusalem by the Romans would have interpreted that event as signaling that the return of Jesus Christ was impending.

The purpose of the Olivet Prophecy was to prevent misinterpretations of world events by future generations of Christ's followers. To do this Jesus Christ unfolded before them something of the state of the world at the end of the age. He set down certain conditions which must exist in the closing period of the age prior to His return. The occurrence of these world conditions will enable the believers to discern the signs of the approaching Second Coming of Jesus Christ. A discussion of the development of certain of these conditions follows below.

238

I. THE PROCLAMATION OF THE GOSPEL

"And this gospel of the kingdom* will be preached throughout the whole world, as a testimony to all nations; and then the end** will come" (Matthew 24:14). There is no implication in these words that Jesus Christ expected His followers to convert the world before His return. As a matter of fact the New Testament teaches that at the end of the age there will be a falling away from the Messianic faith. The following are the words of Christ Himself: "Nevertheless, when the Son of Man comes, will he find faith on earth?" (Luke 18:8). In Phillips' translation the passage is rendered thus: "Yet, when the Son of Man comes, will he find men on earth who believe in him?" In his letter to Timothy the apostle Paul declares: "Now the Spirit [of God] expressly says that in later times some will depart from the faith by giving heed to deceitful spirits, and doctrines of demons" (I Timothy 4:1).

What Christ did say in the Olivet Prophecy is that the New Testament message of the Kingdom of God must be proclaimed to people all over the world before the end of the age. Every nation in the world must be given an opportunity to get to know the essence of the Gospel message before the return of Jesus Christ. This is exactly what is happening, for the first time, in our days. By means of radio and television, the spoken and the printed word, the task of proclaiming the Messianic message of Jesus Christ all over the world is being accomplished in the present period of history. "And this gospel of the kingdom will be preached throughout the whole world, as a testimony to all nations; and then the end will come."

II. WORLD-WIDE DISTRESS

"Then He continued by saying to them, 'Nation will rise against nation, and kingdom against kingdom. And there will be great earthquakes, and in various places plagues and famines; and there will be terrors and great signs from heaven. . . And there will be signs in sun and moon and stars, and upon the earth dismay among nations, in perplexity at the roaring of the sea and the waves. Men fainting from fear and expectation of the things which are coming upon the world; for the powers of the heavens will be shaken. And then they will see the Son of man coming in a cloud with power

---

* The Kingdom of God.
** The end of the age.

and great glory" (Luke 21: 10-11, 25-27). Natural calamities, wars and uprisings of nations, famines and pestilences—these are the elements which will produce an unprecedented world-wide distress at the end of the age.

1. WARS.

According to the Olivet Prophecy wars will form one of the chief elements of a world-wide distress at the end-time of history. But, as we know, wars have always been an inseparable part of human history, and yet they never created a condition of world-wide distress. Up to this century wars were simply incapable of precipitating a world disaster because war casualties had been confined to the battle fields, and the effects of war had been limited to the belligerent parties.

However, events in the 20th century have already furnished a preview of what the Olivet Prophecy has in mind with reference to the catastrophic potentialities of modern warfare. The advent of the airplane in the beginning of this century, and the steady advance of technical science have brought radical changes in the conduct and consequences of warfare. We already had two world wars in this century. At least the First World War was terminated with some sort of a peace treaty. No peace treaty has as yet been concluded after the Second World War. In fact, a recently published book entitled THE VIOLENT PEACE reports that in the 23 years since the end of World War Two there have been over fifty major and numerous minor conflicts in various parts of the world causing the death of hundreds of thousands, or even millions, of people.[1] Today, American cities are more exposed to destruction from an intercontinental missile attack by Russia, which is removed from the American east coast by some 5,000 miles, than the British Isles were in World War Two, though separated from the German war front only by the English Channel.

Not only has the twentieth century witnessed a steep upswing in the frequency of wars and a change from local to world-wide effects of warfare, wars in this century have become increasingly bloodier. In World War Two man came into possession of nuclear weapons. Since then the destructive power of nuclear bombs has been multiplied enormously. We are informed that space ships are being constructed which will fly in outer space, out of reach of any defensive instruments, and capable of discharging their deadly load over any pre-selected area, causing the extermination of the population of whole countries or even continents. The capacity of modern weapons of war to spread world-wide devastation is so great that it imparts a new reality to the awe-inspiring descriptions of the apocalyptic portions of the Bible. If we realize that these nuclear weapons are now in the hands of unscrupulous and irresponsible leaders of nations, it is difficult not to believe that nuclear warfare will take place on this earth before the day of wicked man is over.

2. FAMINE.

"And there will be . . . in various places . . . famines" (Luke 21:11; see also Matthew 24:7, Mark 13:8).

According to the Olivet Prophecy, famine like warfare will be one of the ingredients of a world distress at the end-time of history. Mankind has often experienced famines, but like wars famines have been localized in certain parts of the world. The effects of such local famines have usually been alleviated by the import of food from other areas. For famine to contribute to a world distress it must be a world famine. That this is what the Bible expects to happen at the end-time of history we infer from the following passage in Revelation.

"And I looked, and behold, a black horse; and he who sat on it had a pair of scales in his hand. And I heard as it were a voice in the center of the four living creatures saying, 'A quart of wheat for a danarius, and three quarts of barley for a denarius . . .'" (Revelation 6: 5-6). The world famine at the end-time of history will be so severe that food will be rationed out, and the cost of food will be so high that the price of a quart of wheat will be equivalent to a day's wages.*

There are two factors operating in contemporary history the combined effects of which are capable of producing a world-wide famine of unprecedented severity. These factors are: overpopulation and man's abuse of the earth.

a. Overpopulation.

It is assumed that the primary ingredient in world famine is the present-day exploding population. It is said that the enormous population growth which we witness today poses a threat second in importance to nuclear warfare. From the very beginning of man's existence on earth until the beginning of the twentieth century—

---

* See, marginal note in the *New American Standard Bible*.

hundreds of thousands of years—the population of the world reached about one and a half billion. Within the last sixty years it more than doubled this number. As of this date the population of the world numbers 3.2 billion. At the present rate of growth, in the year of 2000 there will be seven billion people on earth. In 1967 the world population increased by more than 65 million. This increase alone is equal to the combined present population of Bolivia, Cuba, the Dominican Republic, Denmark, Egypt, Hungary, Israel, Norway and Sweden.

The rate of population growth is especially high in the less developed countries, i.e., in those countries which are less able to feed their people. It is said that about 80 percent of the increase of one-half billion of the world population in the decade of the 1950's took place in the less developed countries. As of this date the people of India multiply at a rate of some 55,000 a day. India's annual increase at this time exceeds the total population of Australia.

The reason for this population explosion is the decreased death rate. Until the nineteenth century a high birth rate was effectively balanced by a high death rate. In the latter part of the nineteenth century death rates began to fall off in western countries. In the course of time the same trend spread to the rest of the world due to the introduction of health measures practiced in the West. It is the efficient use of modern medical measures which has disturbed the equilibrium between the birth rate and death rate and which is the primary cause for the present-day population explosion.[2] In nature the excessive multiplication of one animal species is checked by antagonistic and unfavorable agents in its immediate environment. In the case of man no such controls exist. Man was equipped by the Creator with an intelligence capable of instructing him in the fundamentals of his welfare. Indiscriminate multiplication of the human species resulting in the depletion of living space and food resources was never God's intention.

In his discussion of the abuse of the soil which goes back to antiquity, one authority asks, how it is that this damage to his environment was caused by man at a time when the total world population was small. His answer to his own question is, that ancient man had accomplished this damage because of the human reluctance to strike out and develop new areas.[3] It is quite possible that one of the sins of the builders of the Tower of Babel enterprise was this heavy human concentration in a particular area ("Come, let us build ourselves a city . . . lest we be scattered abroad upon the face of the whole earth"); and one of the Divine aims in dispersing them was to prevent the evil consequences of overpopulation in that part of the world ("and from there the LORD scattered them abroad over the face of all the earth", Genesis 11:9)

b. Man's Abuse Of The Earth.

Man's existence is inseparably bound up with the soil, especially the topsoil, on which he lives. Topsoil is the top layer of soil in which grow trees, grass and crops which supply man with the food and fiber he needs. Not only human life, but all life on earth depends for its existence on the topsoil. Trees on slopes prevent the topsoil from being blown away by winds, or washed away by torrential rains. The vegetable cover renders to the plains the same protection against winds. Trees on hillsides and at watersheds allow the melting snows and the rain waters to percolate slowly into the ground and re-plenish the subterranean water resources.

When trees are removed indiscriminately, the topsoil of the hill-sides is blown away by winds, or carried off by the melting snows and rain waters run off into the streams, with the result that river beds are raised causing frequent floods and the lowering of subterranean water levels. When grasslands are denuded of their cover, their soil is carried off by winds and we have duststorms. In the summer of 1934 the people of the United States had a terrible demonstration of the consequences of man's tampering with nature, when they witnessed a vast transcontinental sun-darkening windstorm, laden with a portion of topsoil from five western states—New Mexico, Colorado, Oklahoma, Texas and Kansas. This once fertile portion of the United States was turned into a dust-bowl in the dry season of that year, the result of overgrazing by too large herds of cattle and sheep and by plowing grasslands which were not meant by nature for the raising of crops.

It is this disturbance of the equilibrium in nature, the result of human mismanagement, which has brought about frequent famines throughout history, even at a time when the world's population was small. Man-induced soil erosion is taking place practically all over the world except in northwestern Europe. The dire consequences of man's interference with the economy of nature may be seen from this general survey of this subject as given below.

United States of America

In the 150 years since the Declaration of Independence the United States lost about one-third of its topsoil, more than one-half of its high grade timber, a portion of its reserve waters and a large part of its wild-life.[4] The early European settlers found in the new world one of the richest treasure houses in the history of mankind. In a few decades they caused the ruin of millions of acres. Large areas of Virginia and Maryland were destroyed by the commercial cultivation of tobacco; the lower South suffered the same fate from the cultivation of cotton; corn caused the exhaustion of the soil in the Mississippi Valley; wheat and flax did the same damage to the Northwest part of the country.[5]

How soil erosion is reducing soil fertility may be seen from this example. Virgin soils in the State of Ohio, in the days when there was no insect control and when unimproved seeds were used, yielded a hundred bushels of corn per acre and sixty bushels of wheat per acre. In 1948, when this information was obtained, with insect control and the use of improved seeds crops averaged about forty-two bushels of corn and twenty bushels of wheat. Ohio is one of the most advanced agricultural States in the Union.[6]

About 40 percent of the land in the United States was originally covered with primeval forests. Today, less than 7 percent of the entire land area is covered by virgin forests.[7] Large stretches of forests were completely denuded with no thought given to the vital relationship which exists between forests, water resources and the soil itself.[8]

The rapidly shrinking supplies of underwater living organisms near the coasts of the United States may be seen from the following figures: In 1889 Maine marketed 25 million pounds of fresh lobster. Since 1905 the catch of lobster has seldom been more than six million pounds. From 1845 to 1885 the annual catch of mackerel on the east coast of the United States was about 100 million pounds. Between 1885 and 1930 the annual catch did not exceed 25 million pounds.[9]

"The story of our nation in the last century as regards the use of forests, grasslands, wildlife and water sources is the most violent and most destructive of any written in the long history of civilization."[10]

Mexico and South America

Mexico was once a heavily forested country. Mexican forests have been destroyed through lumbering and burning. The result is marked soil erosion and the drying up of large numbers of wells and springs. Much of Mexico's soil is being washed into the sea.[11]

The story of Mexico is the story of South America. Because of lack of fuel, charcoal and cordwood are used for cooking, heating and even for industrial purposes. This destruction of the forests is producing everywhere extensive areas of soil erosion, converting once fertile lands into deserts. The eroded soil is being deposited in streams producing recurrent floods with enormous damage to property and loss of human lives. About half of the population of South America is underfed.[12]

China

About 100 million people in China died from starvation in the past century. It is estimated that by A. D. 2000 China's population will reach 950 million.[13] Most of the forests are denuded. About 25 percent of its land lost all productive capacity. The Yellow River and Yellow Sea derived their names from the yellow subsoil which has poured into them from the hinterland. The deposition of eroded soil continues to raise the bed of the Yellow River to a higher level than that of the surrounding country giving rise to the world's most disastrous floods. The Yellow River alone is said to transport annually 2,500 million tons of eroded soil ripped away from the hillsides by the rains.[14]

India

The largest part of India is hilly and mountainous. The country has been so much deforested that tens of millions of people use dried cow dung to do their cooking. In many parts of India homes are built of mud, and every available piece of straw, stick and cornstalk is burned as fuel. More than half a billion of people live on the Indian subcontinent, about a third the size of the United States. The population increases at a rate of more than a million a month. Starvation is widespread.

Australia and New Zealand

In the early 19th century a couple decades of experimental sheep breeding produced the quality of wool which England needed. England was then the world's greatest manufacturing center of woolen goods. Sheep breeding opened the Australian continent and became the greatest source of revenue. Enormous destruction of forests ensued, while the grasslands were denuded by the thousands of flocks of sheep and goats. We have here the same story of forests and grass denudation for the purpose of trade and profit, with the same evil consequences as anywhere else.

Africa

Under the administration of the Roman empire North Africa enjoyed a high degree of prosperity. Flourishing cities were built, and the agricultural areas were devoted chiefly to the growing of grains and olives. The deterioration of the region began in the 7th century with the Arab invasion. The cities gradually disappeared and the land turned into a desert.[15]

Africa is said to be one of the most eroded of the continents. Nearly everywhere, forests have been destroyed resulting in erosion of the soil and depletion of the subterranean water resources. In what used to be Belgian Congo, 500,000 acres in the northwest region have been deforested. In 1880 the northern part of Nyasaland was richly forested and irrigated. Today the forests of this entire region have been destroyed. In certain places of Nyasaland whole mountains and hills have lost so much of their soil that they are nothing now but rock. Soil erosion is believed to be Kenya's greatest problem. It is claimed that by changing the native African subsistence agriculture to commercial agriculture European colonists have contributed a great deal to the deterioration of the African continent.[16]

The Near East

The fertility of the land lying between the two rivers of Euphrates and Tigris known under the ancient name of Mesopotamia was such as to make it fit to be called a Garden of Eden. It became the cradle of human civilization. It was here that mankind made the first attempt to establish a world civilization under one government. Here flourishing cities were founded. Advanced agricultural methods were introduced including the use of a complex irrigation system.

Gradually, the forests were cut down, the grasslands laid bare by overgrazing, and all the evil consequences of soil erosion began. Wars played a big part in the devastation of this region. But it is the Arab invasion in the seventh century of our era which accelerated and perpetuated the general ruin. Today, much of this area is desert.

The mountain slopes of European Turkey are treeless. The Turkish province of Anatolia is said to present one of the most glaring spectacles of the consequences of soil erosion. The soil washed into the sea for centuries has choked all the harbors with silt. Tarsus, which in the days of the apostle Paul, was a port city, now lies ten miles inland. The hills around Istanbul, once the proud capital of the eastern part of the Roman empire under the name of Constantinople, are slashed and barren.[17]

These two phenomena—(1) overpopulation made possible by the reduced death rate as a result of modern medical advance, and (2) the effects of manmade soil erosion—are working together in our day to bring on a world famine such as was never known before in human history. Orville L. Freeman, Secretary of Agriculture of the United States Government, stated in 1966 before the House Committee on Agriculture that by 1970 the food shortage in the developing countries will double the need of food aid these countries have been receiving from the United States in 1966. Even if the United States were to turn loose all its facilities for food production the disaster of a world famine could be postponed only for a few years. "The most serious consequence of all," he said, "would come at that time, probably about 1984, when the total U. S. agricultural productive capacity would no longer be sufficient to meet the food needs of the aid-recipient countries. This would lead to a breakdown of the world food economy with consequences that would range from catastrophic famine in many areas to an elemental struggle for the control of food resources."[18]

The authors of a very important book entitled FAMINE—1975! estimate that the world famine will begin in 1975.[19] But no one can be precise as to the exact year. The dates mentioned probably refer to the time when the famine will have assumed its disastrous character. As a matter of fact, the famine, on a smaller scale, is already here. According to estimates made by the United Nations Food and Agriculture Organization ten thousand people are dying of starvation every day.[20]

Gunnar Myrdal, a Swedish economist, predicts a world famine of calamitous proportions in about ten years.[21]

Chester Bowles, American ambassador to India, speaks of the approaching famine as "the most colossal catastrophe in history."[22]

Testifying before a Senate committee, Thomas M. Ware said that "very few grasp the magnitude of the danger that confronts us".[23]

Raymond Ewell, a leading authority on fertilizer and soil chemistry at New York University, says that the world stands on the threshold of the greatest famine in human history which will affect hundreds of millions of people.[24]

William D. McElroy, well-known Johns Hopkins University biologist, stated in an address before the American Institute of Biological Sciences that he agrees with the various predictions by experts concerning a catastrophic famine with which the world will be faced around 1985.[25]

The world famine will affect chiefly the developing nations of Asia and Africa, and probably also many of the nations of South America, which together make up the bulk of the world's population.

The widespread devastation inflicted by man on his earthly home produced intermittent famines in various places at different periods in ages past. The effects of this centuries-old human abuse of nature together with present-day world over-population will precipitate, according to the experts, a world famine of frightful consequences before the twentieth century comes to an end. It is this kind of world famine which is predicted in the Olivet prophecy and in the book of Revelation. "And there will be . . . in various places . . . famines" (Luke 21:11). It is quite possible that the international disturbances recorded in the Olivet prophecy and in Revelation, the "wars and rumors of wars", as well as the epidemics, are related to the world famine. The authors of FAMINE—1975! declare that "revolution and turmoil will be the order of the day in most of the affected countries".[26] The reader will also recall the statement by Secretary of Agriculture Freeman to the effect that one of the consequences of the world famine may well be "an elemental struggle for the control of food resources".

c. "Cursed Is The Ground Because Of You."

Man is the only living being that is bent on destroying his own living quarters. How are we to account for it? Is it greed? Is it a desire for immediate gain without consideration for the welfare of future generations? A Latin American scientist remarked that the number one problem in much of the South American hemisphere is moral erosion.[27] Moral erosion, not only of South America, but of the whole human race, is the Biblical answer. Way back in Genesis earth's coming ruin was predicted as the outcome of man's fallen state. To Adam, the representative of mankind, after he knowingly alienated himself from his Creator, God said: "Cursed is the ground because of you . . . thorns and thistles it shall bring forth to you" (Genesis 3:17-18). The literal fulfillment of these sombre words can be read in the disappearance of the forests, in the depletion or extinction of wildlife, in the pollution and poisoning of streams and rivers, in the "despairing chronicle of ruins buried in sand, of rivers running in channels high above surrounding landscapes, of ever-spreading deltas, of fallen terraces which once held productive fields or rich gardens. It can be seen in man-made deserts and immense reaches of bare stone from which the once fertile soils have been washed or blown away."[28]

We are told that we must institute world-wide population control, and at the same time we must conserve and, wherever possible, restore the precious life-sustaining resources of our earthly environment. We are advised by one of the authorities in this field from whom we have derived much of our information that "economic, political, educational and other measures also are indispensable."[29]

This, of course, brings that writer pretty close to the Biblical position. It is the sense of Biblical revelation that man is the world's problem as well as his own problem. Nature is cursed because of man, and she will continue to suffer until human nature is redeemed, until man's heart is cleansed and renewed. Nature is groaning in her affliction, and she is waiting for man's regeneration before she can be restored. This thought is beautifully expressed in the following passage in Isaiah in connection with Israel's restoration.

"The wilderness and dry land shall be glad; and the desert shall rejoice, and blossom as the rose. It shall blossom abundantly, and rejoice even with joy and singing: the glory of Lebanon shall be given to it, the majesty of Carmel and Sharon; they shall see the glory of the LORD, the majesty of our God.

Strengthen the weak hands, and make firm the feeble knees. Say to those who are of a fearful heart, 'Be strong, feat not! Behold, your God will come with vengeance, with the recompense of God; he will come and save you.'

Then the eyes of the blind shall be opened, and the ears of the deaf unstopped. Then shall the lame man leap like a hart, and the tongue of the dumb sing for joy; for waters shall break forth in the wilderness, and streams in the desert. The burning sand shall become a pool, and the thirsty ground springs of water; the haunt of jackals shall become a swamp, the grass shall become reeds and rushes.

And a highway shall be there, and a road, and it shall be called the Holy Way; the unclean shall not pass over it, even simple ones shall not err therein. No lion shall be there, nor shall any ravenous beast come up on it; they shall not be found there, but the redeemed shall walk there. And the ransomed of the LORD shall return, and come to Zion with singing; everlasting joy shall be upon their heads; they shall obtain joy and gladness, and sorrow and sighing shall flee away" (Isaiah 35:1-10).

With this Old Testament hope of the eventual rejuvenation of nature in the days of the Messiah the New Testament fully agrees. The apostle Peter speaks of the restoration of all things with the return of Christ (Acts 3:21). According to the apostle Paul nature is groaning in its present state and looks forward to its deliverance upon the full redemption of the children of God (Romans 8:19-21).

In his description of the disastrous effects of man-made soil erosion in the various parts of the world, William Vogt makes the following observation concerning Palestine: It is "one of the most hopeful areas not only on the continent [of Asia] but in the entire world. On the raddled hillsides and silt-drifted plains the Jews are repeating the miracle of Lazarus* on the dead land. Once more Palestine demonstrates that 'arable land' is as much a function of the farmer as of the farm. The high intelligence and firm character of the modern Jew is restoring productivity to land that has been sterile desert for hundreds of years in other hands."[30] It seems therefore that what is taking place in the State of Israel today may be the beginning of the fulfillment of the Biblical Messianic hope concerning the redemption of man and the renewal of nature, to take

---

* This refers to the story of the raising of Lazarus from the dead by Jesus Christ as recorded in the New Testament.

place with the coming of the Messiah according to the Old Testament and the Second Coming of Jesus Christ according to the New Testament.

III. The Liberation Of Palestine From Gentile Rule

"And Jerusalem will be trodden down by the Gentiles, until the times of the Gentiles are fulfilled" (Luke 21:24).

Colonel Richard Meinertzhagen, an Englishman, was on Lord Allenby's staff in the Middle East during the First World War. He was also a member of the Peace Delegation, Chief Political Officer in Palestine, and military advisor to the Middle East Department of the British Colonial Office. In his diary entry of February 2, 1918— nine months before the First World War came to an end—he relates that he had lunch with several people among whom was also Mr. Balfour. During the conversation the Balfour Declaration came up for discussion. Colonel Meinertzhagen thought that the Balfour Declaration was ambiguous and he wanted Mr. Balfour to tell him what exactly did the Declaration aim to accomplish. Balfour said: 'Both the Prime Minister and myself have been influenced by a desire to give the Jews their rightful place in the world; a great nation without a home is not right. My personal hope is that the Jews will make good in Palestine and eventually found a Jewish State. It is up to them now; we have given them their great opportunity.' Colonel Meinertzhagen's comment was "that if this declaration did in the end found a Jewish State, it would be the only good thing which came out of this miserable war. . . ."[31]

Many people have been asking what permanent good has come out of the Second World War? True, German Nazism and Japanese militarism have been defeated. But is it not true that a larger portion of the world's population is now deprived of the basic human freedoms than in the Nazi period? The big guns of World War Two stopped firing in 1945. But hardly a year has passed since then without some "little war" being waged here and there. Today, like before the Great Flood in Noah's day, the whole earth is corrupt and filled with violence. Domestic and international turmoil and lawlessness are mounting.

As we contemplate the sombre and distressing state of our world, may we not see in the State of Israel, which sprang into existence as a direct result of World War Two, the Hand of God using people and events to accomplish His Will in the world? That a people which had been deprived of its country, dispersed all over the world, hounded from place to place, that such a people should nevertheless survive, retain its full national identity, and after nineteen hundred years return to its ancient homeland and restore it in such a short time—this is a phenomenon the like of which is unknown in human history. Apart from the Bible and the Biblical faith Israel cannot be accounted for. Shall we not therefore take courage in the fact of Israel's resurrection, knowing that He who has preserved Israel is a faithful God, and that He is the God of all nations, and that He will not rest until He has established His Kingdom on earth?

The following excerpt is from an article by L. Nelson Bell, M.D., the father-in-law of Dr. Billy Graham and executive editor of *Christianity Today.*

"That there is a deep mystery in God's dealings with and plans for Israel is obvious to all students of the Bible. Many wild interpretations have come out of the study of the subject. But there has come rich blessing to those who will let the Scriptures speak for themselves. In the Old Testament and New there are prophecies that speak definitely of Israel as a nation. Many have been fulfilled, and their literal fulfillment strengthens our faith. Other prophecies have yet to be fulfilled.

Our Lord, giving a panorama of the last days (the duration of which is not specifically stated), says in speaking of the Jews, 'They will fall by the edge of the sword, and be led captive among all nations; and Jerusalem will be trodden down by the Gentiles, until the times of the Gentiles are fulfilled' (Luke 21:24). That for the first time in more than 2,000 years Jerusalem is now completely in the hands of the Jews gives a student of the Bible a thrill and a renewed faith in the accuracy and validity of the Bible.

The Jews as a separate people demonstrate a mystery and a hope. Their continuance as a people in the midst of all other nations is in itself a miracle. The cohesiveness of these Jews is demonstrated by the fact that at least ninety-six countries are represented in Israel today—from the ends of the earth, but Jews all.

I have visited Palestine twice, the last time four years ago, and have been amazed to note the resourcefulness, unity of purpose and hard work by which Israel has truly made the desert to 'bloom as the rose' (Isaiah 35:1). These people did not return to Palestine primarily because of religious convictions. It is rather a strong nationalism that has drawn them together. But a small minority in their midst pore over the Old Testament Scriptures and see God's hand working in their behalf.

The entire world has been impressed with the Israeli fighting forces. Military experts have used such terms as 'unbelievable', 'fantastic', and 'overwhelming' in speaking of their brilliant tactics and efficiency in the recent war. We ask, Did this just happen? Pictures show the pinpoint accuracy of the raid on Arab air fields. In many cases planes on the ground were destroyed one by one (over 400 in all) without great damage to the landing strips. Just as the Egyptian army was beginning a retreat through the Milta Pass in Sinai, a perfectly placed bomb destroyed a large Egyptain tank in the pass, completely blocking retreat. Hundreds of Egyptian tanks and trucks were either destroyed or stranded. A veteran of Rommel's retreat at El Alamein* said that this spectacle of destroyed or immobilized heavy equipment beggared anything he had ever seen. The same element of overwhelming military victory is found in every area of the six-day war. We ask again, Did it just happen? One cannot help thinking that in all of this God was working out His own purposes, far above and beyond the capabilities of men and nations! Christians must remember that in events like this we see only a tiny segment of history. Not only does God move in mysterious ways; with Him a day is as a thousand years and a thousand years as a day. For this reason unwarranted dogmatism can lead to foolish conclusions. At the same time, the events in the Middle East certainly fit— at least in some measure—into the picture revealed in the Scriptures. If we say, as the Arabs do, that Israel has no right to exist, we may prove blind to her peculiar destiny under the providence of God.

Isaiah's and Ezekiel's prophecies regarding Egypt seem singularly applicable at this time. Nasser's dire threats still ring in our ears: 'Israel must be destroyed', 'We will swallow you up'; 'You invaders will be driven into the sea'; and 'The Gulf of Akaba is permanently closed to Israeli shipping.' But we read in Isaiah, 'In that day the Egyptians will be like women, and tremble with fear before the hand which the LORD of hosts shakes over them. And the land of

---

* This has reference to the defeat of the German army in North Africa in World War Two.

Judah will become a terror to the Egyptians; everyone to whom it is mentioned will fear because of the purpose which the LORD of hosts has purposed against them' (Isaiah 19: 16-17).

It is thrilling to see a segment of prophecy being fulfilled!"[32]

The following pronouncement was issued by the Board of Directors of Biola Schools and Colleges.

"Recent events have focused the attention of the world upon Biblical prophecies relating to the fulfillment of Israel's destiny. Prominent among predicted end-time events related to the coming of Jesus the Messiah is the return of the Jews to their land and their redemption. It appears that recent developments in the Middle East may be preparing the way for these great prophetic events. Analysts of contemporary developments should exercise caution at this point, however, in equating particular events with fulfillments per se of specific prophecies.

The millions who died in the Nazi holocaust have not been forgotten by Christian people, and there are many upon whose consciences this tragedy still rests painfully. It is true that some atrocities in the past have been committed by some in the church, but there are many in the church who have spoken out against these evils as a violation of the spirit of love in true Christianity, and who have contributed to the rescue, resettlement and rehabilitation of thousands of Jews. God's eternal love for Israel is abundantly delineated in the Holy Scriptures and for many Christians this is an article of faith.

Throughout its history the nation Israel has been the object of opposition and attack by Satan, the arch-enemy of God's purpose and program. Untaught and unholy men have unwittingly cooperated with the devil in this. It is our conviction that the true people of God should not be found in league with those who oppose the will and work of God for Israel.

Antisemitism is anti-Biblical and un-Christian. Recent attempts to equate antisemitism with the New Testament are false and unfounded. Moreover, statements and actions of some professing Christians are not to be viewed as representing the Christian attitude as a whole.

God has an eternal purpose for all the nations and for Israel in particular. He chose this nation to be the channel of world redemption. While mankind failed to cooperate fully in the working out of God's purpose, it is abundantly evident in the Scriptures that His purpose will not on that account be thwarted but will be fully and gloriously accomplished.

God's purpose for the Arab world includes promises of national enlargement and blessing. They along with all Gentiles are the objects of God's love and of the proclamation of His grace. Therefore, we acknowledge our indebtedness to them, as to all nations, and desire to contribute to their spiritual, social, and material needs.

While the Bible discloses and interprets past and present events with regard to God's plan, its basic concern is with the future. The ultimate purpose of God includes the establishment of a perfect kingdom of the nations of the world. Then God will dwell with men and rule over them in the person of His Son, the Lord Jesus Christ, the Messiah of Israel, through whom He has provided personal salvation for all men who put their trust in Him."[33]

IV. A MESSAGE OF HOPE FOR A TIME OF TROUBLE

1. THE HOPE OF CHRIST'S RETURN SHOULD GENERATE FAITHFULNESS AND VIGILANCE.

The aim of the Olivet Prophecy was: To prevent the generation of Christ's followers who were to witness the destruction of Palestine by Rome from identifying that catastrophe with the end of the age; to lay down broad hints of certain trends, movements and developments to occur at the time of the end, which would forewarn the people of God of the nearness of Christ's return. While He refused to fix any definite date for His return, Christ did intimate that a long waiting period would intervene prior to His coming again. This may be inferred from the casual remark in the Parable of the Talents concerning the master who returned after "a long time" (Matthew 25:19); also from the clear statement that before the end of the age the Biblical message of salvation must be disseminated among the nations of the whole inhabited earth, and not merely in the Mediterranean world, which Christ's contemporaries were wont to equate with the whole world (Romans 1:8, Colossians 1:6), a task which only now—19 centuries later—is being completed. Israel was allowed a development of some twelve centuries between the Sinai revelation and the first Advent of Christ. The complex world-wide Gentile civilization needed an even longer period than this to assimilate the more complete revelation of the Old and New Testament.

But a long time interval between Christ's first and second coming was bound to engender undesirable attitudes. In the outside world the long delay of His return would generate an utter disbelief in the second coming of Christ and the world judgment associated with it. Let the world keep in mind what had taken place in the days of the Great Flood, how the severity of Divine judgment fell on all who ignored Noah's warnings (Matthew 24: 37-39).

Even among Christ's followers the long delay of His return would lead to carelessness, unfaithfulness and neglect of the work He entrusted to their care. "But take heed to yourselves lest your hearts be weighed down with dissipation and drunkenness and cares of this life, and that day [of the return of Jesus Christ] come upon you suddenly like a snare" (Luke 21:34; see also Matthew 24:45-51). Hence, the people of God must so live and conduct themselves as if Christ were to return at any moment. We must bend all our efforts to accomplish the work He has committed to us and use all our talents to advance His cause in the hearts and lives of men (The Parable of the Talents, Matthew 25:14-30).

2. "WHEN THESE THINGS BEGIN TO TAKE PLACE, LOOK UP AND RAISE YOUR HEADS, BECAUSE YOUR REDEMPTION IS DRAWING NEAR" (Luke 21:28).

On their way from Bethany to Jerusalem in the early morning following the first "Palm Sunday", Jesus and His apostolic band saw by the roadside a solitary fig tree. It was covered with leaves but it had no figs. It was a barren fig tree. In the Old Testament and Rabinnical literature Israel is compared to a fig tree.[34] Christ Himself, on a previous occasion, used the fig tree to designate Israel (Luke 13: 6-9). To Him, who on the preceding day had wept over Jerusalem because the axe of judgment was already lifted over her (Luke 19: 41-44), the barren fig tree, full of leaves but without any fruit, was symbolic of Israel's pretentious religiosity and her spiritual sterility. Upon Christ's denunciatory word the fig tree by the roadside was withered away (Matthew 21: 18-19).

At the conclusion of the Olivet Prophecy, uttered later in the same week in which the incident of the barren fig tree had taken place, Christ made the following statement: "From the fig tree learn its lesson: as soon as its branch becomes tender and puts forth its leaves, you know that summer is near. So also, when you see all these things, you know that he is near, at the very gates" (Matthew 24: 32-33). In Luke's Gospel the same statement occurs with a slight variation: "And he told them a parable: 'Look at the fig tree, and all the trees. As soon as they come out in leaf, you see for yourselves and know that the summer is already near. So also when you see these things taking place, you know that the kingdom of God is near" (Luke 21: 29-31). As the barren fig tree on the road to Jerusalem was a picture of old Israel on the eve of its destruction by pagan Rome, so the fig tree in the concluding portion of the Olivet Prophecy points to the Israel which was to become resurrected when the Times of the Gentiles are fulfilled. The phrase "and all the trees" in Luke's version may be taken to refer to the other nations which will spring to life simultaneously with Israel. Is it a mere coincidence that the present State of Israel has come into existence together with a multitude of other nations? "And are we not at the present time witnessing a wonderful recovery of the ancient people of the Jews, who, impelled partly by persecution, are seizing the unforseen opportunity of becoming a free and prosperous nation in the land of their inheritance? Indeed, most of the great nations of mankind are astir with nationalistic ambitions and enthusiasms; which accords with St. Luke's version of the Parable: 'Behold the fig tree, and all the trees: when they now shoot forth, you see it and know of your own selves that the summer is nigh.' Are not these signs by which we, even we, may know 'that He is nigh, even at the doors'?"

The above lines are from an article by a Christian clergyman of the Anglican communion. The passage which follows is from the same article. "As the comparatively very slight material achievements of the Graeco-Roman world preceded and facilitated the spiritual advance that sprang from Christ in His first coming, so, by analogy, we may postulate that all that science has accomplished in the past couple of centuries is a preparation for another spiritual advance which Christ will initiate in His second coming. It does appear as if the Times of the Gentiles were nearing their fulfillment, that is as if the civilization of Christendom had almost run its appointed course under the stimulating and moulding influence of the religion that bears His name. The new outlook and the new powers have produced a situation which Christianity, as it has taken shape in the interval, is incapable of satisfactorily dealing with. The problems both of thought and of practice have grown beyond the scope of what we have been brought up to believe and to do. The principles of their solution are, it may be contended, implicit in the pure Gospel of Jesus—the Fatherhood of God, the ideal of absolute love, eternal life, the Kingdom of God. But the application of these to the vast tracts opened up by astronomy and biology and psychology, and to the baffling international and economic complexities of our material civilization, does not lie sufficiently on the surface for the conviction of scientific theorists, or the persuasion of governments and reformers, or the guidance of the multitudes drifting like sheep without a shepherd. The world desperately needs a new revelation, authenticated and compelling, to enable it to escape from the chaos into which it has blundered and proceed along the new and living way to which it is called. There is only One with sufficient authority to deliver that revelation and make evident its saving efficacy . . . . . . With all their shortcomings, the Churches have kept before the world the figure of Jesus, which now exercises its mysterious fascination and appeal more widely over the earth than ever before. For the Gospel has been or is being preached to all the nations and all the tribes. Yet what can He avail, if He be but some one in a remote and ever-receding past? Surely there are some in every inhabited corner of the globe who would welcome Him should He make His presence known.

Never before have there been such enlightened aspirations and well-thought out endeavors for human welfare—large schemes for the consolidation of the nations in peaceful cooperation, careful plans for the improvement of social conditions, constant progress in educational theory and practice, wise and sympathetic dealing with the failures and the unfortunate, determined attempts to eradicate all kinds of maladies, utopian visions of universal brotherhood and well-being—a healthful practical idealism springing from the combination of the principles of Christian ethics with the scientific study of man and his environment. But never before have the forces of evil appeared so mighty and so insidious in thwarting and wrecking hopes and schemes for a better world, fostering in some insatiable greed and ruthless ambition, in others suspicion, fear, and irrational antipathies, and in many shortsighted egoism and cynical apathy. There have been in the past epochs of widespread strife and enmity, wars and revolutions and persecutions: but scientific invention, while greatly augmenting man's ability to help his fellow, has also multiplied his resources to hurt and to destroy. Across the fair face of the earth the approaching tribulation seems to be casting its ominous shadow, with the premonitory mutterings of the tempest about to break forth in devastation. But this to those who understand is a cause, not for dismay, but for exultant hope, as the Master said: 'When these things begin to come to pass, then look up and lift up your heads; for your redemption draweth nigh' . . .

In the approaching crisis there is a special call for fortitude, watchfulness, prayer, and loyalty to our Master, that we 'may prevail to escape all these things that shall come to pass, and to stand before the Son of Man.' "[35]

"The storm clouds that darken the sky
Are the dust of His nearing feet,
Are the signs of the end-time nigh
When hope and fulfillment will meet.
Let the nations rage as they may:
All earth must come under His sway.

He's waited the centuries down
In silence, and hidden in God,
For the hour to put on His crown
And His rights secured by His blood.
He will rise from His heavenly seat;
The clouds are the dust of His feet.

Awake, O my soul, from false dreams;
Let thy garments be always white.
Keep sacred thy troth with thy Lord;
Live constantly in His sight.
Arise, thy Redeemer to meet!
The clouds are the dust of His feet![36]

"Come, Thou long expected Jesus,
Born to set Thy people free;
From our fear and sins release us,
Let us find our rest in Thee.

Israel's Strength and Consolation
Hope of all the earth Thou art;
Dear Desire of every nation,
Joy of every longing heart.

Born Thy people to deliver,
Born a child, and yet a King
Born to reign in us forever,
Now Thy gracious Kingdom bring.

By Thine own eternal Spirit
Rule in all our hearts alone;
By Thine all-sufficient merit
Raise us to Thy glorious throne.[37]

Notes to Chapter 15

[1] See, review in the *Sun* (Baltimore, Md.), June 9, 1968, by Stephen E. Ambrose.

[2] Franklin T. Brayer, *"Population Control,"* article in the *Maryland State Medical Journal* (Baltimore, Md.), July 1965.

[3] Fairfield Osborn, *Our Plundered Planet* (Little, Brown & Company: Boston, 1948), pp. 90-91. Used by permission.

[4] William Vogt, *The Road To Survival* (William Sloane Associates, Inc.: New York, 1948), p. 149. Copyright 1948 by William Vogt. Used by permission of William Morrow & Co., Inc., New York.

[5] Ibid., pp. 114-115.

[6] Ibid., p. 125.

[7] Fairfield Osborn, Op. Cit., pp. 179-180.

[8] Ibid., p. 176.

[9] William Vogt, Op. Cit., pp. 35-36.

[10] Fairfield Osborn, Op. Cit., p. 175.

[11] William Vogt, Op. Cit., pp. 161, 171, 175.

[12] Ibid., pp. 157-158.

[13] Ibid., p. 219.

[14] Ibid., p. 223.

[15] Ibid., pp. 245, 247.

[16] Ibid., pp. 253, 257, 261.

[17] Fairfield Osborn, Op. Cit., pp. 94, 97, 109.

[18] *"Food For Freedom"*, Joint Release of Departments of State and Agriculture, February 10, 1966, p. 16. See also: *"World War on Hunger"*, Hearings before the House Committee on Agriculture, 89th Congress, 2nd Session, February 14-18, 1966, p. 192; Orville L. Freeman, Secretary of Agriculture, *"Food For Freedom Program And Commodity Reserves"*, Hearings, p. 24 (see n. 16).

[19] William and Paul Paddock, *Famine—1975!* (Little, Brown and Company: Boston, 1967, pp. 136-141.

[20] Jesse H. Merrell, *"Ahead Famine"*, article in *These Times* (Nashville, Tenn.), February, 1968.

[21] T. R. B., *"Famine Is Here"*, article in *The New Republic* (Washington, D. C.), September 18, 1965. Reprinted by permission of *The New Republic*. Copyright 1965, Harrison-Blaine of New Jersey, Inc.

[22] Idem.

[23] Idem.

[24] Raymond Ewell, *"Famine and Fertilizer"*, article in *Chemical And Engineering News* (Washington, D. C.), December 14, 1964.

[25] Reported in *The Evening Sun* (Baltimore, Md.), September 3, 1968.

[26] William and Paul Paddock, Op. Cit., p. 211.

[27] William Vogt, Op. Cit., p. 155.

[28] Fairfield Osborn, Op. Cit., p. 89.

[29] William Vogt, Op. Cit., p. 264.

[30] Ibid., pp. 234-235.

[31] Colonel Richard Meinertzhagen, *Middle East Diary 1917-1956* (Thomas Yoseloff: New York, 1960), p. 9. Used by permission of Thomas Yoseloff & A. S. Barnes & Company, Inc.

[32] L. Nelson Bell, *"Unfolding Destiny"*, article in *Christianity Today* (Washington, D. C.), July 21, 1967. Copyright 1967 by *Christianity Today*. Reprinted by permission.

[33] *"A Proclamation Concerning Israel And The Nations"*, issued by the Board of Directors of Biola Schools and Colleges, Inc., La Mirada, California, November 9, 1967. Reprinted by permission.

[34] Hosea 9:10; the *Yalkut* (See *The Jewish Encyclopedia*, art. *"Yudan"*); Agudath Shir Hoshirim, Schechter's edition, line 115.

[35] Frederick A. M. Spencer, *"The Advent Hope"*, The Expository Times, (T. & T. Clark: Edinburgh,), December, 1937.

[36] Max I. Reich, *Sweet Singer Of Israel* (Moody Press: Chicago, 1948) pp. 153-4. Used by permission.

[37] One of the hymns by Charles Wesley.

INDEXES

(1) NAMES

263

(2) SCRIPTURE REFERENCES

270   INDEX

(2) SCRIPTURE REFERENCES